The
Exhaustive Dictionary
of
Bible Names

The
Exhaustive Dictionary
of
Bible Names

by

Stelman Smith, M.M., M.Th.,Th.D.

and

Judson Cornwall, Th.D., D.D.

Bridge-Logos *Publishers*

Gainesville, Florida 32614 USA

All Scripture quotations and names are taken from the *King James Version* of the Bible unless otherwise indicated. Those marked (KJV) are also from the *King James Version* of the Bible.

Scripture quotations and names marked (NIV) are from the *Holy Bible: New International Version.* Copyright © 1973, 1978, 1984 by the International Bible Society. Used by permission of Zondervan Bible Publishers.

The Exhaustive Dictionary of Bible Names
Copyright © 1998 by Stelman Smith\Judson Cornwall
Library of Congress Catalog Card Number: 98-70940
International Standard Book Number: 0-88270-751-5
Reprinted 2001

Published by:
Bridge-Logos *Publishers*
Gainesville, FL 32614
www.bridgelogos.com

Contents

The Authors

Judson Cornwall has been in active ministry for sixty-six years. He pastored churches for more than 30 years, taught in Bible Schools in Washington and Texas and has been a guest lecturer in church Bible Schools through America, Germany, and England. For the past 30 years he has traveled in five of the six continents of the world and spent time teaching in thirty countries in Europe, Asia, Africa, North America, South America, Australia, and New Zealand. Dr. Cornwall is a teacher and a published author who has written 45 books. Some of them have been translated into as many as 15 languages. He did his undergraduate work at Southern California College. His Doctorate degree was taken at Fountain Gate Bible College, Dallas, Texas.

Stelman Smith has been in active ministry since 1969. He has served the Body of Christ as a police chaplain, counselor, pastor, and evangelist. Dr. Smith is retired from the police department and is an active international Bible teacher and published author who enjoys sharing God's Word with the Body of Christ. All his post-graduate degrees were received "Summa Cum Laude" from Trinity Theological Seminary.

Preface

Every Bible name has a meaning. So much so, that sometimes when God changed the nature of a person He also changed his or her name. For example, when Abram believed God's promise of a son, God changed his name to Abraham and changed his wife's name from Sarai to Sarah. Years later, after the angel of the Lord had wrestled with him all night, Jacob's name was changed to Israel. In the New Testament, Saul of Tarsus, whose name meant "demanded," came to be known as Paul, which means "little." And this is what the greatest apostle became in his own eyes as he looked increasingly upon the greatness of Christ. It's amazing how often a Bible character lives up to the meaning of his or her name. Sometimes, as in the case of Paul, they deliberately took a name that meant what they wanted to be.

The Exhaustive Dictionary of Bible Names came into existence as a result of each author's interest in the meaning of places and persons in Bible literature. For some years they shared their research notes with each other, for neither was able to find a single book that contained all the information they wanted. Recently they realized that together they had acquired a wealth of research material that would undoubtedly help others who shared their interests. It was then that they decided to put the material into book form and seek publication.

In addition to an exhaustive listing of Bible names, this dictionary contains the multiple names of God, the many titles for Jesus, the numerous scriptural designations for Christians, the Jewish calendars, and descriptions of the stones in the breastplate of the Old Testament priest.

The authors gratefully acknowledge any and all works of the individuals and references that have been used in compiling this dictionary. Regretfully, there are too many to list, and the names and titles of some of the sources have been lost through the years.

Every effort has been made to make this dictionary easy to use. Where old or outdated language was used in original source material, newer definitions of the words are enclosed in brackets [ ] or parenthesis ( ) within the definition and immediately following the word being defined.

In several cases, the exact meaning of the word could not be determined. When this occurs, the closest possible definition is given, followed by a question mark in parenthesis (?).

An equal (=) sign is used to separate the name or fact being defined from the definition. When the name has several and sometimes even seeming contradictory definitions, the most popular definition is given first and the least accepted definition is given last.

All of the names are from the King James and New International versions of the Bible, with names from the KJV being the primary list. When there is a difference between the King James Version and the New International Version, the name from the NIV is enclosed in brackets [ ] following the name from the KJV.

It is the authors' prayers that *The Exhaustive Dictionary of Bible Names* will save you the many years of research that they spent in finding the definitions, and that it will escalate your understanding of God's holy Word.

Dedicated to
the Glory of God

෧෧

Ask and it will be given to you; seek and you will find; knock and the door will be opened to you (Matthew 7:7).

Aaron (a'-ur-un) = Light; a shining light; a mountain of strength; enlightened; very high; to be high. Teaching; to shine. Chaldean: To be high.

Aaronites (a'-ur-un-ites) = Descendants of Aaron = Light; a shining light; a mountain of strength; enlightened; very high; to be high. Teaching; to shine. Chaldean: To be high.

Ab = Fifth Jewish month (July-August)

Abaddon (ab-ad'-dun) = Destruction.

Abagtha (ab-ag'-thah) = Fortune; happy; prosperous; given by fortune. Father of the winepress.

Abana (ab-ay'-nah) = Stony; rocky; her stones. Constancy; a sure ordinance.

Abarim (ab'-ar-im) = Regions beyond; passages; passing over; (root = *pl.*— beyond; a region on the other side; from beyond).

Abba (ab'-bah) = Father (denotes childlike intimacy and trust. A title of *great* respect.)

Abda (ab'-dah) = Servant or worshiper (of God); (roots = [1] a servant; a slave; {figuratively} a worshiper of God; [2] to labor; to work; to serve; i.e., to worship).

Abdeel (ab'-de-el) = Servant (of God).

Abdi (ab'-di) = Servant of Jehovah; my servant.

Abdiel (ab'-de-el) = Servant of God (El).

Abdon (ab'-dun) =
Servile; hard slavery; a
judge; service or cloud of
judgment. A faithful
servant; a servant; service.

Abednego [Abed Nego]
(ab-ed'-ne-go) = Servant
or worshipper of Nebo;
servant of light; servant of
splendor; i.e., the sun;
worshiper of Mercury. The
servant of Jupiter.

Abel (a'-bel) = A breath;
vanity; vapor; (roots = [1]
vanity; transitoriness;
breath; i.e., breath of the
mouth; fading away; [2]
mourning; from root to
mourn, to lament).
Withering; fading away. A
meadow.

Abelbethmaachah
[Abelbeth Maacah] (a'-
bel-beth-ma'-a-kah) =
Meadow of the house of
Maachah; mourning for
the house of oppression.

Abel Keramim [NIV] (a'-
bel-ker-a'-mim) =
Mourning of the vineyards.

Abelmaim [Abel Maim]
(a'-bel-ma'-im) = Place of
waters; irrigating waters.

Mourning of the waters.

Abelmeholah [Abel
Meholah] (a'-bel-me-ho'-
lah) = Meadow of
dancing; (root = a dance;
dancing; to turn round; to
twist oneself {in pain used
of a woman in labor}; to
dance in a circle).
Mourning for sickness.
Mourning of dancing.

Abelmizraim [Abel
Mizraim] (a'-bel-miz'-ra-
im) = Of Egypt; mourning
of the Egyptians;
mourning of Egypt.

Abelshittim [Abel
Shittim] (a'-bel-shit-tim)
= Plains; meadows of
acacias.

Abez (a'-bez) =
Whiteness; white; to be
white.

Abi (a'-bi) = My father is
Jehovah; the will of God.

Abia (ab-i'-ah) = God my
Father; Jehovah is Father.
Fatherly.

Abiah (ab-i'-ah) = Same
as Abia = God my Father;
Jehovah is Father. My
father is Jah.

Abialbon [Abi-Albon] (ab'-i-al'-bun) = Father of strength; (root = strong). My father is above understanding. Father of understanding.

Abiasaph (ab-i'-as-af) = Father of gathering; remover of reproach; (root = to collect; to gather up; to take away; to vanish).

Abiathar (ab-i'-uth-ur) = Plenty; father of plenty; excellent father; father of superfluity; (root = to abound; to be over and above; to be left; that which is left). Father of the great one.

Abib (a'-bib) = An ear of corn; green ear. First Jewish month (March - April). After the Babylonian exile it was commonly called Nisan.

Abida (ab'-id-ah) = Father of knowledge; my father knows.

Abidah (ab'-id-ah) = Same as Abida = Father of knowledge; my father knows.

Abidan (ab'-id-an) = The father judges; my father judges; father of a judge.

Abiel (a'-be-el) = Father of strength. My father is God (El).

Abiezer (ab-e-e'-zur) = My father will help; in help; father of helps; my father is my help.

Abiezrite [Abi Ezrite] (ab-i-ez'-rite) = Descendants of Abiezer = My father will help; in help; father of helps.

Abigail #1 (ab'-e-gul) = Father of exultation; father of joy; cause of joy; the joy of my father; exultation; joy; gladness; my father is joy.

Abigail #2 (ab'-e-gul) = (2 Samuel 17:25) Father of a heap or billow. Strength

Abihail (ab-e-ha'-il) = Father of might; father or cause of strength; father of splendor; my father is strength.

Abihu (a-bi'-hew) = He (God) is my father; whose father is he; he is my father.

Abihud (a-bi'-hud) =
Father of honor; father of
majesty; father of praise;
my father is majesty.

Abijah (a-bi'-jah) = Same
as Abia and Abiah = God
my Father; Jehovah is my
Father. My father is Jah.

Abijam (a-bi'-jum) =
Father of the sea. Father of
light.

Abilene (ab-i-le'-ne) = A
grassy place.

Abimael (a-bim'-ah-el) =
My father is God. My God
is father.

Abimelech (a-bim'-e-lek)
= Father of the king; my
father is king.

Abinadab (a-bin'-ah-dab)
= Father of nobility; my
father is noble; father or
source of liberality; the
father liberal.

Abiner (ab'-i-ner) = My
father is a lamp.

Abinoam (a-bin'-o-am) =
Father of pleasantness;
father of beauty; father of
grace.

Abiram (a-bi'-rum) =
Father of loftiness; father
is the exalted one; the
renowned father; father of
altitude.

Abishag (ab'-e-shag) =
Father of error; my father
wanders or errs; my father
causes wandering; the
father is a wanderer.

Abishai (ab'-e-shahee) =
Father of a gift; possessor
of all that is desirable; my
father's gift.

Abishaloam (a-bish'-ah-
lum) = Father of peace.

Abishua (a-bish'-u-ah) =
Father of welfare; father
of safety or salvation; my
father is salvation; father
of riches.

Abishur (ab'-e-shur) =
Father of the wall; father
of oxen; my father is a
wall (strong). Father of
beholding; father of the
singer.

Abital (ab'-e-tal) = Father
of dew; whose father is a
dew; my father is dew.

Abitub (ab'-e-tub) =
Father of goodness; father
or source of goodness.

Abiud (a-bi'-ud) = Father of honor; father of trustworthiness.

Abner (ab'-nur) = Father of light. The father's candle.

Abraham (a'-bra-ham) = Father of a multitude; father of a great multitude; father of mercy; a father of many nations.

Abram (a'-brum) = A high father; father of height; the exalted father; high and lofty thinker; high or honored father.

Abrech (Ab'-rech) = I will cause blessing; tender father.

Absalom (ab'-sal-um) = Father of peace; my father is peace.

Accad (ak'-kad) = Fortress; band; chain; i.e., fortress, citadel, castle; (root = to bind; to fortify {a city}). Only a pitcher.

Accho (ak'-ko) = Sand heated; sand made warm by the sun; (root = Arab: To strike; to smite; to be hot {as the day}; to be touched or struck by the sun). His straightness.

Aceldama (as-el'-dam-ah) = Field of blood.

Achaia (ak-ah'-yah) = Trouble. Wailing.

Achaicus (ak-ah'-yah-cus) = Belonging to Achaia = Trouble. Wailing.

Achan (a'-kan) = Serpent; vexation; trouble.

Achar (a'-kar) = Tribulation; trouble; to disturb; to trouble; vexation; (root = to trouble; to disturb).

Achaz (a'-kaz) = Possessor.

Achbor (ak'-bor) = A mouse.

Achim (a'-kim) = Jehovah will establish. Without winter.

Achish (a'-kish) = Serpent charmer; angry; a hard place. I will blacken (or terrify).

Achmetha (ak'-meth-ah) = Fortress; a citadel. Brother of death.

Achor (a'-kor) = Trouble;

tribulation; (roots = [1] to make deep; [2] causing of sorrow).

Achsa (ak'-sah) = Adorned; anklet; an ornament for the feet.

Achsah (ak'-sah) = Same as Achsa = Adorned; anklet; an ornament for the feet. Bursting the veil.

Achshaph (ak'-shaf) = Enchantment. I will be bewitched.

Achzib (ak'-zib) = A deceiver; deceit; lying.

Adadah (ad'-ah-ah) = Festival. Forever adorned.

Adah (a'-dah) = Ornament; to adorn; adornment; beauty; pleasure; (roots = [1] whom Jehovah adorns; [2] ornament from Jehovah).

Adaiah (ad-a-i'-yah) = Jehovah has adorned; pleasing to Jehovah; whom Jehovah adorns; ornament of the LORD. Adorned of Jah.

Adalia (ad-al-i'yah) = Upright; the honor of Ized.

Adam (ad'-um) = Earthy or red earth; of the ground; taken out of the red earth; (root = to be red; ruddy).

Adamah (ad'-am-ah) = Red earth; the ground; (root = the ground; field).

Adami (ad'-am-i) = Human. Man of _____ (add word that follows).

Adar #1 (a'-dar) = Wide; (root = to be wide; to be made great). Height. Glorious. Fire god; fire; adorned. Twelfth Jewish month (February-March).

Adar #2 (a'-dar) = (Joshua 15:3) Exceeding glorious.

Adar Sheni (a'-dar-she-ni) = Thirteenth Jewish month (intercalary month).

Adbeel (ad'-be-el) = Sorrow of God; languishing for God; miracle of God. Chastened of God.

Addan (ad'-dan) = Humble; calamity.

Addar (ad'-dar) = Greatness; height; honorable.

Addi (ad'-di) = My witness; adorned; ornament.

Addon (ad'-don) = Same as Addan = Humble; calamity. Misfortune.

Ader (a'-dur) = A flock. Caretaker.

Adiel (a'-de-el) = Ornament of God.

Adin (a'-din) = Delicate; ornament; slender; soft. Given to pleasure.

Adina (ad'-in-ah) = Pleasant; ornament. Voluptuous.

Adino (ad'-in-o) = Whose pleasure is the spear; his bending of the spear. Delicate; ornament. Luxuriousness.

Adithaim (ad-ith-a'-im) = Two fold ornament. Double ornament.

Adlai (ad'-la-i) = Justice of Jehovah; just; weary. The prey is mine.

Admah (ad'-mah) = Same as Adamah = Earthy; red earth.

Admatha (ad'-math-ah) = God given. Her earthiness.

Adna (ad'-nah) = Pleasure.

Adnah #1 (ad'-nah) = Pleasure; favorite brother.

Adnah #2 (ad'-nah) = (2 Chronicles 12:20) Resting forever.

Adonibezek [Adoni Bezek] (ad'-on-i-be'-zek) = Lord of Bezek; Adoni = Lord; Bezek = A flash of lightning; to be lower; to judge; to domineer). Lord of lightning.

Adonijah (ad-on-i'-jah) = Jehovah is my LORD; LORD of the LORD; my LORD God. My Lord is Jah.

Adonikam (ad-on-i'-kam) = My lord has risen; my Lord has raised me; lord of enemies.

Adoniram (ad-on-i'-ram) = My lord is high; the lord of might; lord of height.

Adonizedek [Adoni Zedek] (ad-on-i- ze'-dek) = Lord of justice; (roots = [1] straightness; rectitude; justice; [2] to be straight;

to be righteous). My lord righteous.

Adoraim (ad-o-ra'-im) = Two chiefs; two fold habitation; (roots = to dwell; to inhabit). Double glory.

Adoram (ad-o'-ram) = Same as Adoniram = My lord is high; the lord of might; lord of height. Adorned; high honor or strength. Their glory.

Adrammelech (a-dram'-mel-ek) = Magnificence of the king; king of fire; the adorned king; honor of the king; Adar is king.

Adramyttium (a-drammit'-te-um) = I shall abide in death. Not in the race.

Adria (a'-dre-ah) = Without wood.

Adriel (a'-dre-el) = Flock of God; honor of flock of God. My Shepherder (the One who is very personally and intensely involved in my life) is God.

Adullam (a-dul'-lam) = Justice of the people; their testimony.

Addulamite (a-dul'-lam-ite) = Same as Adullam = Justice of the people; their testimony.

Adummim (a-dum'-mim) = The red earth. The going up of Adummim = The going up of the red earths; (roots = [1] an ascent; an acclivity; [2] to go up; to be high; [3] *pl.*—red; ruddy).

Aeneas (e'-ne-as) = Praiseworthy; praise.

Aenon (e'-non) = Springs; (Hebrew - fountain). To praise.

Agabus (ag'-ab-us) = A locust. A grasshopper.

Agag (a'-gag) = Flaming; to burn; to blaze as fire; warlike; lofty. I will overtop.

Agagite (ag'-ag-ite) = Same as Agag = Flaming; to burn; to blaze as fire; warlike; lofty.

Agar (a'-gar) = Same as Hagar = Flight; (root = to flee). Came to mean = Fugitive; immigrant. The sojourner.

Agee (ag'-ee) = Fugitive.

Agrippa (ag-rip'-pah) = One who at his birth causes pain. Horse hunter.

Agur (a'-gur) = An assembler; gatherer; (root = to gather in; to collect).

Ahab (a'-hab) = The brother of my father; my father's brother.

Aharah (a-har'-ah) = After a brother; brother of Rach. Brother of breathing; Remaining brother.

Aharhel (a-har'-hel) = Behind the breastwork; what is behind; (root = to be in pain; to tremble; to bring forth {outwork}).

Ahasai (a-ha'-sa-i) = My holder or protector; clear sighted; possessor of God. My possessions.

Ahasbai (a-has'-ba-i) = I flee to the lord; to flee; to take refuge. Shining.

Ahasuerus (a-has-u-e'-rus) = King or mighty man; prince of the people; i.e., lion king; also called Xerxes.

Ahava (a-ha'-vah) = Brotherhood; (Latin = water). I shall subsist.

Ahaz (a'-haz) = Possessor; helper; Jehovah hath seized or sustains.

Ahaziah (a-haz-i'-ah) = Whom Jehovah upholds; Jehovah holds or possesses; taken by God.

Ahban (ah'-ban) = Brotherly; brother of the prudent; brother of intelligence; (roots = [1] brother; [2] to distinguish; to discern; to be prudent). Brother of understanding.

Aher (a'-hur) = Coming slowly; following another; one that is behind; (root = to be behind; to tarry). Another.

Ahi (a'-hi) = Brother; my brother; brother of Jehovah.

Ahiah (a'-hi-ah) = Brother of the LORD; Jehovah is my brother; i.e., friend.

Ahiam (a-hi'-am) = A brother's mother; a mother's brother.

Ahian (a-hi'-an) = Brotherly; fraternal; brother of day. Brother of them.

Ahiezer (a-hi-e'-zer) = Brother of help, (from the idea of surrounding, girding, and defending).

Ahihud (a-hi'-hud) = Brother; friend of the Jews (to make oneself a Jew). Brother of majesty.

Ahijah (a-hi'-jah) = Same as Ahiah = Brother of the LORD; Jehovah is my brother; i.e., friend.

Ahikam (a-hi'-kam) = Brother of rising up; brother of the enemy (in the sense of rising up); my brother has risen or appeared.

Ahilud (a-hi'-lud) = Brother of one born; (root = to bring forth; to bear, as a mother); my brother born.

Ahimaaz (a-him'-a-az) = Brother of anger; a rascal; powerful brother; my brother is counselor.

Ahiman (a-hi'-man) = Brother of gift; who is my brother; my brother is gifted.

Ahimelech (a-him'-el-ek) = Brother of the king; my brother is king.

Ahimoth (a-hi'-moth) = Brother of death.

Ahinadab (a-hin'-ad-ab) = Brother of nobility; brother of liberality.

Ahinoam (a-hin'-o-am) = Brother of grace; the brother pleasant; brother of pleasantries.

Ahio (a-hi'-o) = Brotherly; his brother.

Ahira (a-hi'-rah) = Brother of evil; (root = evil; bad; noxious; to be evil).

Ahiram (a-hi'-rum) = Brother of height; to lift up oneself; exalted brother.

Ahiramites (a-hi'-rum-ites) = Descendants of Ahiram = Brother of height; to lift up oneself; exalted brother.

Ahisamach (a-his'-am-ak) = Brother of support;

(root = to sustain; to be propped).

Ahishahar (a-hish'-a-har) = Brother of the dawn or morning; (root = to break forth).

Ahishar (a-hi'shar) = Brother of firmness; (root = to be firm; hard; to press together).The brother of song; brother of a singer.

Ahithophel (a-hith'-o-fel) = Brother of folly; impiety; (root = unsalted; untempered; to be unseasoned). Brother of supplication.

Ahitub (a-hi'-tub) = Brother of goodness; brother of benevolence; (root = to be good; to be beautiful). The best brother.

Ahlab (ah'-lab) = Fatness; fertility; a fertile place.

Ahlai (ah'-lahee) = Oh that!; O would that!; would to God; (roots = [1] to be polished; smooth; [2] to stroke; to soothe). Jehovah is staying.

Ahoah (a-ho'-ah) = Same as Ahijah and Ahiah =

Brother of the LORD; Jehovah is my brother; i.e., friend. A brother's need. Brother of rest.

Ahohite (a-ho'-hite) = Brother of rest. Same as Ahoah = Same as Ahijah and Ahiah = Brother of the LORD; Jehovah is my brother; i.e., friend. A brother's need.

Aholah (a-ho'-lah) = (She has) her own tent; a tent. (Used to describe Samaria see **Aholibah**).

Aholiab (a-ho'-lee-ab) = Tabernacle of my father; her father's tent; tent of the father.

Aholibah (a-hol'-ib-ah) = My tabernacle in her; my tent is in her; (used to describe Jerusalem see **Aholah**. Together they represent Jerusalem/ Samaria in their adulteries) (Ezekiel 23:4).

Aholibamah (a-hol'-ib-a'-mah) = Tent of the high place; my tent on high.

Ahumai (a-hoo'-mahee) = Brother of waters; dwelling near water.

Ahuzam (a-hoo'-zam) = Their possession; possession; a holding fast.

Ahuzzath (a-huz'-zath) = A possession; holding fast.

Ai (a'-i) = A heap of ruins; (root = to bend; to twist; to distort; to act perversely; to subvert; sin; to contort with pain as in a woman giving birth).

Aiah (a-i'-ah) = A little hawk. A vulture or bird of prey.

Aiath (a-i'ath) = Same as Ai = A heap of ruins; (root = to bend; to twist; to distort; to act perversely; to subvert; to sin; to contort with pain as in a woman giving birth). A steep place or valley.

Aija (a-i'-jah) = Same as Ai and Aiath = A heap of ruins; (root = to bend; to twist; to distort; to act perversely; to subvert; to sin; to contort with pain as in a woman giving birth). A steep place or valley.

Aijalon (a-ij'-el-on) = A large stag; place of gazelles; a swift hind. A deer field.

Aijeleth Shahar (a-ij'-el-eth sha'-har) = Morning hind. (Psalm 22 title).

Ain (a'-in) = Fountain; an eye or fountain.

Ajah (a'-jah) = Same as Aiah = A little hawk. A vulture or bird of prey.

Ajalon (aj'-a-lon) = Same as Aijalon = A large stag; place of gazelle; a swift hind.

Akan (a'-kan) = Torques; acute; twisted; (root = to twist; to wrest). Oppression.

Akkub (ak'kub) = Insidious; cunning; artful; lain in wait; (root = to be behind; to come from behind; to trip up; to supplant). Subtle. Literally: to take by the heel.

Akrabbim (ac-rab'-bim) = Assent of scorpions.

Alameth (al'-am-eth) = Covering; (root = to hide; to cover). Youthful vigor. Concealment.

Alammelech (a-lam'-mel-ek) = Oak of the king; king's oak.

Alamoth (al'-am-oth) = Virgins. (Psalm 46 title). Hiding places.

Alemeth (al-e'-meth) = A hiding place or covering.

Alexander (al-ex-an'-dur) = Defending men; man defender; defender; helper of men; one who turns away evil.

Alexandria(ns) (al-ex-an'-dree-ah) = Same as Alexander = Defending men; man defender; defender; helper of men; one who turns away evil.

Algum (al'-gum) = not drunken ones; not added ones (?).

Aliah (a-li'-ah) = Evil. Same as Alvah = Iniquity. Sublimity.

Alian (a-li'-un) = Tall. Same as Alvan = Unrighteous. Sublime.

Alleluia (al-le-loo'-yah) = Closest definition: Praise ye the LORD.

Allon (al'-lon) = An oak; (root = to roll; to be thick).

Allonbachuth [Allon Bachuth] (al"-lon-bak'-ooth) = Oak of weeping; (root = to flow by drops; to weep for; to bewail).The weeping oak.

Almighty (ol-mit'-e) = Shaddai; the Almighty.

Almodad (al-mo'-dad) = Immeasurable; increasing without measure; extension. The agitator.

Almon (al'-mon) = Hidden; (root = to hide; to conceal).

Almondiblathaim [Almon Diblathaim] (al'-mon-dib-lath-a'-im) = Hiding of the two cakes.

Aloth (a'-loth) = Yielding milk. The heights; mistresses.

Alpha (al'-fah) = The beginning. (First letter of the Greek alphabet).

Alphaeus (al-fe'-us) = Successor. Transient; chief. Produce; gain. Hebrew: My exchanges.

Altaschith (al-tas'-kith) = Do not destroy. (Title of

Psalms 57, 58, 59, 75). You may not destroy.

Alush (a'-lush) = A crowd of men. I will knead (bread).

Alvah (al'-vah) = Iniquity; (root = to turn aside; to distort; to be wicked). Above is Jah. Sublimity; high.

Alvan (al'-vah) = Unrighteous; sublime. Their ascent; iniquitous ones.

Amad (a'-mad) = Eternal people.

Amal (a'-mal) = Troublesome; labor; sorrow; (root = to labor the product of labor; heavy, wearisome labor; trouble; sorrow).

Amalek (am'-al-ek) = A people that lick up or exhaust; people of lapping; a strangler of the people, (a type of the flesh = Exodus 17:8, 13, 16). Warlike; a dweller in the vale.

Amalekites (am'-al-ek-ites) = Descendants of Amalek = A people that

lick up or exhaust; people of lapping; a strangler of the people. Warlike; a dweller in the vale.

Amam (a'-mam) = People; (root = idea of joining together a metropolis). Their mother.

Amana (am-a'-nah) = A confirmation; truth; integrity; (roots = [1] to nurse; to stay; to support; [2] to be faithful). Constancy; a settled provision.

Amariah (am-a-ri'-ah) = Jehovah has said; Jehovah has promised; whom Jehovah spoke of; the speech of the LORD.

Amasa (am'-a-sah) = Burden; burden-bearer. An exalter of the people.

Amasai (am'-as-ahee) = Burden of the LORD; burdensome. My burdens.

Amashai (am'-ash-ahee) = Carrying spoil; burden-bearer. People of my spoilers.

Amasiah (am-a-si'-ah) = Carried of the LORD; burden of Jehovah;

Jehovah is strong. Laden of Jah.

Amaziah (am-a-zi'-ah) = Strength of the LORD; made strong for the LORD; Jehovah strengthens; Jehovah has strength. Strength of Jah.

Amen (a'-men) = So be it; very truly; verily.

Amethyst (am'e-thyst) = Dream stone (Literally, I shall be brought back, as from a dream.)

Ami (a'-mi) = The beginning. Bond-servant.

Aminadab (a-min'-a-dab) = The kinsman is generous.

Amittai (a-mit'-tahee) = Truth of the LORD; true; truthful; (root = to be firm; faithful). My faithfulness.

Ammah (am'-mah) = Beginning. A cubit.

Ammi (am'-mi) = My people.

Ammiel (am'-me-el) = People of God; a devoted ally or kinsman of God.

Ammihud (am-mi'-hud) = People of praise; man of praiseworthiness. People of majesty.

Ammihur (am-mi'-hur) = My people are noble.

Amminadab (am-min'-a-dab) = People of liberality; my liberal people. My people are willing; my kinsman is generous.

Amminadib (am-min'-a-dib) = Same as Amminadab = People of liberality; my liberal people. My people are willing; my kinsman is generous. My people are liberal or princely.

Ammishaddai (am-mi-shad'-dahee) = People of the Almighty; (root = {has concept of strength} most powerful; to be strong; to act violently; to lay waste). An ally is the Almighty.

Ammizabad (am-miz'-a-bad) = People of the bountiful giver. The kinsman has endowed. People of the endower.

Ammon (am'-mon) = Great people; son of my people; pertaining to the nation; people of strength. Tribal.

Ammonite(s) (am'-mon-ites) = Descendants of Ammon = Great people; son of my people; pertaining to the nation; people of strength.

Amnon #1 (am'-non) = Faithful; tutelage; (root = to sustain). A faithful son.

Amnon #2 (a'-mon) = (2 Samuel 13:20) Made faithful.

Amok (a'-mok) = Deep; (root = to be deep; to be unsearchable; to deepen).

Amon (a'-mon) = A nourisher; a nurse or a multitude. Faithful. Security. A workman.

Amorite(s) (am'-o-rite) = Mountaineer. A talker. A slayer.

Amos (a'-mos) = Burden; burden-bearer; one with a burden.

Amoz (a'-moz) = Strong; strength; brass; (root = to be firm; strong). Courageous.

Amphipolis (am-fip'-o-lis) = A city surrounded by the sea; (root = around; *plural* both). Around the city.

Amplias (am'-ple-as) = Enlarged; large.

Amram #1 (am'-ram) Intensely red; (root = to boil up; to ferment). A son of Dishon, a descendant of Esau.

Amram(s) #2 (am'-ram) = People of exaltation; i.e., illustrious; a people exalted; kindred of the Most High; people of the Highest; (i.e., = God). A son of Kohath and father of Aaron and Moses; a son of Bani.

Amramites (am'-ram-ites) = Descendants of Amram #2 = People of exaltation; i.e., illustrious; a people exalted; kindred of the Most High; people of the Highest; i.e., God. A son of Kohath and father of Aaron and Moses; a son of Bani.

Amraphel (am'-raf-el) = One that speaks of dark things; an obscure speech.

The circle of the few. Powerful people. Sayer of darkness; fall of the sayer.

Amzi (am'-zi) = Strong; robust; my strength.

Anab (a'-nab) = A place fertile in grapes.

Anah (a'-nah) = An answer; answering; respond; one who answers or sings; (root = to sing; to cry out; to praise; to reply). One who is poor or afflicted.

Anaharath (an-a-ha'-rath) = Hollow way; pass. The groaning of fear.

Anaiah (an-a-i'-ah) = Answered of the LORD; Jehovah has answered. Afflicted (or answered) of Jah.

Anak (a'-nak) = Long necked; giant. Neck chain.

Anakims (an'-ak-ims) = Descendants of Anak = Long necked; giant. Neck Chain.

Anamim (an'-am-im) = Responding waters. Affliction (or answer) of the waters.

Anammelech (a-nam'-mel-ek) = Idol or statue of the king; the king's answer. The affliction of the king.

Anan (a'nan) = A cloud; he beclouds or covers.

Anani (an-a'ni) = Cloud of the LORD; covered with God. My cloud.

Ananiah (an-an-i'-ah) = Whom Jehovah covers; (cloud of the LORD); Jehovah is a protector.

Ananias (an-an-i'-as) = Jehovah is gracious.

Anath (a'-nath) = An answer to prayer; answer or a granting.

Anathema (a-nath'-em-ah) = Something accursed.

Anathoth (an'-a-thoth) = Answers to prayer. Afflictions.

Andrew (an'-drew) = Manliness.

Andronicus (an-dro-ni'-cus) = Conqueror; conquering men. Victory of man.

Anem (a'-nem) = Two fountains.

Aner (a'-nur) = Exile; to shake out; to drive out. Waterfall; affliction. Chaldean: A lamp; light. A lamp swept away.

Anethothite (an'-e-thoth-ite) = Same as Anathoth = Answers to prayer. Afflictions.

Anetothite (an'-e-toth-ite) = Same as Anathoth = Answers to prayer. Afflictions.

Aniam (a'-ne-am) = Sorrow of the people; sighing of the people.

Anim (a'-nim) = Two fountains.

Anna (an'-nah) = Grace.

Annas (an'-nas) = Grace of Jehovah; humble. Greek form of Hananiah = Whom Jehovah graciously gave.

Antichrist (an'-ti-krist) = Adversary to Christ; against Christ. An opponent of the Messiah. Translated from the Greek word antichristos, (an-tee'-khris-tos).

Antioch (an'-te-ok) = Driven against. (The capitol of the Greek kings of Syria. Later, residence of Roman governors of the province of Antioch).

Antipas (an'-tip-as) = Likeness of his father. Against all; against fatherland.

Antipatris (an-tip'-at-ris) = Same as Antipas = Likeness of his father. Against (or instead of) one's country.

Antothijah (an-to-thi'-jah) = Prayers answered by Jehovah; answer (or afflictions) of Jehovah.

Antothite (an'-to-thite) = A man of Anathoth = Answers to prayer.

Anub (a'-nub) = Bound together; to bind together. Strong; high. Clustered.

Apelles (a-pel'-leze) = Separate; exclude. Without receptacle (hide).

Apharsachites (a-far'-sak-ites) = As causers of division(?)

18

Apharsathchites (a-far'-sath-kites) = I will divide the deceivers(?); investigator(?)

Apharsites (a-far'-sites) = Causers of division(?)

Aphek (a'-fek) = Strength; fortified city; (roots = [1] to be strong; mighty; [2] to hold fast). Restrained.

Aphekah (af-e'-kah) = Strength. Restraint.

Aphiah (af-i'-ah) = Rekindled; refreshed; revivified. I will make to breathe.

Aphik (a'-fik) = Channel; strong; (roots = [1] a channel; bed of a stream; [2] to be strong). Restraint.

Aphrah (af'-rah) = Dust. Dust-heap.

Aphses (af'-seze) = Dispersion; the dispersed; (root = to disperse; to break in pieces; to scatter). The shattering.

Apollonia (ap-ol-lo'-ne-ah) = Belonging to Apollo; (root = to perish; to destroy). Utter destruction. A city of Macedonia named for the pagan deity Apollon.

Apollos (ap-ol'-los) = A destroyer; youthful god of music.

Apollyon (ap-ol'-le-on) = One that exterminates; destroyer.

Appaim (ap'-pa-im) = Face; presence. Two breathing places; i.e., the nostrils or two persons; a double portion. Double-nosed.

Apphia (af'-fee-ah) = That which is fruitful. A dear one.

Appii forum [Forum of Appius] (ap'-pe-i for'-em) = Persuasive mart. Hebrew: I shall be nourished. (The forum or market place of Appius.)

Aquila (ac'-quil-ah) = Hebrew: I shall be nourished; Latin: Eagle. Greek: Immovable.

Ar (ar) = City. Awakening.

Ara (a'-rah) = Congregation; a lion;

(roots = [1] to pluck; to cut down; by plucking; [2] a lion so denominated from its plucking to pieces). Strong. I shall see(?)

Arab (a'-rab) = Fugitive; ambush; to lie in wait; to lie in ambush.

Arabah (ar'-ab-ah) = A plain; a wilderness; a desert. The desert plain.

Arabia (a-ra'-be-ah) = Desert; sterile; (in the OT referred to as the east country; sons of the east). Evening; of the mingled people. Mixed; dusky.

Arabian(s) (a-ra'-be-un) = Dweller in sterile region.

Arad (a'-rad) = Wild ass; fugitive.

Arah (a'-rah) = Wandering; wayfarer; (root = to walk; to travel). Literal: he wandered.

Aram (a'-ram) = High; elevated; lifted up; magnified; exalted.

Aramitess (a'ram-i-tes) = Highlandress; (A female

inhabitant of Aram = High; elevated; lifted up; magnified. The exalted of Jah.

Aramnaharaim [Aram Naharaim] (a'-ram-na-ha-ra'im) = Aram of the two rivers. (Psalm 60 title). Highland of the two rivers.

Aramzobah [Aram Zobah] (a'-ram-zo'-bah) = Exalted station; exalted conflict. (Psalm 60 title, #2).

Aran (a'-ran) = Wild goat; firmness. I shall shout for joy.

Ararat (ar'-ar-at) = Mountain of descent. Chaldean: The trembling light; mount. The curse reversed; precipitation of a curse.

Araunah (a-raw'-nah) = Jehovah is firm. Ash; a large ash or pine; (idea of a tremulous and tinkling or creaking sound, as of a tall tree vibrating). An ark; chest. I will shout for joy. (2 Samuel 24:16 - joyful shouting of Jah).

Arba (ar'-bah) = Foursquare; perfect

stature. The croucher or strength of Baal. Four.

Arbah (ar'-bah) = Same as Arba = Foursquare; perfect stature. The croucher or strength of Baal. Four.

Arbathite (ar'-bath-ite) = Same as Betharabah = House of the desert.

Arbel (ar'-bel) = Same as Betharbel = House of the ambush of God.

Arbite (ar'-bite) = Inhabitants of Arabia = Ambush; to lie in wait; to lie in ambush.

Archelaus (ar-ke-la'-us) = Prince; people's chief. Ruling the people.

Archevites (ar'-ke-vites) = Inhabitants of Erech = Length; to make long; to prolong.

Archi (ar'-kee) = Inhabitants of Erech = Length; to make long; to prolong.

Archippus (ar-kip'-pus) = Master of the horse. Horse chief.

Archite (ar'-kite) =

Inhabitants of Erech = Length; to make long; to prolong.

Arcturus (ark-tu'-rus) = A moth. Consuming.

Ard (ard) = Fugitive; descent. I shall subdue.

Ardites (ar'-dites) = Descendants of Ard = Fugitive; descent. I shall subdue.

Ardon (ar'-don) = Fugitive; descendant.

Areli (a-re'-li) = Lion of my God; heroic; valiant. A lion is my God; he cursed my God.

Arelites (a-re'-lites) = Descendants of Areli = Lion of my God; heroic; valiant. A lion is my god; he cursed my God.

Areopagite (a-re-op'-a-jite) = Martial peak. (Name given to members of the Court of Areopagus [Mars Hill]).

Areopagus (a-re-op'-a-gus) = Martial peak.

Aretas (ar'-e-tas) = A husbandman. Pleasing; virtuous.

21

Argob (ar'-gob) = Heap of stones; a rocky district; strong. A lion's den.

Aridai (a-rid'-a-i) = Gift of the plough or the bull. The lion is enough.

Aridatha (a-rid'-a-thah) = Great or noble birth. The lion of the decree.

Arieh (a-ri'-eh) = Lion. Lion of Jehovah.

Ariel (a'-re-el) = Lion of God; altar of God; God's altar-hearth.

Arimathaea (ar-im-ath-e'-ah) = Same as Ramah = Lofty or high place.

Arioch (a'-re-ok) = The mighty lion. Lionlike; servant; the moon-god.

Arisai (a-ris'-a-i) = Like to a lion. Lionlike; the form of a lion.

Aristarchus (ar-is-tar'-cus) = Best ruling; the best ruler.

Aristobulus (a-ris-to-bu'-lus) = Best counselor.

Arkite (ar'-kite) = Fugitive; (root = to flee; to gnaw). My gnawing.

Armageddon (ar-mag-ed'-don) = Height of Megiddo; hill of Megiddo = Place of crowds. Hill of slaughter.

Armenia (ar-me'-ne-ah) = Same as Ararat. Mountain of descent. Chaldean: The trembling light. The curse reversed; precipitation of a curse.

Armoni (ar-mo'-ni) = Belonging to a palace; pertaining to the palace.

Arnan (ar'-nan) = Nimble; active; strong; agile; (root = to be agile). Lion of perpetuity.

Arni (ar'-ni) = Rejoicing.

Arnon (ar'-non) = Murmuring; roaring; i.e., a sounding torrent; (root = to emit a tremulous sound; to vibrate the voice; to shout for joy {also from root = swift or noisy} suiting the character of the stream).

Arod (a'-rod) = Wild ass; posterity. I will subdue; I will roam.

Arodi (ar'-o-di) = Wild ass.

Arodites (a'-ro-dites) = Descendants of Arod = Wild ass; posterity.

Aroer (ar'-o-ur) = A naked tree; (root = to make naked; to be helpless). Childless; empty. Destitute.

Aroerite (ar'-o-ur-ite) = Descendants of Aroer = A naked tree; (root = to make naked; to be helpless). Childless; empty.

Arpad (ar'-pad) = Support; to prop; rest; strength; (root = to lay out in a bed; to support). I shall be spread out (or supported).

Arphad (ar'-fad) = Same as Arpad = Support; to prop; rest; strength; (root = to lay out in a bed; to support). I shall be spread out (or supported).

Arphaxad (ar-fax'-ad) = One that releases. Boundary of the Chaldeans. A jar pouring forth. I shall fail at the breast.

Artaxerxes (ar-tax-erx'-ees) = A great king; honored king. Possessor of an exalted kingdom. Persian: a quiet light. I will make the spoiled to boil; I will stir myself in water; or I will make the sixth to boil; I will stir myself with drink.

Artemas (ar'-te-mas) = Whole; sound. Safe and sound.

Aruboth (ar'-u-both) = Flood gates; (roots = [1] a window; a chimney; a smoke hole; [2] to lie in wait).

Arumah (a-ru'-mah) = Elevated. I shall be exalted.

Arvad (ar'-vad) = Place of fugitives; wandering. I shall break loose.

Arvadites (ar'-vad-ites) = Inhabitants of Arvad = Place of fugitives; wandering. I shall break loose.

Arza (ar'-zah) = Earth. Firm; delight.

Asa (a'-sah) = Physician. Healer.

23

Asahel (as'-a-hel) = Made of God; God has made; God is doer; whom God made; the work of God; (root = to make; to produce; to labor; to prepare; to appoint).

Asahiah (as-a-hi'-ah) = Made of Jehovah; Jehovah has made.

Asaiah (as-a'-yah) = Same as Asahiah = Made of Jehovah; Jehovah has made. Jehovah is doer.

Asaph (a'-saf) = Collector; to collect together; to draw up; to gather up the rear. He that gathered or removed reproach.

Asareel (a-sar'-e-el) = God is joined. Whom God has bound; bound of God. I shall be prince of God.

Asarelah (as-a-re'-lah) = Upright to God; upright toward God; right before God. Guided towards God.

Asenath (as'-e-nath) = Who belongs to Neith; she who is of Neith (an Egyptian goddess).

Egyptian = Mischief. I shall be hated; she has stored up.

Aser (a'-sur) = Same as Asher = Fortunate; happy.

Ashan (a'-shan) = Smoke.

Ashbea (ash'-be-ah) = I conjure; I adjure; (root = to swear). Man of Baal; let me call as witness. I shall be made to swear.

Ashbel (ash'-bel) = Fire of Bel; vain fire; fire of old age; to waste away; to consume. Man of Baal.

Ashbelites (ash'-bel-ites) = Descendants of Ashbel = Fire of Bel; vain fire; fire of old age; to waste away; to consume. Man of Baal.

Ashchenaz (ash'-ke-naz) = A fire is scattered; a fire that spreads.

Ashdod (ash'-dod) = A fortified place; a strong place; to be strong; powerful; only used in a bad sense to oppress; to spoil; to act violently. A friend to fire.

Ashdodites (ash'-dodites) = Inhabitants of Ashdod = Divided rock; fragment of hewn rock; to divide; to cut up.

Ashdoth (ash'-doth) = Same as Pisgah = Divided rock; fragment of hewn rock; to divide; to cut up.

Ashdothites (ash'-doth-ites) = Same as Ashdodites = Inhabitants of Ashdod = Divided rock; fragment of hewn rock; to divide; to cut up.

Ashdothpisgah (ash'doth-piz'gah) = Springs of Pisgah = Divided rock; fragment of hewn rock; to divide; to cut up. Spoilers of the survey.

Asher (ash'-ur) = Same as Aser = Fortunate; happy. Fortress.

Asherah (ashe'-rah) = She who enriches; (an idol/image of Ashtoreth). Word is also translated "grove" in the KJV; e.g., 2 Kings 21:7; 23:6.

Asherites (ash'-ur-ites) = Descendants of Asher = Fortunate; happy.

Ashima (ash'-im-ah) = A goat without wool; a fault; an offense. Guiltiness; I will make desolate.

Ashkelon (ash'-ke-lon) = Same as Askelon = Migration; taken. The fire of infamy; I shall be weighed.

Ashkenaz (ash'-ke-naz) = Same as Ashchenaz = A fire is scattered.

Ashnah (ash'-nah) = Strong; mighty. I will cause change.

Ashpenaz (ash'-pe-naz) = Horse's nose. I will make prominent the sprinkled.

Ashriel (ash'-re-el) = Same as Asriel = Vow of God; (root = to bind to make fast; to put in chains; to make a prisoner). I shall be prince of God.

Ashtaroth (ash'-ta-roth) = Star; Astartes; i.e., statues of Astarte or Ashtoreth; groves of Ashtoreth. Rich pastures.

Ashterathite (ash'-ter-a-thite) = An inhabitant of Ashtaroth = Star; Astartes;

i.e., statues of Astarte or Astoreth; groves of Astoreth. Rich pastures.

Ashteroth (ash'-ta'roth) = Same as Ashtaroth = Star; Astartes; i.e., statues of Astarte or Ashtoreth; groves of Ashtoreth. Rich pastures.

Ashteroth Karnaim (ash'-te-roth kar-na-im) = Ashtaroth of the two horns; the crescent moons (the new moon). Double horned mind readers.

Ashterothite (ash'-ter-o-thite) = Inhabitants of Ashteroth Karnaim = Ashtaroth of the two horns; the crescent moons (the new moon).

Ashtoreth (ash'-to-reth) = Queen of heaven; she who enriches; (idol represented as a woman with the head of an ox; she was worshiped as the moon). Thought searching.

Ashur (ash'-ur) = Blackness; black; (root = to be black). A watcher. Freeman. I shall be early sought.

Ashurites (ash'-ur-ites) = Inhabitants of Ashur = Blackness; black; (root = to be black). A watcher. Freeman. I shall be early sought.

Ashvath (ash'-vath) = Fabricated. Wrought. Sleek; shinny.

Asia (a'-she-ah) = Orient. Slime; mire. (A Roman province on the western part of Asia Minor).

Asiel (a'-se'-el) = Created by God; God has made.

Askelon (as'-ke-lon) = Same as Ashkelon = Migration; taken. The fire of shame; contempt.

Asnah (as'-nah) = A bramble. A dweller in the thornbush.

Asnapper (as-nap'-pur) = The swift. A dangerous bull. Asnap the great.

Aspatha (as'-pa-thah) = Given by the horse; horse-given. The enticed gathered.

Asriel (as'-re-el) = Vow of God; God is joined; (root = to bind to make fast; to put in chains; to make a prisoner). I shall be prince of God.

Asrielites (as'-re-el-ites) = Descendants of Asriel = The prohibition of God.

Asshur (ash'-ur) = A step; going forward; (root = to go straight on; to be fortunate). Lifted up; exalted. Level plain.

Asshurim (ash'-u-rim) = Steps; going forward; (root = to go straight on). Mighty ones.

Assir (as'-sur) = Captive. Prisoner.

Assos (as'-sos) = Approaching. (A seaport in the Roman province of Asia). Nearer.

Assur (as'-sur) = Same as Asshur = A step; going forward; (root = to go straight on; to be fortunate). Lifted up; exalted. Level plain.

Assyria (as-sir'-e-ah) = The land named for Asshur = A step; (root = to go straight on; to be fortunate). Lifted up;

exalted. Level plain.

Assyrians (as-sir'-e-uns) = Inhabitants of Assyria = The land named from Asshur = A step; (root = to go straight on; to be fortunate). Lifted up; exalted. Level plain.

Astaroth (as'-ta-roth) = Same as Ashtoreth = Queen of heaven; she who enriches.

Asuppim (asup'-pim) = Collected; i.e., a collection (of offerings); (house of) gatherings; storehouse; (root = to gather for any purpose).

Asyncritus (a-sin'-cri-tus) = Incomparable; disciple.

Atad (a'-tad) = Bramble; buck horn. A thorn; a thistle.

Atarah (at'-a-rah) = A crown; (root = to surround).

Ataroth (at'-a-roth) = Crowns.

Atarothadar [Ataroth Adar] (at'-a-roth-a'-dar) = Crowns of greatness; crowns of glory.

Atarothaddar [Ataroth Addar] (at'-a-roth-ad'-dar) = Same as Atarothadar = Crowns of greatness; crowns of glory.

Ater (a'-tur) = Bound; shut; shut up; dumb; (root = to shut; to inclose). Binder, left-handed; i.e., shut as to the right hand.

Athach (a'-thak) = Lodging place. Your due season.

Athaiah (ath-a-i'-ah) = Whom Jehovah made; made opportunity of the LORD; Jehovah is helper. Jah's due season.

Athaliah (ath-a-li'-ah) = Taken away of the LORD; whom Jehovah has afflicted; Jehovah is strong; (root = to handle violently). Due season of Jah.

Athenains (a-the'-ne-uns) = Inhabitants of Athens = Uncertainty.

Athens (ath'-ens) = Uncertainty. (The capitol of Attica. Named after the goddess of wisdom, Athene).

Athlai (ath'-lahee) = Afflicted of the LORD; Jehovah is strong. My due times.

Atroth (a'-troth) = Same as Ataroth = Crowns. Crown of their rapine.

Attai (at'-tahee) = Opportune; opportunity; seasonable. My due seasons.

Attalia (at-ta-li'-ah) = Jah's due season. Gentle father.

Augustus (aw-gus'-tus) = Venerable; sacred; kingly. (Luke 2:1 - radiant).

Ava (a'-vah) = Overturning; (root = to act perversely; to subvert). Perverted.

Aven (a'-ven) = Nothingness. Perverseness.

Avim (a'-vim) = Inhabitants of desert places; (root = to pervert; to sin). Perverters.

Avites (a'-vites) = Perverters.

Avith (a'-vith) = Ruins (of a city), or anything "subverted".

28

Azal (a'-zal) = Noble; root of a mountain; deep rooted; (root = to join together; to put by the side; to separate). He has reserved.

Azaliah (az-a-li'-ah) = Whom Jehovah has reserved; reserved of the LORD; Jehovah is noble; Jehovah has spared; (root = to separate; to reserve).

Azaniah (az-a-ni'-ah) = Whom Jehovah hears; Jehovah is hearer; Jehovah has given ear; heard of the LORD (Jah); (root = to hear and answer).

Azarael (a-zar'-a-el) = Whom God helps; helped of God; God is a helper. The strong one.

Azareel (a-zar'-e-el) = Same as Azarael = Whom God helps; helped of God; God is a helper; (root = to help; to aid).

Azariah (az-a-ri'-ah) = Helped of the LORD; whom Jehovah aids; Jehovah is keeper; Jehovah has helped.

Azaz (a'-zaz) = Strong; (root = to be strong; to be made strong).

Azazel (a-za'-zel) = Goat of departure.

Azaziah (az-a-zi'-ah) = Strengthened of the LORD; whom Jehovah strengthened; Jehovah is strong.

Azbuk (az'-buk) = Strength emptied; (root = to empty; to pour out). Pardon.

Azekah (a-ze'-kah) = Hedged or fenced round. Dug over.

Azel (a'-zel) = Noble; (root = to separate). Reserved.

Azem (a'-zem) = Strength; strenuous; bone.

Azgad (az'-gad) = Worship; supplication; strong of fortune. A mighty troop; strength of God.

Aziel (a'-ze-el) = Comforted of God; whom God strengthens; God is might.

Aziza (a-zi'-zah) = Strong; robust; (root = to be strong). Mightiness.

Azmaveth (az-ma'-veth) = Strong to death; death is strong; counsel.

Azmon (az'-mon) = Strong; (root = to be firm). The mighty.

Aznothtabor [Aznoth Tabor] (az'-noth-ta'-bor) = Ears; (root = to be sharp; to prick up ears). Ears you will purge.

Azor (a'zor) = Helper.

Azotus (a-zo'-tus) = A stronghold. Greek form of Ashdod = A strong place.

Azriel (az'-re-el) = Help of God; God is helper.

Azrikam (az'-ri-kam) = Help against an enemy; my help has risen.

Azubah (a-zu'-bah) = Forsaken; deserted; deserted desolation; (root = to loosen bands; to let go; to leave; to dessert).

Azur (a'-zur) = Same as Azor = Helper.

Azzah (az'-zah) = Strong; fortified.

Azzan (az'-zan) = Very strong; sharp.

Azzur (az'-zur) = Same as Azor = Helper.

Blessed is the nation whose God is the LORD; and the people whom he hath chosen for his own inheritance (Psalms 33:12).

B

Baal (ba'-al) = Lord; master; possessor; controller; possessor of anything; owner.

Baalah (ba'-al-ah) = Mistress; lady; possessing; my master.

Baalath (ba'-al-ath) = Same as Baalah = Mistress; lady; possessing; my master.

Baalathbeer [Baalath

Beer] (ba'-al-ath-be'-ur) = Having a well; lady of the well.

Baalberith [Baal-Berith] (ba'-al-be'rith) = Lord of covenants; master of a covenant.

Baale (ba'-al-eh) = Plural of Baal = Lord; master; possessor; controller; possessor of anything; owner.

Baalgad [Baal Gad] (ba'-al-gad') = Lord of fortune. Master of a troop.

Baalhamon [Baal Hamon] (ba'-al-ha'-mon) = Lord of a multitude; place of a multitude; master of a multitude.

Baalhanan [Baal-Hanan] (ba-al-ha'-nan) = Lord of compassion; the lord is gracious; (roots = [1] lord; [2] to be gracious; to compassionate; to give {anything} graciously). Baal is gracious.

Baalhazor [Baal Hazor] (ba'-al-ha'-zor) = Having a village; fence or castle. Lord of the court; lord of trumpeting.

Baalhermon [Baal Hermon] (ba'-al-her'-mon) = Place of the nose; a devoted master.

Baali (ba'-al-i) = My lord; my master; owner.

Baalim (ba'-al-im) = Idols of Baal; lords; masters.

Baalis (ba'-al-is) = Son of exultation; in rejoicing; the lord of joy or rules. Lord of the banner.

Baalmeon [Baal Meon] (ba'-al-me'-on) = Place of habitation; the master of a dwelling.

Baalpeor [Baal of Peor] (ba'-al-pe'-or) = Lord of the opening; a master of open space.

Baalperazim [Baal Perazim] (ba'-al-per'-a-zim) = Places of breaches; places of overwhelmings; a master of breaches.

Baalshalisha [Baal Shalisha] (ba'-al-shal'-i-shah) = Having a third; the third in rank.

Baaltamar [Baal Tamar] (ba'-al-ta'-mar) = Place of or having palm trees; the master of a palm tree.

31

Baalzebub [Baal-Zebub] (ba'-al-ze'-bub) = Lord of the fly; lord of flies; the master of a fly.

Baalzephon [Baal Zephon] (ba'-al-ze'-fon) = Lord of the north; the master of the north.

Baana (ba'-an-ah) = Son of response; son of grief; son of affliction.

Baanah (ba'-an-ah) = Same as Baana = Son of response; son of grief; son of affliction.

Baara (ba'-ar-ah) = Kindling of the moon; i.e., new moon; (root = to consume with fire; to be kindled; to exterminate). The burning one.

Baaseiah (ba-as-i'-ah) = Work of the LORD; work of Jehovah; Jehovah is bold.

Baasha (ba'-ash-ah) = Wicked; evil; (root = to be evil; to displease). Boldness; offensive; he who lays waste. To compress. Confusion (by mixing).

Babel (ba'-bel) = Confusion; (root = to pour over; to pour together). Greek: to confound. Native etymology is Bab-il = The gate of God.

Babylon (bab'-il-un) = Same as Babel = Confusion; (root = to pour over; to pour together). Greek: To confound.

Babylonians (bab-il-o'-ne-ans) = Inhabitants of Babylon = Confusion; (root = to pour over; to pour together). Greek: To confound.

Babylonish (bab-il-o'-nish) = Of, or belonging to Babylon = Confusion. (root = to pour over; to pour together). Greek: To confound.

Baca (ba'-cah) = Weeping; valley of misery.

Bachrites (bak'-rites) = Descendants of Becher = First born; to come first.

Baharumite (ba-ha'-rum-ite) = Inhabitants of Bahurim = Village (town of) young men.

Bahurim (ba-hu'-rim) = Village (town of) young men. Chosen ones.

Bajith (ba'-jith) = House; place; habitation; the house; temple; i.e., temple of Baal; (root = to build).

Bakbakkar (bak-bak'-kar) = Diligent searching.

Bakbuk (bak'-buk) = A bottle; emptied of everything; (from sound a bottle makes when emptied); (root = to pour out; to empty). A flagon or hollow.

Bakbukiah (bak-buk-i'-ah) = Emptying (i.e., wasting) of Jehovah; wasting by Jehovah. Effusion of Jehovah.

Balaam (ba'-la-am) = Destruction of the people; swallowing up the people; the disturber of the people; (roots = [1] a swallowing; a devouring; destruction; [2] a people). A pilgrim; devouring of the lord of the people.

Balac (ba'-lak) = Same as Balak = Wasting; licking up; to make empty.

Baladan (bal'-adan) = Bel (is his) lord. Having power; a son he has given. Not a lord.

Balah (ba'-lah) = Decayed; (root = to fail; to fall away). Waxed old.

Balak (ba'-lak) = Same as Balac = Wasting; licking up; to make empty. Waster; emptying; destroying.

Bamah (ba'-mah) = High place; (root = a high place; a fortress; a sanctuary {for idols}).

Bamoth (ba'-moth) = High places (for idols).

Bamothbaal [Bamoth Baal] (ba'-moth-ba'-al) = High places of Baal.

Bani (ba'-ni) = Build; built; posterity; (root = to build; to erect; i.e., houses; temples; forts).

Baptist (bap'-tist)= To dip repeatedly; to immerse; to submerge.

Barabbas (ba-rab'-bas) = Son of Abba; son of a father; son of return.

Barachel (bar'-ak-el) = Blessed of God; whom God blesses; God has blessed.

Barachias (bar'-ak-i'-as) = Whom Jehovah blesses.

Barak (ba'-rak) = Lightning; thunder; thunderbolt.

Barhumite (bar'-hu-mite) = Same as Baharumite = Inhabitants of Bahurim = Village (town of) young men. Son of the blackened; in the pitied.

Bariah (ba-ri'-ah) = Fugitive; prince; (roots = [1] a fugitive; a prince; [2] to pass through; to flee away).

Barjesus [Bar-Jesus] (bar-je'-sus) = Son of Jesus.

Barjona [Bar Jona] (bar-jo'-nah) = Son of Jona. Greek: Son of John or Johanan = Jehovah is gracious. Son of a dove.

Barkos (bar'-cos) = Son after his father; partly-colored. The son cut off.

Barnabas (bar'-na-bas) = Son of exhortation; son of prophecy; son of consolation.

Barsabas (bar'-sab-as) = Son of Saba; a son that suspends the water. Man. Son of the host.

Bartholomew (bar-thol'-o-mew) = Son of Talmai = Abounding in furrows.

Bartimaeus (bar-ti-me'-us) = Son of Timaeus; honorable. Son of one esteemed.

Baruch (ba'-rook) = Blessed; (root = to kneel down; to bless God; to be blessed).

Barzillai (bar-zil'-la-i) = Iron of the LORD; i.e., most firm and true; made of iron; strong.

Bashan (ba'-shan) = Soft; sandy soil; i.e., a soft rich soil. The shame of them.

Bashanhavothjair [Bashan Havoth Jair] (ba"-shan-ha'-voth-ja'-ur) = Fruitful village of Jair.

Bashemath (bash'-e-math) = Pleasant smelling; fragrant; perfumed; (root = to smell sweetly; to be pleased). Spice.

Basmath (bas'-math) =
Same as Bashemath =
Pleasant smelling;
fragrant; perfumed. Spice.

Bathrabbim [Bath
Rabbim] (bath-rab'-bim)
= Daughter of many;
daughter of mighty ones.

Bathsheba (bath'-she-
bah) = Daughter of an
oath; (roots = [1] a
daughter; [2] to swear; to
promise by an oath).

Bathshua [Bathsheba]
(bath'-shu-ah) = Daughter
of an oath; daughter of
seven. Daughter of crying;
daughter of opulence.

Bavai (bav'-a-i) = With
the desire of the Lord. By
the mercy of the Lord. My
goings.

Bazlith (baz'-lith) = A
making naked; asking
(root = to peel). Stripping.

Bazluth (baz'-luth) =
Same as Bazlith = A
making naked; asking.
Stripping.

Bdellium (bdel'-li-um) =
In turbidity.

Bealiah (be-a-li'-ah) =
Possession of the LORD;
Jehovah is LORD.
Mastered of Jah.

Bealoth (be'-a-loth) =
City corporations; i.e.,
rulers; daughters of the
city. Mistresses.

Bebai (beb'-a-i) = With
the desire of the Lord;
fatherly. My cavities.

Becher (be'-ker) = First
born; young camel.

Bechorath (be-ko'-rath) =
Offspring of the first born;
first birth.

Bedad (be'-dad) = Son of
Adad; separation; solitary.

Bedan (be'-dan) = Fat;
robust. In judgment. Son
of judgment.

Bedeiah (be-de'-yah) = In
the protection of the
LORD; servant of
Jehovah. Isolated of Jah.

Beeliada (be-e-li'-ad-ah)
= The lord has known;
i.e., for whom the lord
cares; the lord knows;
(roots = [1] lord {Baal};
[2] to perceive; to see; to
know).

Beelzebub (be-el'-ze-bub)

35

= Same as Baalzebub = Lord the fly; lord of flies; the master of a fly.

Beer (be'-ur) = A well.

Beera (be-e'-rah) = A well; expounder.

Beerah (be-e'-rah) = Same as Beera = A well; expounder.

Beerelim [Beer Eelim] (be'-ur-e'-lim) = Well of the mighty ones; well of the heroes. Well of the gods.

Beeri (be-e'-ri) = Well of God; expounder; man of the well. My well.

Beerlahairoi [Beer Lahai Roi] (be'-ur-la'-hahe-ro'-e) = The well of the life of vision; the well of her that lives and of him that sees; i.e., preserves me in life; the well of the living who sees me.

Beeroth (be-e'-roth) = Wells.

Beerothite (be-er'-o-thite) = Inhabitants of Beeroth = Wells.

Beersheba (be-ur'-she-bah) = The well of the oath.

Beeshterah (be-esh'-te-rah) = House or temple of Astarte. In her flock.

Behemoth (be'-he-moth) = The water ox. Beasts.

Bekah (be'-kah) = Part; half; a cleft; division.

Bel (bel) = Lord; (roots = [1] lord; [2] to rule over). Confused; confounded.

Bela (be'-lah) = Devouring; swallowing; destruction; consumption; (root = to swallow down; to devour greedily; to consume; to destroy).

Belah (be'-lah) = Same as Bela = Devouring; swallowing; destruction; consumption; (root = to swallow down; to devour greedily; to consume; to destroy).

Belaites (be'-lah-ites) = Descendants of Bela = Devouring; swallowing; destruction; consumption; (root = to swallow down; to devour greedily; to consume; to destroy).

Belial (be'-le-al) = Worthless; without help.

Belshazzar (bel-shaz'-ar) = Bel, protect the king; the lord's leader. Master of treasure. Lord of destruction straitened.

Belteshazzar (bel-te-shaz'-ar) = Bel, protect his life; the lord's leader. Preserve his life. Lord of the straitened's treasure.

Ben (ben) = Son; edification (of the family).

Benammi [Ben-Ammi] (ben-am'-mi) = Son of my nation; son of my people; son of my own kindred.

Benaiah (ben-ay'-ah) = Whom Jehovah has built; built up of the LORD; Jehovah is intelligent.

Beneberak [Bene Berak] (be'-ne-be'-rak) = Son of lightning, or of Barak.

Benejaakan [Bene Jaakan] (be'-ne-ja'-a-kan) = Son of Jaakan = One who turns. Son of necessity. Sons of one who will oppress them.

Benhadad [Ben Hadad] (ben'-ha-dad) = Son of the most high or most eminent. The beloved son. Son of the god Hadah. Son of the lot-caster; son of the shouter.

Benhail [Ben Hail] (ben-ha'-il) = Son of strength; son of valor; son of might.

Benhanan [Ben Hanan] (ben-ha'-nan) = Son of one who is gracious; son of kind one or very gracious.

Beninu (ben'-i-nu) = Our son or posterity; our edification. Son of us.

Benjamin (ben'-ja-min) = Son of the right hand; son of my days; i.e., son of old age.

Benjamite(s) (ben'-ja-mite) = Descendants of Benjamin = Son of the right hand; son of my days; i.e., son of old age.

Beno (be'-no) = His son.

Benoni [Ben-Oni] (ben-o'-ni) = Son of my sorrow; son of my strength.

Benzoheth [Ben Zoheth] (ben-zo'-heth) = Son of most violent transportation.

37

Corpulent; strong. Son of releasing.

Beon (be'-on) = House of habitation. Indwelling.

Beor (be'-or) = Torch; lamp; burning; (root = to consume; to burn up). Shepherd.

Bera (be'-rah) = Son of evil; (root = to be evil; to do evil; to be wicked). Gift; excellence. In the evil.

Berachah (ber'-a-kah) = Blessing; benediction.

Berachiah (ber-a-ki'-ah) = Whom Jehovah has blessed; blessed of the LORD; Jehovah is blessed; bending the knee.

Beraiah (ber-a-i'-ah) = Created of the LORD; whom Jehovah has created; Jehovah has created.

Berea (be-re'-a) = To stabilize; stable; steadfast; sure; (root = to walk). The pierced; the beyond.

Berechiah (ber-e-ki'-ah) = Same as Berachiah = Whom Jehovah has

blessed; blessed of the LORD; Jehovah is blessing; bending the knee.

Bered (be'-red) = Place of hail; hail; seed; (root = to be cold).

Beri (be'-ri) = Expounder; man of the well; well of God.

Beriah (be-ri'-ah) = In calamity; i.e., a calamity in his house; in evil; unfortunate.

Beriites (be-ri'-ites) = Inhabitants of Beriah = In calamity; i.e., a calamity in his house; in evil; unfortunate.

Berites (be'-rites) = Inhabitants of Beri = Expounder; man of the well; well of God.

Berith (be'-rith) = A Covenant; (root = to eat together).

Bernice (bur-ni'-see) = Victorious; carrying off victory.

Berodachbaladan (ber-o'-dak-bal'-ad-an) = Same as Merodachbaladan =

Berodach (same as Merodach) has given a son. Baladan = Bel is his lord. Bold. The causer of oppression is not a lord.

Berothah (ber-o'-thah) = Wells of the LORD. The place of wells.

Berothai (ber'-o-thahee) = My wells.

Berothite (be'-ro-thite) = Inhabitants of Beeroth = Wells.

Beryl (ber'-yl) = She will impoverish.

Besai (be'-sahee) = A sword; victory; treading down.

Besodeiah (bes-o-di'-ah) = In the council of the LORD. Familiar with Jehovah. In Jah's secret.

Besor (be'-sor) = Fresh; cool; cold. The bringer of good tidings.

Betah (be'-tah) = Confidence; security.

Beten (be'-ten) = Belly; (root = the belly; the womb).

Bethabara (beth-ab'-ar-ah) = House of passage. A ferry-house.

Bethanath [Beth Anath] (beth'-a-nath) = House of response; i.e., a place of echo.

Bethanoth [Beth Anoth] (beth'-a-noth) = Same as Bethanath = House of response.

Bethany (beth'-a-ny) = House of affliction (or response). House of dates or figs. (Out of affliction comes fruit.)

Betharabah [Beth Arabah] (beth-ar'-ab-ah) = House of the desert.

Betharam [Beth Haram] (beth'-a-ram) = House of the lofty or of the exalted. The house of their hill.

Betharbel [Beth Arbel] (beth-ar'-bel) = House of the ambush of God.

Bethaven [Beth Aven] (beth-a'-ven) = House of vanity; i.e., idols. The house of iniquity.

Bethazmaveth [Beth

Azmaveth] (beth-az'-maveth) = House strong with death.

Bethbaalmeon [Beth Baal Meon] (beth-be'-al-me'-on) = House or place of habitation of Baal. House of the lord of the dwelling.

Bethbarah [Beth Barah] (beth-ba'-rah) = Place of the ford; i.e., a place of cutting through. House of eating or choice.

Bethbirei [Beth Biri] (beth-bir-e-i) = House of my creation. House of my creator.

Bethcar [Beth Car] (beth'-car) = House of battering rams; house of pasture. House of measure.

Bethdagon [Beth Dagon] (beth-da'-gon) = House of Dagon. House of a fish (an idol). House of the fish god.

Bethdiblathaim [Beth Diblathaim] (beth-dib-lath-a'-im) = House of two cakes of figs. The house of dried figs. House of the double fig-cake.

Bethel (beth'-el) = House of God.

Bethelite (beth'-el-ite) = Inhabitants of Bethel = House of God.

Bethemek [Beth Emek] (beth-e'-mek) = House or place of the valley.

Bether (be'-thur) = Dividing; separation. A place cut off.

Bethesda (beth-ez'-dah) = House of mercy; place of the flowing of water.

Bethezel [Beth Ezel] (beth-e'-zel) = House of firmness. The house close by. The neighbor's house; the next house.

Bethgader [Beth Gader] (beth-ga'-der) = House of the wall; walled place.

Bethgamul [Beth Gamul] (beth-ga'-mul) = House of the recompensed; house of the weaned.

Bethhaccerem [Beth Hakkerem] (beth-hak'-se-rem) = House of the vineyard; house of the vine.

Bethharan [Beth Haran]

(beth-ha'-ran) = House of the lofty. House of joyful shouter.

Bethhogla [Beth Hogla] (beth-hog'-lah) = House of the partridge; i.e., place abounding in partridges.

Bethhoglah [Beth Hoglah] (beth-hog'-lah) = Same as Bethhogla = House of the partridge; i.e., place abounding in partridges. House of the languished feast.

Bethhoron [Beth Horon] (beth-ho'-ron) = House or place of the great cavern or holes. The house of wrath. Consumer's house; cavernous house.

Bethjesimoth [Jesimoth] (beth-jes'-im-oth) = House of the deserts; i.e., a place situated in barren wastes. House of the wastes.

Bethjeshimoth [Beth Jeshimoth] (beth-jesh'-im-oth) = Same as Bethjesimoth = House of the deserts; i.e., a place situated in barren wastes. House of the wastes.

Bethlebaoth [Beth Lebaoth] (beth-leb'-a-oth) = House or place of lionesses; i.e., a place abounding in lions.

Bethlehem (beth'-le-hem) = House of bread.

Bethlehemite (beth'-le-hem-ite) = Inhabitants of Beth-lehem = House of bread.

Bethlehemjudah [Bethlehem Judah] (beth'-le-hem-ju'-dah) = House of bread and praise.

Bethmaachah [Beth Maachah] (beth-ma'-a-kah) = House of oppression.

Bethmarcaboth [Beth Marcaboth] (beth-mar'-cab-oth) = House of chariots.

Bethmeon [Beth Meon] (beth-me'-on) = House of habitation.

Bethnimrah [Beth Nimrah] (beth-nim'-rah) = House of pure water. House of the leopardess.

Bethpalet [Beth Pelet] (beth-pa'-let) = House or

place of escape; i.e., place of refuge or asylum.

Bethpazzez [Beth Pazzez] (beth-paz'-zez) = House of dispersion.

Bethpeor [Beth Peor] (beth-pe'-or) = House or temple of the hiatus. A house wide open; i.e., a place for idol worship.

Bethphage (beth'-fa-je) = House of unripe figs. Green fig house.

Bethphelet [Beth Pelet] (beth'-fe-let) = Same as Bethpalet = House or place of escape; i.e., a place of refuge or asylum.

Bethrapha [Beth Rapha] (beth'-ra-fah) = House of Rapha; house of a giant; place of fear. House of the healer.

Bethrehob [Beth Rehob] (beth'-re-hob) = House of breadth; region of wideness. House of the broad way.

Bethsaida (beth-sa'-dah) = House of fish. House of provision; house of hunting.

Bethshan [Beth Shan]

(beth'-shan) = House of quiet; house of rest. House of the sharpener.

Bethshean [Beth Shan] (beth-she'-an) = Same as Bethshan = House of quiet; house of rest.

Bethshemesh [Beth Shemesh] (beth'-she-mesh) = House of the sun; the house of the light of the sun.

Bethshemite [Beth Shemesh] (beth'-shem-ite) = Inhabitants of Beth-shemesh = House of the sun; the house of the light of the sun.

Bethshittah [Beth Shittah] (beth-shit'-tah) = House of acacia; i.e., abounding in acacias. House of the scourge.

Bethtappuah [Beth Tappuah] (beth-tap'-pu-ah) = House of apples; i.e., abounding in apples. House of the breather.

Bethuel (beth-u'-el) = Virgin of God; separated of God. A relation to God. Abode of God; dweller in God.

Bethul (beth'-ul) = Virgin. Separated.

Bethzur [Beth Zur] (beth'-zur) = House of the rock; place of rock.

Betonim (bet'-o-nim) = Cavities; (pistachio) nuts.

Beulah (be-u'-lah) = Married; a married woman.

Bezai (be'-zahee) = In the labor of the LORD; i.e., birth; root = [1] to hasten; to honor; [2] Jehovah). Shinning; high. My fine linen (garments).

Bezaleel (be-zal'-e-el) = In the shadow of God; under God's shadow.

Bezek (be'-zek) = Flash of lighting; a spark.

Bezer (be'-zer) = Gold ore; defense. Strong; gold one. Munition.

Bichri (bik'-ri) = Juvenile; first born; youthful; first fruits.

Bidkar (bid'-kar) = Son of thrusting through. A piercer. Servant of Kar; in sharp pain. In stabbing.

Bigtha (big'-thah) = Given by fortune. In the winepress.

Bigthan (big'-than) = Gift of fortune; giving meat. A giver of pastry. In their winepress.

Bigthana (big'-than-ah) = Given of fortune. In their winepress.

Bigvai (big'-vahee) = Happy; of the people. In my bodies.

Bildad (bil'-dad) = Son of contention; contender. Lord Adad; old friendship; with love. Confusing (by mingling) love.

Bileam (bil'-e-am) = Same as Balaam = Destruction of the people; swallowing up the people; (roots = [1] a swallowing; a devouring; destruction; [2] a people).

Bilgah (bil'-gah) = Consolation; reviving; cheerful; bursting forth.

Bilgai (bil'-gahee) = Consolation of the LORD; bursting forth; first born. My comforts.

Bilhah (bil'-hah) =

Timidity; in weakness; (root = to terrify; to trouble). In languishing; decrepitude.

Bilhan (bil'-han) = Modest; tender; bashful. Their decrepitude.

Bilshan (bil'-shan) = Son of tongue; son of eloquence; searcher; inquirer. In slander.

Bimhal (bim'-hal) = Son of circumcision. In circumcision; in weakness (by mixture).

Binea (bin'-e-ah) = Gushing forth; wanderer.

Binnui (bin'-nu-ee) = Building up; a building of familyship.

Birsha (bur'-shah) = Son of wickedness; in wickedness; thick; strong.

Birzavith (bur'-za-vith) = Selection of olives; i.e., choice olives; (root = to select; to separate; to purge). Olive well; wounds.

Bishlam (bish'-lam) = In peace; peaceful; son of peace; i.e., born in a time of tranquillity.

Bithiah (bith-i'-ah) = Daughter (worshiper) of Jehovah; a daughter of Jehovah. Daughter of Jah.

Bithron (bith'-ron) = Great division; i.e., a region divided by mountains and valleys; the broken or divided place; a broken place.

Bithynia (bith-in'-e-ah) = A violent pushing. (A Roman province in Asia Minor).

Bizjothjah (biz-joth'-jah)= Contempt of Jehovah; (root = to despise).

Biztha (biz'-thah) = Eunuch. Booty.

Blastus (blas'-tus) = A shot; a sprout; a sucker; a bud.

Boanerges (bo-an-er'-jees) = Sons of thunder; sons of rage.

Boaz (bo'-az) = In Him (the Lord) is strength. Come in strength; strength; fleetness.

Bocheru (bok'-er-u) = His first born; youth; first born.

Bochim (bo'-kim) = Weepers; (root = to weep; to lament).

Bohan (bo'-han) = Thumb; stumpy.

Booz (bo'-oz) = In him is strength.

Boscath (bos'-cath) = Elevated ground.

Bosor (bo'-sor) = Burning; torch. Greek form of Beor = Torch; lamp; burning; (root = to consume; to burn up).

Bozez (bo'-zez) = Shinning; glistening; surpassing white; blooming.

Bozkath (boz'-kath) = Same as Boscath = Elevated ground. A swelling (as of dough).

Bozrah (boz'-rah) = Fortification; a vintage; a sheep fold; (root = to gather the vintage; to render inaccessible). Besieged.

Bukki (buk'-ki) = Emptying of the LORD; wasting from Jehovah; mouth of Jehovah; devastation sent by Jehovah; wasting.

Bukkiah (buk-ki'-ah) = Same as Bukki = Emptying of the LORD; wasting from Jehovah; mouth of Jehovah; devastation sent by Jehovah; wasting.

Bul (bul) = Rain. Withering. Increase; produce.

Bunah (boo'-nah) = Prudence; understanding; (root = to understand; to be prudent; to consider).

Bunni (bun'-ni) = My understanding; built. I am built.

Buz (buz) = Contempt; to despise; (root = to despise).

Buzi (boo'-zi) = Contemned of Jehovah; my contempt.

Buzite (boo'-zite) = Descendants of Buz = Contempt; to despise; (root = to despise).

Come unto me, all ye that labour and are heavy laden, and I will give you rest. (Matthew 11:28)

Cabbon (cab'-bon) = Cake. As the prudent; as the builder.

Cabul (ca'-bul) = Fetter; bound; (root = to bind).

Caesar (se'-zur) = One cut out. Severed.

Caesar Augustus (se'-zur aw-gus'-tus) = Caesar = One cut out. Augustus = Venerable; sacred; kingly.

Caesarea (ses-a-re'-ah) = Severed.

Caesarea Philippi (ses-a-re'-ah fil-ip'-pi) = Caesarea = Severed. Philippi = Lover of horses.

Caiaphas (cah'-ya-fus) = A searcher; he that seeks with diligence. As comely.

Cain (cain) = Possession; acquisition; fabrication; (root = to possess; to acquire). A purchase. Maker.

Cainan (ca'-nun) = Possessor; acquisition; a purchase; being purchased. Their smith.

Calah (ca'-lah) = Old Age; completion; (root = to be completed). Seasonable. Full age.

Calamus (cal'-a-mus) = Sweet stalk; reed.

Calcol (cal'-col) = Sustenance; sustaining; who nourishes; (root = to sustain with food; to nourish). Comprehended.

Caleb (ca'-leb) = Bold; impetuous. A dog. Whole-hearted. Hearty.

Calebephratah [Caleb Ephratah] (ca'-leb-ef'-ra-tah) = Caleb = Bold; impetuous. A dog. Hearty. Ephratah = Fruitful.

Calneh (cal'-neh) = Fortified dwellings. The wall is complete.

Calno (cal'-no) = Same as

Calneh = Fortified dwellings. His perfection.

Calvary (cal'-va-ry) = Skull; place of a skull.

Camon (ca'-mon) = Abounding in stalks; standing corn. A riser up.

Cana (ca'-nah) = Place of reeds. Zealous; acquired.

Canaan (ca'-na-an) = Merchants; trader; servant; low region; lowland; low; humbled; (root = to be humble; to be subdued; to be brought low). A trafficker.

Canaanite(s) (ca'-na-an-ites) = Inhabitants of Canaan = Merchants; trader; servant; low region; lowland; (root = to be humble; to be subdued; to be brought low). A trafficker.

Canaanitish (ca'-na-an-i-tish) = Referring to Canaan = Merchants; trader; servant; low region; lowland; (root = to be humble; to be subdued; to be brought low). A trafficker.

Candace (can'-da-see) = Queen or ruler of children.

Canneh (can'-neh) = Surname; flattering title.

Capernaum (ca-pur'-na-um) = City of consolation. Village of comfort.

Caphthorim (caf'-tho-rim) = Same as Caphtorim = Pomegranates; crowns; (place of rock towers).

Caphtor (caf'-tor) = Crown; knop; pomegranate. A button. As if to interpret; he bowed down to spy out.

Caphtorim (caf'-to-rim) = Pomegranates; crowns; (place of rock towers).

Cappadocia (cap-pa-do'-she-ah) = Province of good horses. Branded unreal.

Carbuncle (car'-bun-cle) = Lighting stone (literally, she shot forth). I will kindle.

Carcas (car'-cas) = Severe; an eagle, (characteristics = strength, velocity, longevity, clearness of vision). As the bound (one).

Carchemish (car'-ke-mish) = Fortress of refuge; (root = to surround; to fortify). A fed lamb; cut off.

Careah (ca-re'-ah) = Bald; bald head.

Carmel (car'-mel) = Fruitful field; park; fertile.

Carmelite (car'-mel-ite) = Inhabitants of Carmel = Fruitful field; park.

Carmelitess (car'-mel-i-tess) = Inhabitants of Carmel = Fruitful field; park.

Carmi (car'-mi) = Vinedresser; my vineyard; noble.

Carmites (car'-mites) = Descendants of Carmi = Vinedresser; my vineyard; noble.

Carpus (car'-pus) = Fruit; the wrist.

Carshena (car-she'-nah) = Illustrious; spoiler; slender.

Casiphia (cas-if'-e-ah) = Silver of the LORD; (root = to desire; to long for). Desirable. Longing of Jah.

Casluhim (cas'-loo-him) =

Their boundary protected. As forgiven ones.

Castor (cas'-tor) = Castor and Pollux - twin sons of Jupiter and Leda; name means = A girl; damsel; maiden.

Cedron (se'-drun) = Same as Kidron = Very black; full of darkness, (intense form); turbid; (root = black). Great obscurity; a wall. (Brook and ravine near Gethsemane frequented by our Lord).

Cenchrea (sen'-kre-ah) = Millet; small pulse. Granular.

Cephas (se'-fas) = A stone.

Chalcedony (chal-ced'-o-ny) = Copperlike; flowerlike.

Chalcol (kal'-kol) = Same as Calcol = Sustenance; sustaining; who nourishes; (root = to sustain with food; to nourish). Maintaining; supplying.

Chaldaeans #1 (kal-de'-uns) = As clod breakers.

Chaldea (kal-de'-ah) =

The land of the Chaldeans = Astrologer. Wanderers.

Chaldean(s) #2 (kal-de'-uns) = Astrologer. Wanderers.

Chaldeans #3 (kal-de'-uns) = As it were demons; (root = to lay waste; to destroy). Astrologer. Wanderers

Chaldees (kal'-dees) = Same as Chaldeans = Astrologer. Wanderers.

Chanaan (ka'-na-un) = Another form of Canaan = Merchants; servant; low region; (root = to be humble; to be subdued; to be brought low).

Chapmen (chap'-men) = The search-men.

Charashim (car'-a-shim) = Craftsmen.

Charchemish (car'-ke-mish) = Same as Carchemish = Fortress of refuge; (root = to surround; to fortify).

Charran (car'-ran) = Same as Haran #2 =Very dry; (place parched with the sun); (root = to be dry;

to kindle; to burn). Grievous.

Chebar (ke'-bar) = Abundant; vehement; great; (root = to make much; to multiply; to have in abundance). A river.

Chedorlaomer (ke'-dor-la'-o-mer) = Handful of sheaves; to bind sheaves; sheaf band; servants of the god Lagamar; to make merchandise; glory of Laomer.Chedorlaomer king of Elam. (Elam was the son of Shem, Genesis 10:22). He that dwells in a sheaf.

Chelal (ke'-lal) = Completion; completeness.

Chelluh (kel'-loo) = Consumed of the LORD; union; (root = to consume; to make an end). Determine ye Him; consume ye Him.

Chelub (ke'-lub) = Binding together (like a basket); wicker basket; bird's cage; Boldness. A coop.

Chelubai (ke-loo'-bahee) = Binding together of the Lord. My baskets.

Chemarims (kem'-a-rims) = Persons dressed in black attire. To be warm; affectionate. As changed ones.

Chemosh (ke'-mosh) = The swift; subduer. Cut off. As if departing or fleeing.

Chenaanah (ke-na'-a-nah) = Merchant; i.e., one who bends the knee. Subduer; flat. As if afflicted.

Chenani (ken'-a-ni) = Perfecter; firm; creator; (root = to perfect; to protect). As my perpetuator.

Chenaniah (ken-a-ni'-ah) = Established of the LORD; whom Jehovah supports; Jehovah is firm; preparation. As perpetuated of Jah.

Chepharhaammonai (ke'-far-ha-am'-mo-nahee) = Village of the Ammonites; (roots = [1] a village; [2] to cover over; to make atonement for; to be forgiven).

Chephirah (ke-fi'-rah) = Village. A young lioness; covert.

Cheran (ke'-ran) = Lamb; union; lute. As shouting for joy.

Cherethims (ker'-e-thims) = Executioners; exiles. Those cut off.

Cherethites (ker'-e-thites) = Same as Cherethims = Executioners; exiles. He that is cut off.

Cherith (ke'-rith) = Separation; gorge. Cut off.

Cherub (ke'-rub) = Celestial. As if contending.

Cherubim (cher'-u-bims) = Plural of Cherub = Celestial.

Chesalon (kes'-a-lon) = Firm confidence; hope. Foolish confidence; as extolled.

Chesed (ke'-sed) = Increase; conqueror; a devil. As harrower.

Chesil (ke'-sil) = Orion; constellations; a fool.

Chesulloth (ke-sul'-loth) = Confidences.

Chezib (ke'-zib) = Lying; deceptive; false.

Chidon (ki'-don)= Great destruction; javelin; dart.

Chileab (kil'-e-ab) = Accomplished of the father; perfection of the father; like to a father.

Chilion (kil'-e-on) = Pining; consuming; wasting away; complete. Consumption.

Chilmad (kil'-mad) = As learned. As a disciple.

Chimham (kim'-ham) = Great desire; longing; pining. As confusion.

Chinhan (kin'-ham) = (feminine) Their longing.

Chinnereth (kin'-ne-reth) = Harp; a lyre.

Chinneroth (kin'-ne-roth) = Harps. (Plural of Chinnereth).

Chios (ki'-os) = Snowy. An unlucky throw of the dice. (An island in the Mediterranean).

Chisleu (kis'-lew) = Like a quail. His confidence.

Chislon (kis'-lon) = Firm confidence; hope; trust; strong; confidence.

Chislothtabor [Chisloth Tabor] (kis'-loth-ta'-bor) = Confidence of Tabor; i.e., in its fortifications. Foolish confidences you will purge.

Chittim (kit'-tim) = Subduers; smiters; bruisers. Breakers in pieces.

Chiun (ki'-un) = Statue; image. Established. Pillar (as set up).

Chloe (clo'-e) = Green herb; covered with green vegetation.

Chorashan (cor-a'-shan) = Smoking furnace.

Chorazin (co-ra'-zin) = A furnace of smoke. (A city that Christ denounced.)

Chozeba (ko-ze'-bah) = Lying; deceiver. Falsehood.

Christ (krist) = Anointed.

Christians (kris'-tyans) = Christ like; a follower of Christ.

Restorative Titles of Believers

Abraham's Seed	John 8:37
Anointed	2 Corinthians 1:21
Apostles	Acts 11:1
Assembly of the saints	Psalm 89:7
Assembly of the upright	Psalm 111:1
Believers	1 Timothy 4:12
Beloved	Romans 12:19
Body of Christ	1 Corinthians 12:27
Born again	1 Peter 1:23
Branches	John 15:55
Branch of God's planting	Isaiah 60:21
Brethren	Hebrews 2:11
Bride	Revelation 21:9
Building	1 Corinthians 3:9
Children of God	Galatians 3:26
Christ's	1 Corinthians 3:23
Chosen ones	John 15:16
Chosen generation	1 Peter 2:9
Children of the day	1 Thessalonians 5:5
Children of light	1 Thessalonians 5:5
Christians	Acts 11:26
Church	Ephesians 1:22
Church of God	Acts 20:28
Church of the Living God	1 Timothy 3:15

Church of the firstborn	Hebrews 12:23
City of the Living God	Hebrews 12:22
Clay	Isaiah 64:8
Complete in Him	Colossians 2:10
Congregation of saints	Psalm 149:1
Creature, new	2 Corinthians 5:17
Disciples	John 13:35
Evangelists	Ephesians 4:11
Epistles	2 Corinthians 3:2
Faithful	1 Timothy 6:2
Family in heaven and earth	Ephesians 3:15
Fellow citizens	Ephesians 2:19
Firstborn	Hebrews 12:23
Firstfruit	Romans 11:16
Flock of God	1 Peter 5:2
Fold of Christ	John 10:16
Friends	John 15:14
General assembly	Hebrews 12:23
God's building	1 Corinthians 3:9
Golden lampstand	Revelation 1:20
God's building	1 Corinthians 3:9
God's elect	Romans 8:33
God's heritage	1 Peter 5:3
God's inheritance	Psalm 28:9
Habitation of God	Ephesians 2:22

Heirs of God	Romans 8:17
Hidden ones	Psalm 83:3
His own house	Hebrews 3:6
Holy priesthood	1 Peter 2:5
Holy nation	1 Peter 2:9
House of God	1 Timothy 3:15
Husbandry, God's	1 Corinthians 3:9
Image of God	Genesis 9:6
Israel of God	Galatians 6:16
Joint heirs	Romans 8:17
Justified	1 Corinthians 6:11
Kings unto God	Revelation 1:6
Kings	1 Timothy 2:2
Lamb's wife	Revelation 19:7
Light of world	Matthew 5:14
Lively stones	1 Peter 2:5
Ministers of our God	Isaiah 61:6
Mount Zion	Hebrews 12:22
New Jerusalem	Revelation 21:2
One body	Romans 12:5
One bread	1 Corinthians 10:17
Pastors	Ephesians 4:11
Peace makers	2 Corinthians 1311
Peculiar people	1 Peter 2:9
Peculiar treasure	Exodus 19:5

Pillar	Revelation 3:12
Pillar and ground of truth	1 Timothy 3:15
Priests	Revelation 5:10
Priests of the Lord	Isaiah 61:6
Prophets	Ephesians 4:11
Purchased	1 Corinthians 7:23
Ransomed	Isaiah 35:10
Righteous	1 Peter 3:12
Royal priesthood	1 Peter 2:9
Sanctified	1 Corinthians 1:2
Saints	Hebrews 6:10
Salt of the earth	Matthew 5:13
Saved	1 Corinthians 1:18
Sent ones	John 20:21
Servants	Romans 6:22
Sheep	John 10:27
Sheepfold	John 10:1
Sons of God	Philippians 2:15
Teachers	Ephesians 4:11
Temple of God	1 Corinthians 3:16
Temple of the Living God	2 Corinthians 6:16
Vineyard, My	Jeremiah 12:10
Virgins	Revelation 4:14
Washed	1 Corinthians 6:11
Wife	Revelation 19:7

Witnesses   Acts 1:8

Work of Thy Hand   Isaiah 64:8

Yokefellows   Philippians 4:3

Zion   Zechariah 8:2

Chrysolyte (chry'-so-lyte) = Gold stone.

Chrysoprasus (chry'-so-pra'-sus) = Golden green; golden achievement.

Chub (cub) = Christ's thorn. Clustered; a horde.

Chun (kun) = Firm; to establish.

Chushanrishathaim [Chushan-Rishathaim] (cu'-shan-rish-a-tha'-im) = Two fold malicious Ethiopian; the wickedness of Ethiopia; blackness of iniquities.

Chuza (cu'-zah) = Modest. A mound; a Chrysolyte (chry'-so-lyte) = Gold stone.

Cilicia (sil-ish'-yah) = Hair Cloth. The land of Celix. (A city in the southeast province of Asia Minor).

Cinneroth (sin'-ne-roth) = Same as Chinneroth/Chinnereth = Harp; a lyre.

Cis (sis) = Same as Kish = Snaring; bird catching.

Clauda (claw'-dah) = Lame. Surging(?).

Claudia (claw'-de-ah) = Same as Clauda = Lame.

Claudius (claw'-de-us) = Lame. Whining. (The fourth emperor of Rome).

Claudius Lysias (claw'-de-us lis'-e-as) = Claudius = Lame. Lysias = He who has the power to set free; releaser, (A captain in the army of Rome).

Clement (clem'-ent) = Kind; merciful; mild.

Cleopas (cle'-o-pas) =
The whole glory;
renowned father. Famed of
all.

Cleophas (cle'-o-fas) =
My exchanges. Same as
Cleopas = The whole
glory; renowned father.

Cnidus (ni'-dus) = Nettle.

Colhozeh [Col-Hozeh]
(col-ho'-zeh) = All-seer;
every one that sees; the
all-seeing one; wholly a
seer.

Colosse (co-los'-see) =
Also Colossae =
Monstrosities. (The city to
which the Epistle of
Colossians was written).

Colossians (co-los'-yuns)
= Monstrosities.

Conaniah (co-na-ni'-ah) =
Jehovah hath established;
stability of the LORD.

Coniah (co-ni'-ah) =
Established of the LORD;
whom Jehovah has set up.

Cononiah (co-no-ni'-ah)
= Same as Conaniah =
Jehovah has established;
stability of the LORD.

Coos (co'-os) = Summit.
A public prison.

Coral (co'-ral) = Heights.

Core (co'-ree) =
Baldness; bald. Greek
form of Korah = Ice; hail;
hard. Baldness; bald.

Corinth (cor'-inth) =
Satiated—(to fill full; to
satisfy).

Corinthians (co-rin'-the-
uns) = Inhabitants of
Corinth = Satiated—(to
fill full; to satisfy).

Corinthus (co-rin'-thus)
= Another spelling for
Corinth = Satiated—(to
fill full; to satisfy).

Cornelius (cor-ne'-le-us)
= The beam of the sun.
Pitiless full.

57

Delight thyself also in the LORD; and he shall give thee the desires of thine heart (Psalms 37:4).

Dabareh (dab'-a-reh) = A sheep walk; manner of speaking; pasture; (root = to lead flocks to pasture; to speak; to promise).

Dabbasheth (dab'-ba-sheth) = Flowing with honey.

Daberath (dab'-e-rath) = Same as Dabareh = A sheep walk; manner of speaking; pasture. A subject.

Dabrasheth (dab'-ra-sheth) = Hump of a camel. He whispered shame.

Dagon (da'-gon) = Honored fish; A national idol and god of the Philistines it had the head, arms and body of a man, but the body terminated in a fish; (roots = [1] fish; [2] to increase; to multiply).

Dalaiah (dal-a-i'-ah) = Whom Jehovah has delivered; Jehovah is deliverer. Drawn of Jah.

Dalmanutha (dal-ma-nu'-thah) = Slow firebrand. (A town on the west side of the Sea of Galilee). Hebrew: Poor portion.

Dalmatia (dal-ma'-she-ah) = Deceitful.

Dalphon (dal'-fon) = Proud; strenuous. Dropping.

Damaris (dam'-a-ris) = Calf; a heifer. A yoke-bearing wife.

Damascenes (dam-as-senes') = Inhabitants of Damascus = Activity; moist with blood. Silent is the sackcloth weaver.

Damascus (da-mas'-cus) = Activity; moist with blood. Sackcloth (weaver) is going about (or dwelling). (The oldest standing city in the world).

Dan (dan) = Judging; judge; he that judges; (root = to judge; to rule; to execute judgment; to contend).

Daniel (dan'-yel) = Judge of God; i.e., one who delivers judgment in the name of God; my judge is God; God is my judge; he that judges.

Danites (dan'-ites) = Descendants of Dan = Judging; judge; he that judges.

Danjaan [Dan Jaan] (dan-ja'-an) = Judge of the woodland. The judge will afflict; the judge is greedy.

Dannah (dan'-nah) = You have judged; judgment. Low land.

Dara (da'-rah) = Bearer. The arm.

Darda (dar'-dah) = Pearl of wisdom. He compassed knowledge; dwelling of knowledge.

Darius (da-ri'-us) = A restrainer; governor. A possessor by succession. He that informs himself; a king. Investigation; the dwelling will be full of heaviness.

Darkon (dar'-kon) = Thrusting through; (root = to pierce through). Bearer; scattering. The dwelling of lamentation.

Dathan (da'-than) = Belonging to a fountain; belonging to law or fount. Judgment; law. Their law; their decree.

David (da'-vid) = Beloved.

Debir (de'-bur) = An oracle; speaker; a recess; i.e., the inner part of the temple where the ark of the covenant was placed and where responses were given.

Deborah (deb'-o-rah) = Eloquent; an orator; bee; (roots = [1] a bee; [2] to speak). Her speaking.

Decapolis (de-cap'-o-lis) = Ten cities.

Dedan (de'-dan) = Leading forward; (root = to go forward; to go softly). Low; their friendship. In judgment. Their love.

Dedanim (ded'-a-nim) = Same as Dedan = Leading

forward; (root = to go forward; to go softly). Low; their friendship. In judgment.

Dehavites (de-ha'-vites) = Villagers. The sickly.

Dekar (de'-kar) = Thrusting through; lance bearer; piercing; perforation. The piercer.

Delaiah (del-a-i'-ah) = Drawn up of the LORD; whom Jehovah has freed; Jehovah is deliverer. Delicate; Dainty one.

Delilah (de-li'-lah) = Delicate; (root = to be brought low; to hang down; to be languid). A drawer of water.

Demas (de'-mas) = Popular; ruler of people.

Demetrius (de-me'-tre-us) = Belonging to Demeter. (Demeter was the goddess of agriculture and rural life). Mother earth.

Derbe (der'-by) = Tanner; tanner of skin; covered with skin.

Deuel (de-oo'-el) = Invocation of God; God is

knowing. Know ye God.

Deuteronomy (doot'-er-an'-e-me) = Transliteration from the Greek: Second law.

Diamond (dia'-mond) = He will smite down.

Diana (di-an'-ah) = Justice; one who judges. Flow restrained; complete light.

Diblaim (dib'-la-im) = Two cakes of figs; double embrace; twin balls.

Diblath (dib'-lath) = Cake. Place of the fig cake.

Diblathaim (dib-lath-a'-im) = Same as Diblaim = Two cakes of figs; double embrace; twin balls.

Dibon (di'-bon) = Weeping; pining; wasting; (root = to mourn; to be sorrowful). Full of understanding. The waster.

Dibongad [Dibon Gad] (di'-bon-gad') = Wasting of Gad.

Dibri (dib'-ri) = Promise (of the LORD); on the

pasture born. My word.

Didymus (did'-i-mus) = Double; i.e., a twin.

Diklah (dik'-lah) = A palm tree; palm grove. The beaten-small fainted.

Dilean (dil'-e-an) = A large gourd; cucumber field. Brought low in affliction.

Dimnah (dim'-nah) = Dunghill.

Dimon (di'-mon) = Secure fast; undisturbed silence. (root = to be silent; to be dumb). The quieter. Abundance of blood.

Dimonah (di-mon'-nah) = Sufficient numbering. Feminine of Dimon.

Dinah (di'-na) = Judged; i.e., vindicated; justice; she that is judged.

Dinaites (di'-na-ites) = Judgment. (Name of Cuthaean colonists placed in Samaria).

Dinhabah (din'-ha-bah) = She gives judgment; giving judgment.

Dionysius (di-on-ish'-yus)

= Divinely touched. (The God of wine).

Diotrephes (di-ot'-re-feez) = Loves preeminence; nourished by Jupiter.

Dishan (di'-shan) = Gazelle; wild goat; antelope; leaping. Their threshing; their treading.

Dishon (di'-shon) = Same as Dishan = Gazelle; wild goat; antelope; leaping. A thresher.

Dizahab (diz'-a-hab) = A place abounding with gold.

Dodai (do'-dahee) = Beloved of the LORD.

Dodanim (do'-da-nim) = Leaders; a leader.

Dodavah (do'-da-vah) = Love of the LORD; Jehovah is loving.

Dodo (do'-do) = Same as Dodai = Beloved of the LORD; Jehovah is loving. His beloved.

Doeg (do'-eg) = Fearful; anxious; timid; sorrowful; root = to fear; to be afraid; to be sorrowful).

Dophkah (dof'-kah) = Knocking; (root = to knock; to beat). Beating (literally: you have beaten).

Dor (dor) = Habitation; circle; i.e., circle of the years of life; dwelling. Generation.

Dorcas (dor'-cas) = Gazelle. (An emblem of beauty).

Dothan (do'-than) = Two wells or cisterns. Judgment; law. Their decree; their sickness.

Drusilla (dru-sil'-lah) = Watered by the dew.

Dumah (doo'-mah) = Silence; resemblance.

Dura (doo'-rah) = Circle. Habitation

Exalt the LORD our God, and worship at his holy hill; for the LORD our God is holy (Psalms 99:9).

Easter (east'-er) = Passover.

Ebal (e'-bal) = Stone; stony; a heap of ruins; heap of bareness; bare. Heaps of confusion.

Ebed (e'-bed) = Servant; slave; (root = to labor; to toil; to serve).

Ebedmelech [Ebed-Melech] (e'-bed-me'-lek) = Servant of the king; slave of the king.

Ebenezer (eb-en-e'-zur) = Stone of help; the Lord helped us. (Stone raised in memory of the defeat of the Philistines.)

Eber (e'-bur) = He who passed over; the region beyond. A passer over. A shoot. (root = to pass over a river; to go through a land; to pass by). Beyond: the other side (as having crossed over).

Ebiasaph (e-bi'-a-saf) = Father of increase; the father that gathers together; the father of gathering; (roots = [1] father; [2] to add; to increase; to repeat).

Ebronah (eb-ro'-nah) = Passage; i.e., of the sea; (root = to pass over). Crossing over.

Ecclesiastes (e-kle'-ze-as'-tez) = Preacher.

Ed (ed) = Witness.

Edar (e'-dar) = Flock; (root = to keep in ranks; to keep in order; to lack nothing).

Eden (e'-dun) = Paradise; a place of delight; delight; pleasantness.

Eder (e'-dur) = Same as Edar = Flock; (root = to keep in ranks; to keep in order; to lack nothing).

Edom (e'-dum) = Red; red earth.

Edomites (e'-dum-ites) = Inhabitants of Edom = Red; red earth.

Edrei (ed'-re-i) = Strong.

A valley for a flock. Goodly pasture.

Eglah (eg'-lah) = A girl; a heifer; (roots = [1] a calf; [2] to go round).

Eglaim (eg'-la-im) = Two pools. Drops of dew. Double reservoir.

Eglon (eg'-lon) = A fine bull calf; i.e., large and fat. A strong heifer. Circle; chariot.

Egypt (e'-jipt) = Black; oppressors. Double straits.

Egyptian (e-jip'-shun) = An oppressor. Double straits.

Ehi (e'-hi) = My brother; unity.

Ehud (e'-hud) = Joined together; strong; union. He that praises.

Eker (e'-ker) = Offspring; a shoot; one transplanted.

Ekron (ec'-ron) = Uprooting; emigration; a rooter out; (root to root up).

Ekronites (ek'-ron-ites) = Inhabitants of Ekron = Uprooting; emigration.

Eladah (el'-a-dah) = God adorns; ornament of God; whom God clothes; God has adorned.

Elah (e'-lah) = Oak. An oak tree; like a tree. The denunciation of a curse. Also a proper name for God = ELAH (El-aw, #426) = Root Oak, tree symbolizes durability, The everlasting God. (e.g., Ezra 5:1 rebuilding the house of God). About 90 times. Indicates the living and true God who identifies with His people in captivity (43 times in Ezra; 46 times in Daniel). Arab word Allah.

Elam (e'-lam) = Hidden time; eternity. Youth; high. Their heaps; suckling them; eternal.

Elamites (e'-lam-ites) = Inhabitants of Elam = Hidden time; eternity. Youth; high. Their heaps; suckling them; eternal.

Elasah (el'-a-sah) = Whom God made; God is doer.

Elath (e'-lath) = Terebinths; a grove. An oak tree; an imprecation. Mightiness.

Elbethel [El Bethel] (el-beth'-el) = Strong house of God. The God of the house of God. God of God's house.

Eldaah (el'-da-ah) = Whom God called. God has known.

Eldad (el'-dad) = Whom God loves; the love of God; God has loved; God is a friend.

Elead (e'-le-ad) = Whom God praises; God is witness; God continues.

Elealeh (el-e-a'-leh) = Whither God ascends; the ascension of God.

Eleasah (el-e'-a-sah) = Same as Elasah = Whom God made; God is doer. God is helper.

Eleazar (el-e-a'-zar) = Whom God helps or aids; the help of God; God is helper.

Elelohe [El Elohe] (el-el-o'-he) = God of gods.

Elelohe-Israel [El Elohe Israel] (el-el-o'-he-iz'-rahel) = God is the God of Israel.

Eleph (e'-lef) = A great multitude; i.e., the abode of; (roots = [1] a thousand; a great number; the abode of a tribe; [2] to bring forth thousands). A disciple.

Elhanan (el-ha'-nan) = Whom God graciously gave; God was gracious; God has been generous; mercy of God.

Eli (e'-li) = Jehovah is high; my God; a foster son; adopted of the LORD. My ascension. My God; Elevated. (The high priest in Samuel's time).

Eliab (e'-le-ab) = My God is Father; whose Father is God; God, my Father; God is a Father.

Eliada (e-li'-a-dah) = Whom God knows; i.e., acknowledges and cares for; God is knowing; God kindly regarded.

Eliadah (e-li'-a-dah) =

Same as Eliada = Whom God knows; i.e., acknowledges and cares for; God is knowing; God kindly regarded.

Eliah (e-li'-ah) = Same name as Elijah = God-LORD; strength of the LORD. God is Jehovah. My God is Jah.

Eliahba (e-li'-ah-bah) = Whom God hides; God does hide.

Eliakim (el-li'-a-kim) = Whom God sets up; i.e., establishes and causes to stand; God will raise up; God does establish.

Eliam (e'-le-am) = God's people; the people of my God; God is one of the family; God's founder of the people.

Elias (e-li'-as) = Same as Elijah = God-LORD; strength of the LORD; God is Jehovah; God, Himself.

Eliasaph (e-li'-a-saf) = Whom God added; God has added; God is gathered.

Eliashib (e-li'-a-shib) = Whom God restores; whom God leads back again; God will restore; God is requiter; God has restored.

Eliathah (e-li'-a-thah) = God comes; to whom God comes; God has come. God of the coming (one).

Elidad (e-li'-dad) = Whom God loves; God has loved; God is a friend. My God is lover.

Eliel (e'-le-el) = To whom God is God; to whom God is strength; God is God.

Elienai (e-li-e'-nahee) = God of my eyes; unto Jehovah my eyes are raised; unto God are my eyes.

Eliezer (e-li-e'-zur) = God of help; my God is help; God is my help.

Elihoenai (e-li-ho-e'-nahee) = Same as Elioenai = God the LORD of my eyes; to Jehovah are my eyes.

Elihoreph (e-li-ho'-ref) = God of the reward; to

whom God is the reward. The God of winter. God of harvest rain; God is a reward.

Elihu (e-li'-hew) = Whose God is He. He is my God. He is God, Himself. My God is Jehovah.

Elijah (e-li'-jah) = God-LORD; strength of the LORD; my God is Jehovah; the LORD God.

Elika (e-li'-kah) = God of the congregation; strength of the congregation. God is rejector; God has spewed out.

Elim (e'-lim) = A grove of oaks; palms; (roots = [1] a strong robust tree; [2] to strengthen). Mighty ones.

Elimelech (e-lim'-e-lek) = God of the king. My God the king. God is king.

Elioenai (e-li-o-e'-nahee) = God the LORD of my eyes; i.e., to whom my eyes are directed.

Eliphal (el'-i-fal) = Whom God judges; God the judge; God is judge;

God has judged. The God of deliverance.

Eliphalet (e-lif'-a-let) = God of salvation; God the Savior; to whom God is salvation. The God of deliverance; God of escape.

Eliphaz (el'-if-az) = My God is fine gold; God the strong; to whom God is strength. My precious God; God is dispenser. My God has refined.

Elipheleh (e-lef'-e-leh) = God distinguishes him; i.e., makes him eminent; Jehovah is distinction; distinguished. My God, set thou apart.

Eliphelet (e-lif'-e-let) = Same as Eliphalet = God of salvation; God the Savior; to whom God is salvation. God of escape.

Elisabeth (e-liz'-a-beth) = Greek form of Elisheba = God of the oath; i.e., God is her oath, a worshiper of God; to whom God is the oath; God of the covenant; oath of my God; my God has sworn.

Eliseus (el-i-se'-us) = God, his salvation. Greek form of Elisha = God the Savior; to whom God is salvation; God of salvation; God is Savior.

Elisha (e-li'-shah) = God the Savior; to whom God is salvation; God of salvation; God is Savior.

Elishah (e-li'-shah) = Same as Elisha = God the Savior; to whom God is salvation; God of salvation; God is Savior. My God has disregarded.

Elishama (e-lish'-a-mah) = God the hearer; my God will hear; God is hearer; God has heard.

Elishaphat (e-lish'-a-fat) = God the judge; God judges; i.e., defends him; whom God judges; God is judge; God has judged.

Elisheba (e-lish'-e-bah) = God of the oath; i.e., God is her oath, a worshiper of God; to whom God is the oath. God of the covenant; oath of my God; my God has sworn.

Elishua (e-lish'-oo-ah) = God the rich; God of affluence; God is rich; God is salvation. God of crying. God of supplication, opulence.

Eliud (e-li'-ud) = God of Judah; God is majesty; God is my praise.

Elizaphan (e-liz'-a-fan) = God hides; i.e., defends him; whom God protects; God is protector; God has concealed.

Elizur (e-li'-zur) = God the Rock; God is my rock; God is a rock.

Elkanah (el-ka'-nah) = God has redeemed; possession of God; whom God possessed; (root = to possess; to acquire; to redeem). God hath created; God is jealous; God is possessing.

Elkoshite (el'-ko-shite) = God my bow; i.e., my defense. The gathered of God.

Ellasar (el'-la-sar) = Declension of God. God is chastener.

Elmodam (el-mo'-dam) = Same as Almodad = Immeasurable; increasing; without measure; extension. The God of measure.

Elnaam (el-na'-am) = God of pleasantness; whose pleasure God is; God is pleasant.

Elnathan (el-na'-than) = God gave; whom God gave; God has given; God is giving.

Eloi (e-lo'-ee) = My God.

Elon (e'-lon) = Magnificent oak; an oak tree; strong. Might.

Elonbethhanan [Elon Bethhanan] (e'-lon-beth-ha'-nan) = Oak of the house of grace. Might of the house of the gracious giver.

Elonites (e'-lon-ites) = Descendants of Elon = Magnificent oak; an oak tree; strong.

Eloth (e'-loth) = Same as Elath = Terebinths; a grove. Mightiness.

Elpaal (el-pa'-al) = God the maker; to whom God

is the reward; God is a reward; God is working.

Elpalet (el-pa'-let) = God is deliverance. Same as Eliphalet = God of salvation; God the Savior; to whom God is salvation. God is escape.

Elparan [El Paran] (el-pa'-ran) = Strong (applied to a State, with the idea of robust: of a tree, as a terebinth or pistacia); terebinths or turpentines abounding in foliage; (The terebinths live a thousand years - loaded with foliage and are evergreens); (roots = [1] strong; [2] to beautify; to adorn; to be glorified). The power of their adorning.

Eltekeh (el'-te-keh) = God fearing; whose fear is God. Let God spue you out.

Eltekon (el'-te-kon) = God the foundation; whose foundation is God; i.e., a place established on God. Made straight of God.

Eltolad (el-to'-lad) = God of the generation; God's race; whose posterity is from God; (root = to bring forth; to bear [as a mother]; to begot [as a father]; to be born; to make fruitful). May God cause you to forget.

Elul (e'-lul) = A vain thing. Nothingness. Sixth Jewish month (August - September)

Eluzai (e-loo'-zahee) = God of my congregation; God is my praise; God is my strength. God is my gathering strength (for flight).

Elymas (el'-i-mas) = A wise man; a magician; a sorcerer.

Elzabad (el'-za-bad) = God gave; i.e., whom God gave; God has endowed; God has bestowed.

Elzaphan (el'-za-fan) = Same as Elizaphan = God hides; i.e., defends him; whom God protects. God has concealed; God has protected.

Emerald (em'-er-ald) = Enameled.

Emims (e'-mims) = Terrors; horrors; terrible men; giants; the fearful.

Emmanuel (em-man'-uel) = God with us.

Emmaus (em'-ma-us) = Hot springs. In earnest longing.

Emmor (em'-mor) = Same as Hamor = Ass; an ass; (root = to be red; to be inflamed).

Enam (e'-nam) = Two fountains.

Enan (e'-nan) = Having eyes; a fountain.

Endor (en'-dor) = Fountain of habitation. The eye of a generation.

Eneas (e'-ne-as) = I praise; praise of Jehovah. Uttering praise.

Eneglaim [En Eglaim] (en-eg'-la-im) = Fountain of two calves. The eye of a heifer.

Engannim [En Gannim] (en-gan'-nim) = Fountain of the gardens.

Engedi [En Gedi] (en-ghe'-di) = Fountain of the kid. The eye of a kid.

Enhaddah [En Haddah] (en-had'-dah) = Fountain of sharpness; fountain of swiftness. Fountain of joy.

Enhakkore [En Hakkore] (en-hak'-ko-re) = Fountain of the calling; i.e., of prayer; (root = to cry out; to call; to proclaim).

Enhazor [En Hazor] (en-ha'-zor) = Fountain of Hazor. Fountain of the village; fount of trumpeting.

Enmishpat [En Mishpat] (en-mish'-pat) = Fountain of judgment. The eye of judgment.

Enoch (e'-nok) = Initiated; initiating; teacher; dedicated; consecrated;experienced.

Enos (e'-nos) = Man; man in his frailty; feeble; mortal.

Enosh (e'-nosh) = Same as Enos = Man; man in his frailty; feeble; mortal.

Enrimmon [En Rimmon]

(en-rim'-mon) = Fountain of the pomegranate.

Enrogel [En Rogel] (en-ro'-ghel) = Fountain of the fuller; (roots = [1] a fountain; [2] a treader {on garments to be washed}; a fuller). Fount of the spy.

Enshemesh [En Shemesh] (en-she'-mesh) = Fountain of the sun.

Entappuah [En Tappuah] (en-tap'-poo-ah) = Fountain of the apple tree.

Epaenetus (ep-en'-e-tus) = Laudable; worthy of praise.

Epaphras (ep'-a-fras) = Commended; charming; foamy.

Epaphroditus (e-paf-ro-di'-tus) = Lovely; handsome; charming.

Epenetus (ep-en'-e-tus) = Same as Epaenetus = Laudable; worthy of praise.

Ephah (e'-fah) = Darkness; obscurity. A measure.

Ephai (e'-fahee) =

Wearying of the Lord; i.e., great languishing; fatigued; obscured; (root = faint; weary; thirsty). My coverings; my shadows; my fowls.

Epher (e'-fur) = A young hart; calf. Mule; young calf. Dustiness.

Ephesdammim [Ephes Dammim] (e'-fes-dam'-min) = 1 Samuel 17:1, Extremity of bloods; boundary of blood; nothing but blood. (Called Pas-dammim in 1 Chronicles 11:13.)

Ephesian(s) (e-fe'-zheuns) = Inhabitants of Ephesus = Desirable; beloved. A giving away; to relax; loosening. (A city on the western coast of Asia Minor noted for the worship of the goddess Diana.)

Ephesus (ef'-e-sus) = Desirable; beloved. A giving away; to relax; permitted; loosening. (A city on the western coast of Asia Minor noted for the worship of the goddess

Diana.) Full purposed; a throwing at.

Ephlal (ef'-lal) = Judgment; judicious; judging; (root = to judge; to pray; to intercede).

Ephod (e'-fod) = Covering; Vestment (of the high priest); (root = to gird on; to bind on).

Ephphatha (ef'-fath-ah) = Be opened.

Ephraim (e'-fra-im) = Two fold increase; very fruitful; doubly fruitful. Double ash-heap.

Ephraimite(s) (e'-fra-im-ites) = Inhabitants of Ephraim = Two fold increase; very fruitful; doubly fruitful.

Ephrain (e'-fra-in) = Same as Ephron = A great and choice fawn. Double dust.

Ephratah (ef'-rat-ah) = Fruitful. Ash heap.

Ephrath (e'-frath) = Same as Ephratah = Fruitful. Fruitful land. A shyness.

Ephrathite(s) (ef'-rath-ites) = Inhabitants of Ephrath = Fruitful.

Ephron (e'-fron) = A great and choice fawn; of or belonging to a calf. Full of dust. Strong.

Epicureans (ep-i-cu-re'-ans) = A helper; defender.

Er (er) = Watcher; awake; on the watch; (root = to awake). Stirring up.

Eran (e'-ran) = Watchful (intensive form of Er). Their awaking; their stirring up.

Eranites (e'-ran-ites) = Descendants of Eran = Watchful.

Erastus (e-ras'-tus) = Beloved.

Erech (e'-rek) = Length.

Eri (e'-ri) = Watcher of the LORD; i.e., worshiper of Jehovah; my watcher. My awakening; my stirring up.

Erites (e'-rites) = Descendants of Eri = Watcher of the LORD; i.e., worshiper of Jehovah; my watcher.

Esaias (e-sah'-yas) = Same as Isaiah = Salvation of the LORD; Jehovah is helper; salvation is of the LORD. Jehovah has saved.

Esarhaddon (e'-zar-had'-dun) = Gift of fire. A restrainer of joy. Victorious; Ashur has given brothers. Captivity of the fierce; I will chastise the fierce.

Esau (e'-saw) = Covered with hair; hairy.

Esek (e'-sek) = Strife; contention. Oppression.

Eshbaal [Esh Baal] (esh'-ba-al) = Fire of Baal; a man of Baal.

Eshban [Esh Ban] (esh'-ban) = Very red. Intelligence; man of understanding. Fire of discernment.

Eshcol (esh'-col) = A cluster of grapes or flowers; cluster of grapes.

Eshean (esh'-e-an) = Support; i.e., a place of confidence; (root = to lean upon; to rely upon; to put confidence in).

Eshek (e'-shek) = Oppression; strife; violence; (root = to oppress; to defraud; to deceive).

Eshkalonites (esh'-ka-lon-ites) = Same as Ashkelon = Migration.

Eshtaol (esh'-ta-ol) = Woman requesting. I will be entreated.

Eshtaulites (esh'-ta-u-lites) = Inhabitants of Eshtaol = Woman requesting.

Eshtemoa (esh-te-mo'-ah) = Woman of fame; obedience. I will make myself heard.

Eshtemoh (esh'-te-moh) = Same as Eshtemoa = Woman of fame; obedience. I will soar aloft; I will cause my own ruin.

Eshton (esh'-ton) = Womanly; rest.

Esli (es'-li) = Same as Azaliah = Reserved of the LORD; Jehovah has reserved. God at my side.

Esrom (es'-rom) = Same

as Hezron = Enclosed; enclosure; surrounded by a wall.

Esther (es'-thur) = Star. She that is hidden.

Etam (e'-tam) = A place of ravenous creatures; wild beasts' lair.

Etham (e'-tham) = Boundary of the sea. Their plowshare.

Ethan (e'-than) = Firmness; strength; ancient; perplexity.

Ethanim (eth'-a-nim) = Gifts.

Ethbaal (eth'-ba-al) = Living with Baal; a man of Baal; with him is Baal; Baal's man.

Ether (e'-ther) = Abundance; plenty.

Ethiopia (e-the-o'-pe-ah) = Same as Cush = A black countenance; full of darkness; region of burnt faces; blackness.

Ethiopian (e-the-o'-pe-en) = Same as Cush = A black countenance; full of darkness; region of burnt faces; blackness.

Ethnan (eth'-nan) = A gift; i.e., of an harlot; hire. Hire of unchastity.

Ethni (eth'-ni) = Reward; bountiful; my gift. My hire.

Eubulus (yu-bu'-lus) = Good counselor; well advised; prudent.

Eunice (yu-ni'-see) = Conquering well. Literally - happy victory.

Euodias (yu-o'-de-as) = Success; prosperous journey.

Euphrates (yu-fra'-teze) = Fruitfulness; fruitful; the fertile river; (root = to bear fruit).

Euroclydon (yu-roc'-lid-on) = Storm from the east; a wind. An easterly tempest.

Eutychus (yu'-tik-us) = Fortunate; happy. Well off.

Eve (eev) = Life; life-giving; living; (root = to live; to prosper; to keep alive; to give life). Mother of all who have life.

Evi (e'-vi) = Desire; (root = to desire; to lust).

Evilmerodach [Evil-Merodach] (e'-vil-mer'-o-dak) = The fool of Merodach; (root = to be foolish). Chaldean: A rebellious fool. (Also see Merodach). Foolish is your rebellion.

Exodus (ek'-so-dus) = Departure.

Ezar (e'-zar) = Treasure.

Ezbai (ez'-bahee) = Spoil; (root = to seize; to spoil; to take spoil; to rob). Beautiful. My humblings(?).

Ezbon (ez'-bon) = Great beauty; splendor. Hastening to discern; I will be enlargement.

Ezekias (ez-e-ki'-as) = Same as Hezekiah = Strength of the LORD; Jehovah is strength.

Ezekiel (e-zeke'-yel) = Strength of God; whom God will strengthen; God is strong; the man God strengthens.

Ezel (e'-zel) = Departure; running.

Ezem (e'-zem) = Same as Azem = Strength; bone.

Ezer (e'-zur) = Treasury; treasure; help; (root = to lay up; to treasure up; to store up). A help.

Eziongaber [Ezion Gaber] (e'-ze-on-ga'-bur) = Same as Ezion-geber = The backbone of a man (intense form). Counsel of a man.

Eziongeber [Ezion Geber] (e'-ze-on-ge'-bur) = The backbone of a man (intense form).

Eznite (ez'-nite) = Same as Adino the Eznite = Whose pleasure is the spear; his bending of the spear; (roots = [1] a spear; [2] to be mighty; strong). The stiff-backed.

Ezra (ez'-rah) = Help; assistance; my helper.

Ezrahite (ez'-rah-hite) = Sprung up. A native (as arising out of the soil).

Ezri (ez'-ri) = Help (of the Lord); God is a help.

F aithful is he that calleth you, who also will do it (1 Thessalonians 5:24).

Felix (fe'-lix) = Delusive. Latin - Happy; prosperous.

Festus (fes'-tus) = Joyful; festal; prosperous.

Fortunatus (for-chu-na'-tus) = Prosperous. Well freighted.

Frankincense (frank-in'-cense) = Whiteness.

Give unto the LORD the glory due unto his name; worship the LORD in the beauty of holiness (Psalms 29:2).

Gaal (ga'-al) = Loathing; an abhorrence; rejection; contempt.

Gaash (ga'-ash) = Shaking; earthquake; (root = to shake, especially the earth; to be moved).

Gaba (ga'-bah) = Hill; highlander.

Gabbai (gab'-bahee) = An exacter of tribute; in-gatherer; tax gatherer. My eminences.

Gabbatha (gab'-ba-thah) = Height; elevated; platform.

Gabriel (ga'-bre-el) = Man of God. God my strength.

Gad (gad) = Good

fortune; good luck; a troop; (root = to gather in troops; to cut through). A seer.

Gadarenes (gad-a-renes') = Reward at the end.

Gaddi (gad'-di) = Fortunate; belonging to fortune.

Gaddiel (gad'-de-el) = God is a fortune bringer; God has given fortune; my fortune. Troop of God.

Gadi (ga'-di) = Fortune sent from God; fortunate. Troop of God.

Gadites (gad'-ites) = Descendants of Gad = Good fortune; good luck; a troop; a seer; (root = to gather in troops; to cut through).

Gaham (ga'-ham) = Having large and flaming eyes; sunburnt; flaming; blackness. The devastator waxed hot; the valley was lost.

Gahar (ga'-har) = Hiding place; prostration. The valley burned.

Gaius (gah'-yus) = I am glad. On earth.

Galal (ga'-lal) = He has rolled away (the reproach of the parents); worth; influential. Rolling of one's day upon the Lord.

Galatia (ga-la'-she-ah) = Land of the Gali or Gauls. (Root same as Galilee = Circuit; rolling; revolving). Milky(?).

Galatians (ga-la'-she-uns) = Inhabitants of Galatia = Land of the Gali or Gauls. (Root same as Galilee = Circuit; rolling; revolving).

Galeed (ga'-le-ed) = Hill of witness; witness; heap, of witnesses or testimony.

Galilaean (gal-i-le'-un) = Same as Galilee = Circuit; rolling; revolving.

Galilee (gal'-i-lee) = Circuit - as enclosed, or rolled around; rolling; revolving.

Gallim (gal'-lim) = Fountains. Heaps. Billows (as heaps of water).

Gallio (gal'-le-o) = He that sucks.

Gamaliel (gam-a'-le-el) = Recompense of God; benefit of God; God is the one who brings recompense; the gift or reward of God.

Gammadims (gam'-ma-dims) = Warriors. Cutters; additional garments.

Gamul (ga'-mul) = Weaned; matured; recompensed.

Gareb (ga'-reb) = Scabby; leprous; reviler; rough.

Garmite (gar'-mite) = Bony.

Gashmu (gash'-mu) = Same as Geshem = Rain. Corporealness.

Gatam (ga'-tam) = Great fatigue; (root = to labor; to be weary). Puny; burnt valley. Reach thou the end; their touch.

Gath (gath) = Winepress.

Gathhepher (gath-he'-fer) = Winepress of the well.

Gathrimmon [Gath Rimmon] (gath-rim'-mon) = Winepress of the pomegranate.

Gaza (ga'-zah) = Same as Azzah = Strong; fortified.

Gazathites (ga'-zath-ites) =Inhabitants of Gaza = Strong; fortified.

Gazer (ga'-zur) = Place cut off; precipice; (roots = [1] a piece; a part {from the idea of dividing asunder}; [2] to cut off; to divide).

Gazez (ga'-zez) = Shearer; (root = to shear; to cut off; to shave).

Gazites (ga'-zites) = Inhabitants of Gaza = Strong; fortified.

Gazzam (gaz'-zam) = Violently torn off; swaggerer; devourer. Palmerworm - literally, their shearing.

Geba (ghe'-bah) = Same as Gaba = Hill. A drinking cup.

Gebal (ghe'-bal) = Boundary; (root = to set bounds; to make a boundary). A border.

Geber (ghe'-bur) = Warrior; hero; strong.

Gebim (ghe'-bim) = Pits; trenches. Grasshoppers.

Gedaliah (ghed-a-li'-ah) = Magnified of the LORD; whom Jehovah has made great; Jehovah is great. Brought up by God.

Gedeon (ghed'-e-on) = The cutter down. Greek form of Gideon = Feller; cutter down; one who cuts down; a hewer down; a cutting down. He that bruises; great warrior.

Geder (ghe'-dur) = A wall; a walled place.

Gederah (ghed'-e-rah) = Enclosure; sheepfold.

Gederathite (ghed'-e-rath-ite) = Inhabitants of Gederah = Enclosure; sheepfold.

Gederite (ghed'-e-rite) = Inhabitants of Geder = A wall.

Gederoth (ghed'-e-roth) = Folds; fortifications; sheepfolds.

Gederothaim (ghed-e-ro-tha'-im) = Two folds; two fortified places; two sheepfolds.

Gedor (ghe'-dor) = Fortified; a fortress; wall.

Gehazi (ghe-ha'-zi) = Valley of vision; the valley of sight. Denier.

Gehenna (ge-hen'-na) = Hell (from "the valley of Hinnon').

Geliloth (ghel'-il-oth) = Regions. Circles; borders.

Gemalli (ghe-mal'-li) = Possessor of camels; camel owner; rider of a camel.

Gemariah (ghem-a-ri'-ah) = Perfected of the LORD; whom Jehovah has completed; Jehovah has fulfilled; accomplishment of the LORD; God has finished; (root = to perfect; to perform; to bring to an end).

Genesis (jen'-e-sis) = Generation; beginning.

Gennesaret (ghen-nes'-a-ret) = A harp; harp shaped.

Gentiles (jen'-tiles) = A people or nation, other than the Jews.

Genubath (ghen'-u-beth) = Theft; (root = to steal; to take away anything secretly; to acquire by stealth).

Gera (ghe'-rah) = Rumination (the food which ruminating animals bring up to chew, commonly called the cud); grain; (root = to ruminate; to chew [the cud]; to saw; to destroy). Excitement. Enmity; pilgrimage.

Gerah (ghe'-rah) = A piece; a bit. (The twentieth part of a shekel.)

Gerar (ghe'-rar) = Sojourning; journeying; a lodging place; (root = to turn aside [from the way]; to tarry; to sojourn; to dwell; to fear; to be a stranger). Annoyance. Dragging away.

Gergesenes (ghur'-ghes-enes') = A stranger drawing near.

Gerizim (gher'-iz-im) = Cutters down; fellers; cuttings off. Divisions. (The mount of blessing.)

Gershom (ghur'-shom) = A stranger there; exile; expulsion. A sojourner there.

Gershon (ghur'-shon) = Same as Gershom = A stranger there; exile; expulsion. Driven out. An outcast.

Gershonite(s) (ghur'-shon-ites) = Descendants of Gershon = A stranger there; exile; expulsion. Driven out. An outcast.

Gesham (ghe'-sham) = Large clod; firm; strong.

Geshem (ghe'-shem) = Rain; (root = to rain; to cause to rain).

Geshur (ghe'-shur) = Expulsion. A bridge. Proud; beholder.

Geshuri (ghesh'-u-ri) = Exiles.

Geshurites (ghesh'-u-rites) = Inhabitants of Geshuri = Exiles.

Gether (ghe'-ther) = Fear

(of the enemy); vale of trial. A proud spy.

Gethsemane (gheth-sem'-a-ne) = Oil press.

Geuel (ghe-u'-el) = Majesty of God; salvation of God; (root = to lift up; to triumph gloriously). Exalt ye God.

Gezer (ghe'-zur) = Same as Gazer = Place cut off; precipice; (root = to cut off; to divide). A piece; a portion (as cut off).

Gezrites (ghez'-rites) = Inhabitants of Gazer = Place cut off; precipice; (roots = [1] a piece; a part {from the idea of dividing asunder}; [2] to cut off; to divide).

Giah (ghi'-ah) = Breaking forth; i.e., of a fountain; gushing forth. To draw out; extend.

Gibbar (ghib'-bar) = Hero; mighty; mighty man.

Gibbethon (ghib'-be-thon) = A lofty place; (root = to be high; to be lifted up; to be exalted).

Gibea (ghib'-e-ah) = Same as Gaba = Hill; highlander.

Gibeah (ghib'-e-ah) = The hill; a hill.

Gibeath (ghib'-e-ath) = Same as Gibeah = The hill. Hilliness.

Gibeathite (ghib'-e-ath-ite) = Hilliness.

Gibeon (ghib'-e-on) = High hill; a dweller on a hill.

Gibeonite(s) (ghib'-e-on-ites) = Inhabitants of Gibeon = High hill; a dweller on a hill.

Giblites (ghib'-lites) = Inhabitants of Gebal = Boundary; (root = to set bounds; to make a boundary).

Giddalti (ghid-dal'-ti) = I have trained up; I have increased; I have magnified; I magnify God.

Giddel (ghid'-del) = He has become great; very great; gigantic; he has magnified.

Gideon (ghid'-e-on) =

Feller; cutter down; one who cuts down; a hewer down; a cutting down. He that bruises; great warrior.

Gideoni (ghid-e-o'-ni) = Same as Gideon = Feller; cutting down; one who cuts down; a hewer down; a cutting down. He that bruises; great warrior. A cutting of.

Gidom (ghi'-dom) = Cutting down.

Gihon (ghi'-hon) = Great breaking forth, (of waters); a river.

Gilalai (ghil'-a-lahee) = Rolled off of the Lord. Weighty.

Gilboa (ghil-bo'-ah) = Bubbling water of a fountain; (root = swelling up; gushing up; boiling up). Literally - rolling, pouring out. A flow of joy.

Gilead (ghil'-e-ad) = Perpetual fountain. A heap of testimony; a witness; mass of testimony; strong.

Gileadite(s) (ghil'-e-ad-ites) = Inhabitants of Gilead = Perpetual

fountain. A heap of testimony; a witness; mass of testimony; strong.

Gilgal (ghil'-gal) = Liberty; rolling away; a circle; (root = a wheel).

Giloh (ghi'-loh) = Exodus of a great multitude; (root = to lead into exile; to lead into captivity; to make bare; to depopulate [a land]; to uncover; to reveal). His joy.

Gilonite (ghi'-lo-nite) = Inhabitants of Giloh = Exodus of a great multitude.

Gimzo (ghim'-zo) = Sycamores. Swallowing this.

Ginath (ghi'-nath) = Protection. Similitude; (root = my garden).

Ginnetho (ghin'-ne-tho) = Great protection. Garden; gardener.

Ginnethon (ghin'-ne-thon) = Same as Ginnetho = Great protection. Garden; gardener.

Girgashite(s) (ghur'-gash-ites) = Dwellers in a clayey soil. Driven out. A stranger drawing near(?).

Girgasite (ghur'-ga-site) = Same as Girgashite = Dwellers in a clayey soil. Driven out.

Gispa (ghis'-pah) = Soothing; flattery; (root = to soothe tenderly). Attentive; banishment.

Gittahhepher [Gath Hepher] (ghit'-tah-he'-fer) = Winepress of the well.

Gittaim (ghit-ta'-im) = Two winepresses.

Gittite(s) (ghit'-tites) = Inhabitants of Gath = Winepress.

Gittith (ghit'-tith) = Same as Gath = Winepress.

Gizonite (ghi'-zo-nite) = Stone quarrier; (root = to cut out [of any place]).

Goath (go'-ath) = Fatigue; (root = to weary; to labor).

Gob (gob) = Pit; snare. The back.

GOD = self-revealing names of GOD in the Old Testament. (Scripture references are the first place the word is used in the Bible.)

Adon = To rule; sovereign; controller. In KJV printed as Lord (capital "L" small case "ord") Used about 31 times in the OT when referring to God.

Adonai = (Genesis 15:2). =Master; Lord; Owner. When printed as Lord (capital "L" small case "ord") in KJV to refer to Deity, the name usually refers to Jesus (Genesis 15:2).

Adon-Adonai = Jehovah our Ruler. A vigorous name of God expressing divine dominion; reveals God as the absolute Owner and Lord.

Adoni-Jah = Jehovah is LORD

EL = (Genesis 14:18); Root = to be strong. The Strong One. Indicates the great power of God. In the singular it emphasizes the essence of the

Godhead. It has been translated as "Mighty, Prominent, The First One."

Elah = (elahh) (Ezra 4:24); oak; an oak tree; like a tree. The denunciation of a curse. Root = an oak; tree symbolizes durability; the EVERLASTING God (Ezra 5:1 rebuilding the house of God). Indicates the living and true God who identifies with His people in captivity (used 43 times in Ezra; 46 times in Daniel).

Eloah = (elowahh) (Deuteronomy 32:15). Used 54 times in Scripture (40 times in Job alone). Root = to fear; to worship; to adore. The adorable or worshipful One, (Job 19:25-26). The name for *absolute Deity*. The only living and true God, in all His being. The object of all testimony and worship. It is the singular of Elohim. It speaks of the totality of His being; the finality of His decisions.

Elohim = (*El-lo-heem*) (Genesis 1:1); Root = to swear; name indicates God, under the covenant of an oath with Himself to perform certain conditions (Hebrews 6:13). Name implies: One in covenant; Fullness of might. Refers to absolute, unqualified, unlimited energy. A plural name revealing God in the unity and trinity of *all* His divine personality and power.

El Elohe-Israel = (Genesis 33:18-20); God of Israel; God, the God of Israel

El Elyon = (Genesis 2); Most high God; God most high; combines the idea of God's highness with His might. (The Possessor [or framer] of heaven and earth.)

El Olam = (Genesis 20:13); God of eternity; KJV the everlasting God. The God without a beginning; the God who never will cease to be;

the God who will never grow old; the God to whom eternity is what present time is. Describes God as He who extends beyond our greatest vision of who we think God is (no matter how great our concept of God is, He is always greater).

El Roi = (Genesis 16:13,14 only time used); the well of Him that lives and sees. Roi = root = that sees; of sight.

El Shaddai = (*el shad-di*) = Almighty God; all-sufficient God; (first used in Genesis 17:1; last used in Revelation 19:15). In Him all fullness dwells, and out of His constant fullness His own receive all things. **EL** sets forth God's Almightiness, and **Shaddai,** His exhaustless bounty; i.e., the all-bountiful One. The psalmist reveals God's supremacy and sufficiency with His eternalness; He that dwelleth in the secret place of El Elyon, shall abide under the shadow of El Shaddai (Psalm 91:1). ". . . from everlasting to everlasting, Thou art God (Psalm 90:2).

Shaddai = (Genesis 17:1) Almighty; used 48 times 31 times in Job; about 10 times in the New Testament where it speaks of the all powerful One, the absolute Sovereign. In Scripture, the term Almighty (used about 58 times) is applied only to God. Shaddai speaks of God Almighty; the mighty One of resource or sufficiency; the pourer forth of blessings (temporal and spiritual); the breasted One; the mighty One of resource of sufficiency; root = shad = a breast; Genesis 49:25 *the blessings of the breasts* presents God as the One who nourishes, supplies, and satisfies. God, all bountiful; God all sufficient.

Heleyon or **Eleyon** = most high; highest; Jehovah most high (Psalm 7:17; 47:2; 83:18; 97:9). Reveals God as the high and lofty One who inhabits eternity (Isaiah 57:15). The title has to do with the Most High as the ascended One who is in the highest place, guarding and ruling over all things and making everything work to one given end (Daniel 4:25).

Jah = (Psalm 68:4); found 50 times in Exodus, Psalms, and Isaiah. A shortened, poetic, form of Jehovah; the Independent One; the LORD most vehement; root = to be; to breathe. The name signifies, He is; present tense of the verb to be. (It foreshadows Jesus as the I AM in John.) He will be; i.e., the Eternal who always is; the Eternal One; the name of the LORD everlasting. First used in Exodus 15:2; this song of salvation shows Jah to be a present and perpetual support and security (Isaiah 26:4). The name suggests Jehovah as the *present Living God* the presence of God in daily life; His present activity and oversight on behalf of His own. Jah reveals God as the One intensely and personally interested in us, and who sits on the circuit of the earth observing our every action.

Jehovah = (Genesis 2:4). Self-existent; the eternal, ever-loving One; He will be; i.e., the Eternal who always is; the eternal One; the I AM THAT I AM; (He) was, is, will be, the LORD God; root = to be; to exist; being; to breathe). In Hebrew this name is written as YHVH (called a Tetragrammaton or four-lettered name).

This name reveals God as the One Who is absolutely self-existent, and who, in Himself, possesses essential life and permanent existence. A name of covenant relationship; God's signature when He entered into a covenant with man. The name is first used as Jehovah-Elohim in Genesis 2:4, denoting that Elohim, the God of relationship, now requires order and obedience. The name is first used alone in God s revelation to Moses in Exodus 6:3. **Jehovah** is derived from the Hebrew verb "havah" = to be; to exist; being; to breathe. The name Jehovah brings before us the idea of being or existence and life. Jehovah is the Being who is absolutely self-existent, the One who in Himself possesses essential life, the One who has permanent existence, He who is without beginning or end (Isaiah 43:10, 11; Psalm 102:27). Jehovah is the ever existent One; the Eternal; the Everlasting One - that is; the One continually revealing Himself and His ways and purposes. In the KJV, the Father, Jehovah, is printed as LORD or GOD (all caps); i.e., the Lord GOD, Ezekiel 16:8,30,{Adonai-Jehovah}. The only departure from this is found in Deuteronomy 28:58 in the phrase: "THE LORD THY GOD" {Jehovah-Elohim}. Middle-Ages Jewish commentator, Moses Maimonides, stated that, "All the names of God which occur in Scripture are derived from His works except one, and that is Jehovah, and this is called the plain name, because it teaches plainly and unequivocally of the substance of God. In the name Jehovah the personality of the Supreme is distinctly expressed. It is everywhere a proper name denoting the person of God and Him only."

Jehovah-Elohay = The LORD my God. Similar to Adhon or Adhonay; a personal name meaning My LORD; likewise emphasizing divine sovereignty (Judges 6:15; 13:8). Elohay, however points to the personal pronoun as being expressive of a personal faith in the GOD of power (Zechariah 14:5). Wherever the title is used, it is in the individual, personal sense, and not a general one as in The LORD our God.

Jehovah-Elobeenu =The LORD our God; suggesting the common wealth of God's people in Him.

Jehovah-Eloheka = The LORD your God. This title is found 20 times in Deuteronomy 16. Taking its use from Exodus (Exodus 20:2) where it is often used, this divine name denotes Jehovah s relationship to His people, and their responsibility to Him. This name is more personal than His previous name,

Jehovah-Eloheenu = The LORD our God.

Jehovah-Elohim = Reveals the majestic omnipotent God, combining the majesty and meaning of both names (Zechariah 13:9; Psalm 118:27). Together they imply man's place of conscious intelligent relationship to his creator. Reveals man's accountability to God. Name first used in Genesis 2:4 (LORD God, twenty times in Genesis 2 and 3) reveals the nature of (Elohim) the God of relationship and

(Jehovah) the GOD of holiness and order who requires sacrifice (Genesis 8:20) and obedience (Exodus 6:3) based on relationship.

Jehovah-Gmolah = (Jeremiah 51:7,8); The GOD of recompenses.

Jehovah-Heleyon = (Psalm 97:9, ASV; 7:17; 47:2; 83:18); reveals God as the high and lofty One that inhabits eternity (Isaiah 57:15).

Jehovah-Hoseenu = (Psalm 95:6); The Lord our maker. Refers to God's ability to fashion something out of what already exists (Hebrews 11:10; Ephesians 2:22), not to His ability to speak and create out of nothing.

Jehovah-Jireh = (Genesis 22:14); the LORD is provision; the LORD will see and provide.

Jehovah-Makkeh = (Ezekiel 7:9); The LORD shall smite you.

Jehovah-M'Kaddesh = (*M-kad-desh*) =

(Leviticus 20:8); the LORD is sanctification; the LORD who sanctifies; the LORD does sanctify (sanctify = to set apart); root = M'Kaddesh = sanctify; holy; hallow; consecrate; dedicate; sanctuary; Holy One.The term "holiness" from the Hebrew "kodesh" is allied to sanctify, which is translated by words such as dedicate, consecrate, hallow, and holy in the Scriptures. GOD wants us to know Him as Jehovah-M'Kaddesh, Jehovah who sets us apart unto Himself. In connection with man, Jehovah M'Kaddesh (Jehovah who sanctifies), empowers us with His presence to set us apart for His service. The Lord wants us to be a holy nation (Exodus 19:5, 6) that appreciates our high, holy, and heavenly calling (Exodus 31:13). We have no inherent holiness or righteousness apart from Him. God's command, "Sanctify yourselves" can be fulfilled only in the imparted and imputed righteousness of Christ, for, "I am the LORD which sanctify you."

Jehovah-Nissi (nis-see) = (Exodus 17:8-15); the LORD is a Banner; the LORD my banner; the LORD our banner; root = "Nissi" = Banner; an ensign; a standard (Isaiah 5:26; 49:22; 62:10; compare Psalm 20:5; 60:4). A sign, (Numbers 26:10); and a pole in connection with the brazen serpent (Numbers 21:9). Jesus is our victory over Amalek (the flesh) through the Cross; He is our banner leading us to victory. Dr. F. E. Marsh says: "The Lord in His death for us is our Banner in victory our Standard in life our Ensign in testimony our Sign to all that He is the Triumphant Lord."

Jehovah-Rohi (*Ro -ee*) = (Psalm 23:1); the LORD is a Shepherd; the LORD my Shepherd; (root = Rohi = shepherd; feed; to lead to pasture; tend a flock.)

Jehovah-Rophe (*Rophi*) (*Ro'-phay*) = (Exodus 15:22-26); the LORD is healing (physical and spiritual); the LORD who heals you; the LORD the Physician; (root = Rophi = heals; healing; restore; repair; make whole.) Verse 26 can be "I Am Jehovah, thy Healer. Heals or healeth = to mend (as a garment is mended); to repair (as a building is constructed); and to cure (as a diseased person is restored to health) (Compare Psalm 103.3; 147:3; Jeremiah 3:22; Genesis 20:17; 2 Kings 20:5.)

Jehovah-Sabaoth = Hebrew Tsebaoth; Greek: Sab-a-oth,

(Romans 9:29; James 5:4); Sabaoth = host or hosts, with special reference to warfare or service. The LORD of Hosts (1 Samuel 1:3; Jeremiah 11:20; used about 260 times in the Old Testament); LORD of all power and might (material or spiritual), LORD of heaven and earth, sole God and ruler of the world; LORD of all angels, men, demons; the absolute monarch of this universe (Daniel 4:33). The LORD of powers the LORD all possessing, all-controlling.

Jehovah-Shalom (*Shallom*) = (Judges 6:24); the LORD is peace; the LORD my peace; the LORD our peace; the LORD is or sends peace; (root = Shalom = peace; welfare; good health; whole; favor; perfect; full; prosperity; rest; make good; pay or perform in the sense of fulfilling or completing an obligation.)

Jehovah-Shammah (Shamah) (Ezekiel 48:35); the LORD is there; the LORD is present: (Root = Shammah = presence).

Jehovah-Tsebaoth = Same as Jehovah-Sabaoth = LORD of hosts; Hebrew: "Sabaoth" [Saw-Baw], (1 Samuel 1:3); Word literally means hosts; combines the ideas of divine maker and controller with special reference to warfare; implies divine revelation and authority; armies; a gathering together in His name.

Jehovah-Tsidkenu (*tsidkay'-noo*) = (Jeremiah 23:5, 6; 33:16); the Lord is righteous; the LORD our righteousness; the LORD my righteousness; root = **Tsidkenu** = straight; right; righteous; just; justify. This word represents God s dealing with men under the ideas of righteousness, justification, and acquittal.

Gog (gog) = Extension; a roof; a mountain; (root = a roof [of a house]; surface of the altar; top of the house).

Golan (go'-lan) = Great exodus; exile; (root = a band of exiles). Their captivity; their rejoicing.

Golgotha (gol'-go-thah) = Place of a skull.

Goliath (go-li'-ath) = Exile; the exile; soothsayer. Taken captive. Stripped (as a captive).

Gomer (go'-mer) = Complete; completion; heat; perfect; conclusion; i.e., filling up of the measure of idolatry or ripeness of consummate wickedness.

Gomorrah (go-mor'-rah) = People of fear; fear of the people; a rebellious people; (roots = [1] a people; [2] to be fearful; to tremble).

Depression; (root = to bind; to subdue). Bondage.

Gomorrha (go-mor'-rah) = Same as Gomorrah = People of fear; fear of the people; a rebellious people; (roots = [1] a people; [2] to be fearful; to tremble). Depression; (root = to bind; to subdue). Bondage.

Gopher (go'-pher) = Covered; pitch-wood.

Goshen (go'-shen) = The place or temple of the sun. Approaching. Drawing near.

Gozan (go'-zan) = Cut through; (root = to cut off; to pass through). A fleece.

Grecia (gre'-sha) = A defrauder. Unstable; the miry one.

Grecians (gre'-shuns) = Same as Greeks = Same as Javan (Hebrew): Supple; clay. He that deceives; a defrauder. (In NT, a Hellenist or Greek-speaking Jew.)

Greece (gres) = (OT) = Same as Grecia = A

defrauder; (root = to effervesce; i.e., wine).

Greece (gres) = (N.T.) = Unstable; the mirey one.

Greek(s) (greks) = Same as Greece = Unstable; the mirey one.

Gudgodah (gud-go'-dah) = Same as Horhagidgad = Cavern of thunder. The slashing place.

Guni (gu'-ni) = My garden; protected; painted with colors.

Gunites (gu'-nites) = Descendants of Guni = My garden; protected; painted with colors.

Gur (gur) = Same as Gerar = Sojourning; journeying; a lodging place; (root = to turn aside [from the way]; to tarry; to sojourn; to dwell; to fear; to be a stranger).

Gurbaal [Gur Baal] (gur-ba'-al) = Sojourning of Baal.

ope thou in God: for I shall yet praise him for the help of his countenance (Psalms 42:5).

Haahashtari (ha-a-hash'-te-ri) = Muleteer. From root word meaning = I will diligently observe the searching.

Habaiah (hab-ah'-yah) = Hidden of the LORD.

Habakkuk (hab'-ak-kuk) = Embracing (as a token of love); (root = to embrace; to fold [the hands together]). Ardently embraced.

Habaziniah (hab-az-in-i'-ah) = Light of Jehovah. The hiding of Jah's thorn.

Habor (ha'-bor) = Uniting together; (rot = to join together; to couple together; to make a league).

Hacerem = [NIV] See Bethhaccerem.

Hachaliah (hak-a-li'-ah) = Dark-flashing of the Lord; (root = to be dark [as regards the eyes]). The waiting on Jah.

Hachilah (hak'i-lah) = Dark; dusky.

Hachmoni (hak'-mo-ni) = Very wise; (root = to be wise; to be cunning; to be skillful).

Hachmonite (hak'-mo-nite) = Same as Hachmoni = Very wise; (root = to be wise; to be cunning; to be skilful).

Hadad (ha'-dad) = Chief; most eminent; most high. Sharpness. Noisy. 1 Kings 11:17 - I shall move softly; I shall love. (1 Chronicles 1:30) - sharp.

Hadadrimmon [Hadad Rimmon] (ha'-dad- rim'-mon) (Zechariah 12:11). Hadad = Chief; most eminent; most high. Sharpness. Rimmon = A Pomegranate; very high;

(roots = [1] a pomegranate; [2] to be high). Bursting of the pomegranate. Great shouting.

Hadadezer (had-a-de'-zer) = Whose help is Hadad; mighty is the help; Hadar is a help; beauty of assistance.

Hadah = [NIV] See Enhaddah.

Haddon = [NIV] See Esarhaddon.

Hadar (ha'-dar) = Ornament; honor; (root = to honor; to deck oneself with ornaments and glorious apparel). Privy chamber (Genesis 25:18).

Hadarezer (had-a-re'-zer) = Majesty of help. Whose help is Hadad. Honor of the helper.

Hadashah (had'-a-shah) = New; (root = to renew; to repair). Renewal.

Hadassah (ha-das'-sah) = Myrtle. (Jewish name for Esther).

Hadattah (ha-dat'tah) = Newness. Sharpness.

Hadid (ha'-did) = Sharp; (root = to be sharp).

Hadlai (had'-la-i) = Forsaken of the LORD; frail; lax; (root = to forsake; to leave; to leave off; to cease; to forbear).

Hadoram (ha-do'-ram) = Noble generation or race. Their glory. Hadar is high.

Hadrach (ha'-drak) = Spherical. Chaldean: A gentle voice. Your privy chamber.

Hagab (ha'-gab) = Grasshopper; a locust; bent; (root = a leaper; a locust).

Hagaba (hag'-a-bah) = Grasshopper; leaper; a locust.

Hagabah (hag'-a-bah) = Same as Hagaba = Grasshopper; leaper; a locust.

Hagar (ha'-gar) = Same as Agar = Flight; (root = to flee). Came to mean = Fugitive; immigrant. The sojourner. Ensnaring.

Hagarenes (hag-a-renes') = Fugitives. Sojourners.

Ensnaring.

Hagarites (hag'-a-rites) = Same as Hagarenes = Fugitives. Sojourners.

Hagerite (hag'-e-rite) = Same as Hagarenes = Fugitives. Sojourners.

Haggai (hag'-ga-i) = Festival of the LORD; festal; born of a festival day; (root = to keep a feast, with the idea of dancing; to dance; to leap with joy; to reel to and fro). My solemn feast.

Haggeri (hag'-gher-i) = Wanderer. Same as Hagarenes = Fugitives. Sojourners.

Haggi (hag'-ghi) = Exultation (of the LORD); festive; born of a festival. My feast.

Haggiah (hag-ghi'-ah) = Exultation; festival of Jehovah. Feast of Jehovah.

Haggites (hag'-ghites) = Same as Haggi = Exultation (of the LORD); festive; born of a festival.

Haggith (hag'-ghith) = Same as Haggi =

exultation (of the LORD); festive; born of a festival; festival of the LORD. Festival; dancer. A solemnity.

Hai (ha'-i) = Same as Ai = A heap of ruins; (root = to bend; to twist to distort; to act perversely; to subvert; to sin; to contort with pain as in a woman giving birth).

Hakkatan (hak'-ka-tan) = Little; smallness; the younger; the little one.

Hakkoz (hak'-koz) = Same as Coz = Thorn. Nimble; the thorn of the nimble.

Hakupha (ha-ku'-fah) = Bent; curved; incitement; (root = to bend one's self). Decree on the month.

Halah (ha'-lah) = Same as Calah = Old Age; completion; (root = to be completed). Painful; fresh anguish.

Halak (ha'-lak) = Smooth.

Halhul (hal'-hul) = Trepidation; trembling; (root = to twist oneself; to writhe in pain; to tremble; to bring forth).

Hali (ha'-li) = Necklace; ornament; jewel.

Halleluiah (hal-le-loo'-i-yah) = (Alleluia) Closest definition (KJV) = Praise ye the LORD. Praise ye Jah.

Hallelujah (hal-le-loo'-yah) = (Alleluia) Closest definition (KJV) = Praise ye the LORD.

Hallohesh (hal-lo'-hesh) = The whisperer; enchanter; (root = to mutter; to whisper; to use enchantments). The charmer.

Halohesh (hal-lo'-hesh) = Same as Hallohesh = The whisperer; enchanter; (root = to mutter; to whisper; to use enchantments). The charmer.

Ham #1 (ham) = Heat; hot; warm; black; dark; (root = to wax warm; to wax hot; to inflame). (The second son of Noah).

Ham #2 (ham) = Noisy;

(root = to make noise; to rage; to roar, like the sea). (The region of Zuzim near Ammon).

Haman (ha'-man) = Alone; solitary. Well disposed. A rioter. The rager; their tumult.

Hamath (ha'-math) = Defense; citadel; fortress; (root = to guard; to join together). Furious. Enclosure of wrath. Warm; hot springs.

Hamathite (ham'-a-thite) = Same as Hamath = Defense; citadel; fortress; (root = to guard; to join together). Furious. Enclosure of wrath. Warm; hot springs.

Hamathzobah [Hamath Zobah] (ha'-math-zo'-bah) = Fortress of Zobah. Same as Hamath = Defense; citadel; fortress; (root = to guard; to join together). Furious. Warm; hot springs. Swelling hosts enclosure of wrath.

Hammath (ham'-math) = Warm baths; warm springs. Hot place.

Hammedatha (ham-med'-a-thah) = he that troubles the law; double. Chaldean: The opposer of justice or law. Persian: Twin. Measurement.

Hammelech (ham'-me-lek) = The king.

Hammoleketh (ham-mol'-e-keth) = The queen or regent.

Hammon (ham'-mon) = Hot; great hot baths; (root = to be hot).

Hammothdor [Hammoth Dor] (ham'-moth-dor') = Same as Hamath = Defense; citadel; fortress. Warm springs of Dor. Hot places of the dwelling (or generation).

Hamonah (ha-mo'-nah) = Multitude.

Hamongog [Hamon Gog] (ha'-mon-gog') = Multitude of Gog. A crowd upon the roof.

Hamor (ha'-mor) = Ass; an ass; (root = to be red; to be inflamed).

Hamuel (ha-mu'-el) = Heat (wrath) of God; God

is a sun; warmth of God. They were heated of God.

Hamul (ha'-mul) = Who has been favored; who has experienced mercy; pity; pitied.

Hamulites (ha'-mu-lites) = Same as Hamul = Who has been favored; who has experienced mercy; pity; pitied.

Hamutal (ha-mu'-tal) = Akin to the dew; refreshing like dew; kinsman of the dew; father-in-law of dew.

Hanameel (ha-nam'-e-el) = Gift of God; the grace of God; God has pitied. Place of God's favor.

Hanan (ha'-nan) = Compassionate; merciful; gracious. A gracious giver.

Hananeel (ha-nan'-e-el) = Graciously given of God; whom God graciously gave; God was gracious; God is gracious; the mercy of God.

Hanani (ha-na'-ni) = Graciously given of the Lord; gracious to me; gracious; the mercy of God.

Hananiah (han-a-ni'-ah) = Jehovah is gracious; gift of the LORD; graciously given of the LORD.

Hanes (ha'-nees) = Grace has fled; to bring down; to lead down; (root = to bring; to level). (A town located in lower Egypt also called ahpanes = The beginning of the age; Head of the age.)

Haniel (ha'-ne-el) = Favor of God; grace of God.

Hannah (han'-nah) = Gratuitous gift; i.e., grace, mercy; gracious; graciousness; favor. Bestowed. She was gracious.

Hannathon (han'-na-thon) = Extraordinary free gift. Graciously regarded.

Hanniel (han'-ne-el) = Same as Haniel = Favor of God; grace of God.

Hanoch (ha'-nok) = Dedicated. Same as Enoch = initiated; initiating; dedicated; experienced.

Hanochites (ha'-nok-ites) = Descendants of Enoch = Initiated; initiating; dedicated; experienced.

Hanun (ha'-nun) = Giving for nought; enjoying favor; gracious; he that rests; whom God pities.

Haphraim (haf-ra'-im) = Two wells; two pits. Double digging.

Hara (ha'-rah) = Mountainous.

Haradah (har'-a-dah) = Fear (of an host); (root = to be afraid; to tremble).

Haran #1 (ha'-ran) = Mountaineer; very high; enlightened; strong. (Generally refers to a man).

Haran #2 (ha'-ran) = Very dry, (place parched with the sun); (root = to be dry; to kindle; to burn). Grievous. (Generally refers to a place).

Hararite (har'-a-rite) = Same as Haran #1 = Mountaineer; very high; enlightened; strong. 2

Samuel 23:33 - the curser. 2 Samuel 23:11 - my mountain.

Harbona (har-bo'-nah) = Warlike; martial; a destroyer. Ass driver; the anger of him who builds.

Harbonah (har-bo'-nah) = Same as Harbona = Warlike; martial. Ass driver; the anger of him who builds. Chaldean: A destroyer. Drought.

Hareph (ha'-ref) = Maturity; i.e., the flower of life; plucking; plucking off; early born. Reproachful.

Hareth (ha'-reth) = A cutting; thicket; (root = to engrave; to cut).

Harhaiah (har-ha-i'-ah) = Anger of the LORD; (roots = [1] to be angry; to wax hot; to burn; [2] Jehovah). Jehovah is protecting. Dried up. Kindled of Jah.

Harhas (har'-has) = Glitter; splendor. He burned; he pitied.

Harhur (har'-hur) =

99

Extreme burning; inflammation. Nobility; distinction.

Harim (ha'-rim) = Snub nosed; flat nosed; bent upwards; consecrated; (root = to have a flat nose; to destroy utterly; to devote; to consecrate).

Hariph (ha'-rif) = Early born; autumnal rain or showers.

Harnepher (har-ne'-fur) = Panting. The frustrator; burnt.

Harod (ha'-rod) = Trembling; fear; terror.

Harodite (ha'-ro-dite) = Inhabitants of Harod = Trembling; fear; terror.

Haroeh (ha-ro'-eh) = Seeing; seer; vision; the seer.

Harorite (ha'-ro-rite) = Same as Hararite = Haran #1 = Mountaineer; very high; enlightened; strong.

Harosheth (har'-o-sheth) = Manufactory; carving; i.e., cutting, carving, and working in stones, wood, or iron; (root = to engrave; to work in brass; to keep silent; to plow). A plowed field.

Harsha (har'-shah) = Enchanter; magician. Artifice; deviser; secret work.

Harum (ha'-rum) = High; i.e., illustrious; exalted; elevated.

Harumaph (ha-ru'-maf) = Flat; nose; flat nosed.

Haruphite (ha'-ru-fite) = Matured.

Haruz (ha'-ruz) = Sharpened; decided; industrious; (root = to cut; to decree; to bring to a point; to be determined).

Hasadiah (has-a-di'-ah) = Love of the LORD; whom Jehovah loves; Jehovah is kind; Jehovah has shown kindness.

Hasenuah (has-e-nu'-ah) = Light. She that is hated; the violated. The thorny.

Hashabiah (hash-a-bi'-ah) = Esteemed of the LORD; whom Jehovah esteems; Jehovah is associated; Jehovah has devised.

Hashabnah (hash-ab'-nah) = Jehovah is a friend. Same as Hashabiah = Esteemed of the LORD; whom Jehovah esteems; Jehovah is associated; Jehovah has devised. (roots = [1] to esteem; to regard; to imagine; to impute; [2] Jehovah). Inventiveness; the device was lamented.

Hashabniah (hash-ab-ni'-ah) = Jehovah is a friend. Same as Hashabiah = Esteemed of the LORD; whom Jehovah esteems; Jehovah is associated; Jehovah has devised. (roots = [1] to esteem; to regard; to imagine; to impute; [2] Jehovah). The devising of Jah.

Hashbadana (hash-bad'-a-nah) = Reason; thought in judging; wise judge; thought. He hasted in the judgment; considerate in the judgment.

Hashem (ha'-shem) = Astonished; shining. Dull; sleepy. To make desolate.

Hashmonah (hash-mo'-nah) = Very fat; fatness; fat soil. He hasted the numbering.

Hashub (ha'-shub) = Much esteemed; thoughtful; associated.

Hashubah (hash-u'-bah) = Highly esteemed; esteemed; association. Consideration.

Hashum (ha'-shum) = Great; wealthy; rich; shining. The desolate hasted.

Hashupha (hash-u'-fah) = Exhaustion; made bare; nakedness; (root = to make bare; to discover; to uncover; to draw out). Stripped.

Hasrah (has'-rah) = Extremely poor; extreme poverty; root = to lack [bread, understanding]; to be in need; to be destitute; to suffer want).

Hassenaah (has-se-na'-ah) = Same as Senaah = Elevated, (idea of lifting up); thorny; the thorn hedge.

Hasshub (hash'-ub) = Same as Hashub = Much

esteemed; thoughtful; associated.

Hasupha (has-u'-fah) = Same as Hashupha = Exhaustion; made bare; nakedness; (root = to make bare; to discover; to uncover; to draw out).

Hatach (ha'-tak) = Gift; a gift. Why will you smite.

Hathath (ha'-thath) = Terror; casting down; bruised; terror; (root = to be broken; to be dismayed; to be amazed; to be terrified).

Hatipha (hat'-if-ah) = Seized; captivated; captive; (root = to seize hold of; to take with violence).

Hatita (hat'-it-ah) = Exploring; digging. My sin removed.

Hattil (hat'-til) = Inquietude; wavering; decaying; vacillating. Sin cast out.

Hattush (hat'-tush) = Assembled; gathered together; contender. Sin was hated.

Hauran (hau'-ran) = Very white.

Havilah (hav'-il-ah) = Bringing forth; trembling (with pain); circle; (root = pang; pain; sorrow; especially of a pregnant woman). To declare to her.

Havothjair [Havoth Jair] (ha'-voth-ja'-ir) = Villages of the enlightener. Living places; producers.

Hazael (ha'-za-el) = He who sees God; whom God watches over; God sees; God has seen.

Hazaiah (ha-za-i'-ah) = Seen of the LORD; whom Jehovah watches over; Jehovah is seeing; Jehovah has seen.

Hazaraddar [Hazar Addar] (ha'-zar-ad'-dar) = Village of greatness. Enclosures of glory.

Hazarenan [Hazar Enan] (ha'-zar-e'-nan) = Village of fountains. Enclosure of their fountains; (Ezekiel 47:17 - enclosure of the one with eyes).

Hazargaddah [Hazar

Gaddah] (ha'-zar-gad'-dah) = Village of fortune or luck. Enclosure of conflict; enclosure of fortune.

Hazarhatticon [Hazar Hatticon] (ha'-zar-hat'-ti-con) = The middle village. The middle enclosure.

Hazarmaveth (ha-zar-ma'-veth) = The court of death; death town. The enclosure of death.

Hazarshual [Hazar Shual] (ha'-zar-shoo'-al) = Village of the fox or jackal. Enclosure of the jackal.

Hazarsusah [Hazar Susah] (ha'-zar-soo'-sah) = Village of the houses. Mare enclosure.

Hazarsusim [Hazar Susim] (ha'-zar-soo'-sim) = Same as Hazarsusah = Village of the houses. Enclosure of horses.

Hazazontamar [Hazazon Tamar] (haz'-a-zon-ta'-mar) = Pruning of the palm; (root = to cut off; to divide; to be in divisions).

Hazelelponi (haz-el-el-po'-ni) = The shadow looking on me; the shade turns toward me; (roots = [1] shadow; [2] to turn towards; to turn away; to look).

Hazerim (haz'-e-rim) = Villages. Enclosures.

Hazeroth (haz'-e-roth) = Same as Hazerim = Villages. Enclosures.

Hazezontamar [Hazezon Tamar] (haz'-e-zon-ta'-mar) = Same as Hazazontamar = Pruning of the palm.

Haziel (ha'-ze-el) = The vision of God; God is seeing.

Hazo (ha'-zo) = Vision; seer.

Hazor (ha'-zor) = Fence; castle; a court. To trumpet; enclosure.

Hazarhadatah (ha'-zor-ha-dat'-tah) = New castle; (root = to be new). Enclosure of rejoicing; new enclosure.

Heber (he'-bur) = Fellowship; a companion;

production; one that passes; (root = to confederate). A company; enchantment.

Heberites (he'-bur-ites) = Sam as Heber = Fellowship; a companion; production; one that passes; (root = to confederate).

Hebrew(s) (he'-broos) = He who passed over; from the other side; passer over. (Descendants of Abraham).

Hebrewess (he'-broo-ess) = Same as Eber (feminine) = One who passes over, a Jewess (Jewess: a Jewish woman who is a believer - word now considered to be offensive by many).

Hebron (he'-brun) = Confederation; conjunction; alliance; associating; joining together; union; company.

Hebronites (he'-brun-ites) = Same as Hebron = Confederation; conjunction; alliance; associating; joining

together; union; company.

Hegai (he'-gahee) = Venerable. A speaker. My meditations.

Hege (he'-ghe) = Same as Hegai = Venerable. A speaker. Meditation.

Helah (he'-lah) = Scum; sick; (root = to be diseased).

Helam (he'-lam) = An army; their strength. Stronghold.

Helbah (hel'-bah) = Fatness; i.e., fertile.

Helbon (hel'-bon) = Fat; i.e., fertile. The fat one.

Heldai (hel'-dahee) = Life; age; my endurance; enduring; durable. My time.

Heleb (he'-leb) = Fat; i.e., fertile; fatness; endurance.

Heled (he'-led) = Life; duration; enduring; durable; (root = to be lasting). The age.

Helek (he'-lek) = Portion; smoothness; (root = to be divided; to separate; to flatter)

Helekites (he'-lek-ites) = Same as Helek = Portion; smoothness; (root = to be divided; to separate; to flatter).

Helem #1 (he'-lem) = (1 Chronicles 7:35) = One who hammers; hammer; (root = to smite; to hammer; to beat; to break; to break down). *A son of Heber, grandson of Asher.*

Helem #2 (he'-lem) = (Zec. 6:14) = Robust; dream; manly vigor; strong; (root = to be strong; to dream).

Heleph (he'-lef) = Exchange; (root = to pass away; to change; to pierce through; to sprout).

Helez (le'-lez) = Liberation; strength; alertness; (root = to deliver; to draw out; to arm; i.e., for war). Stripped - as for battle.

Heli (he'-li) = Elevation; ascending. Greek form of the Hebrew name, Eli = Jehovah is high; my God; a foster son; adopted of the LORD. My ascension.

Helkai (hel'-kahee) = Portion of the LORD; Jehovah is a portion.

Helkath (hel'-kath) = Same as Helek = Portion; smoothness; (root = to be divided; to separate; to flatter). A possession.

Helkathhazzurim [Helkath Hazzurim] (hel'-kath-haz'-zu-rim) = Field of swords. The portion of the rocks. Possession of the besieger.

Helon (he'-lon) = Very strong; strong.

Hemam (he'-mam) = Same as Homam = Destruction; (root = to destroy; to discomfit; to crush). The south.

Heman (he'-man) = Faithful; raging. *A son of Zerah, a descendant of Judah.* Right-handed.

Hemath (he'-math) = Warmth. Same as Hamath = Defense; citadel; fortress; (root = to guard;

to join together). Furious.

Hemdan (hem'-dan) = Desire; desirable; delight; pleasant.

Hen (hen) = Gracious gift; grace; favor; (root = grace; favor; goodwill).

Hena (he'-nah) = Depression; low land. The shaken.

Henadad (hen'-a-dad) = The favor of Hadad; Hadad is gracious.

Henoch (he'-nok) = Same as Enoch = Initiated; initiating; dedicated; experienced.

Hepher (he'-fer) = Well; pit; digging.

Hepherites (he'-fer-ites) = Descendants of Hepher = Well; pit.

Hephzibah (hef'-zi-bah) = My delight is in her; in whom is my delight.

Heres (he'-res) = Sun.

Heresh (he'-resh) = Silence; artificer; work.

Hermas (her'-mas) = Interpreter; Mercury; i.e.,

herald or messenger of the gods. Sand bank.

Hermes (her'-mees) = Gain. (Messenger or herald of the Greek gods, especially Zeus). Bringer of good luck; teacher for gain.

Hermogenes (her-moj'-e-nees) = Begotten of Mercury; generation of Lucre. Born lucky.

Hermon (her'-mon) = Devoted; (root = to extirpate; to devote). A prominent summit of a mountain (mountain of snow).

Hermonites (her'-mon-ites) = Same as Hermon = Devoted; (root = to extirpate; to devote).

Herod (her'-od) = Heroic; son of the hero; the glory of the skin.

Herodians (he-ro'-de-uns) = A political party active during the time of the Herodian dynasty.

Herodias (he-ro'-de-as) = Heroic. (Feminine form of Herod).

Herodion (he-ro'-de-on) = Conqueror of heroes. Valiant.

Hesed (he'-sed) = Mercy; kindness; pity; (root = mercy; kindness; goodness; good deeds).

Heshbon (hesh'-bon)= Reason; device; counting; an account.

Heshmon (hesh'-mon) = Very fat; fatness, (fruitful soil). Hasting the separation.

Heshvan = Eighth Jewish month (October - November)

Heth (heth) = An annoyance; an annoyer; dread; fear; terrible.

Hethlon (heth'-lon) = Hidden place; a place wrapped up. Swaddled.

Hezeki (hez'-e-ki) = Strength or might of Jehovah; Jehovah is strength. My strong (one).

Hezekiah (hez-e-ki'-ah) = The LORD my strength; the might of Jehovah; strength of the LORD; a strong support is Jehovah.

Hezion (he'-zi-on) = Vision.

Hezir (he'-zur) = Returning home; a swine.

Hezrai (hez'-rahee) = Bulwark of the LORD; enclosed wall; enclosed; beautiful.

Hezro (hez'-ro) = Same as Hezrai = Bulwark of the LORD; enclosed wall; enclosed; beautiful.

Hezron (hez'-ron) = Enclosed; surrounded by a wall; shut in;blooming; dart of joy. His court.

Hezronites (hez'-ron-ites) = Descendants of Hezron = Enclosed; surrounded by a wall; shut in; blooming; dart of joy.

Hiddai (hid'-dahee) = Echo of the LORD; the rejoicing of Jehovah; joyful; mighty. My noises; my echoes.

Hiddekel (hid'-de-kel) = The rapid swift; the rapid Tigris; (roots = [1] a swift horse; [2] to be light; to be swift; to be cursed). Riddle of the (date) palm; riddle of lightness.

Hiel (hi'-el) = God lives; the life of God.

Hierapolis (hi-e-rap'-o-lis) = Sacred city. Temple city.

Higgaion (hig-gah'-yon) = Meditation.

Hilen (hi'-len) = Same as Holen = Sandy. Pain them.

Hilkiah (hil-ki'-ah) = Same as Helkai = Portion of the LORD; the LORD my portion. Jehovah is protection.

Hillel (hil'-lel) = Praise; i.e., of God; praised greatly; (root = to praise [the Lord]; to make bright, clear; to make mad, foolish).

Hinnom (hin'-nom) = Lamentation; (root = to mourn; to roar). Gratis. Behold them (a valley). To make self drowsy; behold them.

Hirah (hi'-rah) = Nobility; noble race; destination. Paleness; hollowness.

Hiram (hi'-ram) = Consecration. Same as

Huram = Exalted in life; most noble; (root = noble; freeborn). Their paleness.

Hittite (hit'-tite) = Same as Heth = An annoyance; an annoyer; dread; fear.

Hittites (hit'-tites) = Descendants of Heth = An annoyance.

Hivites (hi'-vites) = A declarer; pronouncer; villagers. Showers of life; livers.

Hizkiah (hiz-ki'-ah) = Jehovah is strong. Same as Hezekiah = The LORD my strength; the might of Jehovah; strength of the LORD.

Hizkijah (hiz-ki'-jah) = Jehovah is strong. Same as Hezekiah = The LORD my strength; the might of Jehovah; strength of the LORD.

Hobab (ho'-bab) = Beloved; most beloved; lover; favored.

Hobah (ho'-bah) = Hiding place. Affectionate.

Hod (hod) = Glory; majesty; splendor; (root =

glory; majesty; honor).

Hodaiah (ho-da-i'-ah) = Praise of the LORD; the splendor of Jehovah; honored of Jehovah.

Hodaviah (ho-da-vi'-ah) = Praise of the LORD; Jehovah is his praise.

Hodesh (ho'-desh) = The new moon; i.e., beautiful as the new moon.

Hodevah (ho-de'-vah) = Jehovah is honor. Same as Hodaviah = Praise of the LORD; Jehovah is his praise.

Hodiah (ho-di'-ah) = Same as Hodaiah = Praise of the LORD; the splendor of Jehovah; honored of Jehovah.

Hodijah (ho-di'-jah) = Same as Hodaiah = Praise of the LORD; the splendor of Jehovah; honored of Jehovah.

Hoglah (hog'-lah) = Partridge. The feast has languished.

Hoham (ho'-ham) = A multitude of a multitude; i.e., a great multitude;

Jehovah protects the multitude; (root = to make a noise; the motion of people; to destroy). He crushed.

Holon (ho'-lon) = Sandy. Anguished.

Homam (ho'-mam) = Destruction; raging; destroyer; strong; (root = to destroy; to discomfit; to crush).

Hophni (hof'-ni) = Boxer; pugilist; a little fist; a handful; strong; (roots = [1] two fists full; two hands full; [2] to take with both hands; to fill both hands).

Hophra (hof'-rah) = Priest of the sun. To cover evil.

Hor (hor) = Mountain. Chaldean: White (a mount). Progenitor.

Horam (ho'-ram) = High spirited; elevated; lofty. Their progenitor.

Horeb (ho'-reb) = Arid; desert; desolation; (root = to dry up; to lie waste; to be destroyed).

Horem (ho'-rem) = Devoted. Banned.

Horhagidgad [Haggidgad] (hor-hag-id'-gad) = A mount of Galgad. Cavern of thunder. The slashing hole.

Hori (ho'-ri) = Cave dweller; a cave man; free; noble.

Horims (ho'-rims) = Descendants of Hori = Cave dweller; a cave man; free; noble.

Horites (ho'-rites) = Same as Hori = Cave dwellers; a cave man; free; noble.

Hormah (hor'-mah) = Anathema; i.e., devoted to destruction; a devoting; a place laid waste. Excommunication.

Horonaim (hor-o-na'-im) = Grievous; vexatious. Two caverns. Double caves.

Horonite (ho'-ron-ite) = Same as Horonaim = Grievous; vexatious. Two caverns.

Hosah (ho'-sah) = A place of refuge; fleeing for refuge; fleeing to Jehovah for refuge; (root = to put trust in [God, man, or anything]; to flee for refuge).

Hosanna (ho-zan'-nah) = Greek: Save us we pray. Hebrew: God, make it rain.

Hosea (ho-se'-ah) = Jehovah is help or salvation; salvation; causing to save.

Hoshaiah (ho-sha-i'-ah) = Whom Jehovah has set free; set free of the LORD; God has saved. Saved of Jah.

Hoshama (ho-sha'-mah) = The LORD has heard; i.e., his parents' prayers; Jehovah has heard.

Hoshea (ho-she'-ah) = Same as Hosea = Jehovah is help or salvation; salvation; causing to save.

Hotham (ho'-tham) = Signet ring; determination; (root = to seal; to complete; to shut up).

Hothan (ho'-than) = Same as Hotham = Signet

ring; determination; (root = to seal; to complete; to shut up).

Hothir (ho'-thur) = Abundance; [whom God] let remain; (root = to be undaunted). A surplus.

Hozai = Jehovah is seeing.

Hukkok (huk'-kok) = Appointed portion; decreed; (roots = [1] appointed portion; a decree; a statute; [2] to engrave; to inscribe; to decree). The law (as graven, or appointed).

Hukok (hu'-kok) = Same as Hukkok = Appointed portion; decreed; (roots = [1] appointed portion; a decree; a statute; [2] to engrave; to inscribe; to decree). The engraving.

Hul (hul) = Writhing; trembling; circle.

Huldah (hul'-dah) = Weasel; i.e., from its quickness in getting into holes. Endurance. Perpetuity.

Humtah (hum'-tah) = A place of lizards; fortress; (roots = [1] to lie on the ground; [2] a defense).

Hupham (hu'-fam) = Inhabitants of the sea shore; (roots = [1] the shore; haven of the sea; [2] to wash off; to rub off; to cover). Protected; a covering.

Huphamites (hu'-fam-ites) = Descendants of Hupham = Inhabitants of the sea shore; (roots = [1] the shore; haven of the sea; [2] to wash off; to rub off; to cover). Protected; a covering.

Huppah (hup'-pah)= Nuptial bed; covering; protected.

Huppim (hup-pim) = Same as Hupham = Inhabitants of the sea shore; (roots = [1] the shore; haven of the sea; [2] to wash off; to rub off; to cover.) Protected; a covering.

Hur (hur) = Cavern; (root = a hole; a cavern, with the idea of hollowing or boring). Noble; splendor. White.

Hurai (hu'-rahee) = Linen worker; a linen weaver; noble; (root = to be white; i.e., splendid or noble). My caves.

Huram (hu'-ram) = Exalted in life; most noble; ingenious; (root = noble; freeborn). Their whiteness.

Huri (hu'-ri) = Linen worker; linen weaver; nobleman. My whiteness.

Hushah (hu'-shah) = Haste; i.e., in being born; passion; (root = to make haste; to hasten; to flee).

Hushai (hu'-shahee) = Hasting of the LORD; hasting; quick; (root = to haste).

Husham (hu'-sham) = Great haste; i.e., a son born prematurely; haste; passion.

Hushathite (hu'-shath-ite) = Inhabitants of Hushah = Haste; i.e., in being born; passion; (root = to make haste; to hasten; to flee).

Hushim (hu'-shim) = Those who hasten their birth; those who make haste; to hasten; hasting opulent.

Huz (huz) = Firm. Counselor.

Huzzab (huz'-zab) = It is decreed. He was established.

Hymenaeus (hy-men-e'-us) = Nuptial; belonging to marriage. From Hymen, the god of marriage. A wedding song.

J *will say it again: Rejoice!*·(Philippians 4:4, NIV).

I

Ibhar (ib'-har) = Whom God elects; God does choose; chosen; chooser. He will choose.

Ibleam (ib'-le-am) =

Devouring the people; he destroys the people; (root = to swallow; to devour).

Ibneiah (ib-ne-i'-ah) = He will be built up of the LORD; whom Jehovah will build up; Jehovah does build. Jah will build.

Ibnijah (ib-ni'-jah) = Same as Ibneiah = He will be built up of the LORD; whom Jehovah will build up; Jehovah does build. Jehovah is builder. He will be built of Jah.

Ibri (ib'-ri) = Beyond at the river; i.e., born beyond the river; passer over; a Hebrew. Literally: one who has crossed.

Ibzan (ib'-zan) = Great fatigue; i.e., of the mother at birth; active; splendid. Their witness.

Ichabod (ik'-a-bod) = Inglorious; the glory is departed; the glory is not; where is the glory; (roots = [1] glory; glorious; honor; [2] to be heavy; to be honored; to be glorified). Where is honor. Woe.

Iconium (i-co'-ne-um) = Little image. Yielding; the comer.

Idalah (id'-a-lah) = Place of execration; snares; (root = an oath; a covenant confirmed by an oath; a curse; an execration). He will fly to her; hand of imprecation.

Idbash (id'-bash) = He will be as agreeable as honey; honeyed; honey sweet; corpulent. Hand of shame.

Iddo #1 (id'-do) = Great calamity; (root = to fall, as misfortune). Chief of Casiphia—Ezra 8:17.

Iddo #2 (id'-do) = Love of Him; i.e., the Lord affectionate; festal; favorite; his power; (root = to love; beloved; loves; well beloved). An ornament. Son of Zechariah and ruler the half tribe of Manasseh.

Iddo #3 (id'-do) = Time of Him; i.e., the Lord; (root = to espouse; to meet according to appointment; to come together). A prophet of God—2 Chronicles 9:29.

Idumaea (i-doo-me'-ah) = Same as Edom = Red.

Idumea (i-doo-me'-ah) = Same as Edom = Red.

Igal (i'-gal) = He will redeem; i.e., God His people; whom God will avenge; deliverer; He will vindicate; (root = to redeem; to buy back; to do the kinsman's part; i.e., revenge blood).

Igdaliah (ig-da-li'-ah) = Whom Jehovah shall make great; great is Jehovah; greatness of the LORD.

Igeal (ig'-e-al) = Same as Igal = He will redeem; i.e., God His people; whom God will avenge; deliverer; He will vindicate; (root = to redeem; to buy back; to do the kinsman's part; i.e., revenge blood).

Iim (i'-im) = Ruinous heaps.

Ijeabarim [Iye Abarim] (i'-je-ab'-a-rim) = Ruinous

heaps of Abarim. Heaps of the regions beyond or of "those who have crossed."

Ijon (i'-jon) = A great heap; ruin.

Ikkesh (ik'-kesh) = Perverse; deceitful; subtle; perverseness of mouth; (root = to pervert; to make crooked).

Ilai (i'-lahee) = Most high; elevated; supreme.

Illyricum (il-lir'-ic-um) = The lyric band.

Imla (im'-lah) = He will fill up; whom (God) will fill up; God does fill; fulfilling; plentitude; (root = to fill; to fulfill; to consecrate; to expire).

Imlah (im'-lah) = Same as Imla = He will fill up; whom (God) will fill up; God does fill; fulfilling; plentitude; (root = to fill; to fulfill; to consecrate; to expire).

Immanuel (im-man'-u-el) = (Emmanuel) God with us.

Immer (im'-mur) = He promised; i.e., of the Lord; talkative; prominent.

Imna (im'-nah) = He [God] will retain; whom (God) assigns; God does restrain; withdrawing; holding back; (root = to withhold; to keep back; to deny).

Imnah (im'-nah) = Prosperity; he allots; success. Right-handed; the right side; he will number.

Imrah (im'-rah) = He will extol himself; stubborn; height of Jehovah; (root = to rebel; to be rebellious; to disobey).

Imri (im'-ri) = Promised of the Lord; eloquent; projecting. My saying.

India (in'-de-ah) = Praise ye. Give ye thanks; flee ye away.

Iphedeiah (if-e-di'-ah) = The LORD will redeem [him]; whom Jehovah frees; Jehovah does deliver; redemption of the LORD. Jah will redeem.

Iphtah El (NIV) = See Jiphthahel.

Ir (ur) = Citizen; watcher; (root = a city; a camp; a watch tower).

Ira (i'-rah) = Watchful; watcher; city watch; (root = to be awake).

Irad (i'-rad) = City of witness. Wild ass. A descent to a valley.

Iram (i'-ram) = Belonging to a city; watchful. Their city.

Iri (i'-ri) = Same as Ir = Citizen; watcher; (root = a city; a camp; a watch tower). Jehovah is watcher. My city.

Irijah (i-ri'-jah) = Whom Jehovah looks on; he will see the LORD; God does see; fear of the LORD; My fear of the LORD. Fear thou Jah; Jah will see me.

Irnahash [Ir Nahash] (ur-na'-hash) = City of serpents; snake town; serpent city; magic city; (root = to hiss; to whisper; to use sorcery; to augur; to divine; to forebode).

Iron (i'-ron) = Reverence; pious; (root = to fear; to be afraid). Tearful.

Irpeel (ur'-pe-el) = God will restore; which God heals.

Irshemesh [Ir Shemesh] (ur-she'-mesh) = City of the sun; sun-town.

Iru (i'-ru) = Same as Iram = Belonging to a city. Watch. They were awake; awake ye.

Isaac #1 (i'-za-ak) = Laughing; laughter; he laughs; laughing one; (root = to laugh; to sport).

Isaac #2 (i'-za'ak) = He will laugh (in mockery)— Psalm 105:9; Jeremiah 33:26; Amos 7:9, 16).

Isaiah (i-za'-yah) = Salvation of the LORD; Jehovah is helper; salvation is of the LORD. Save thou Jehovah.

Iscah (is'-cah) = She will look out, as to God; she will see. Sheltered; protected. He will pour out; he will anoint her; he will screen her.

Iscariot (is-car'-e-ot) = Man of Kerioth; a man of murder. He will be hired.

Ishbah (ish'-bah) = He will praise [God]; praising; he praises; (root = to praise [the Lord]; to glory; to make smooth). Appeaser.

Ishbak (ish'-bak) = Free; empty; exhausted; he releases. He will leave (alone). Chaldean: Forsaken.

Ishbibenob [Ishbi-Benob] (ish'-bi-be'-nob) = Dweller on the mount; he that predicts. One who dwells at Nob = high places. His seat is in the high places.

Ishbosheth [Ish-Bosheth] (ish-bo'-sheth) = Man of shame; (root = to be ashamed; to be confused; to be confounded).

Ishi (i'-shi) = Salvation; my husband; my help; saving; (roots = [1] to dwell; to abide; to be inhabitants; [2] to be prominent; to be high). Literally: my man—Hosea 2:16.

Ishiah (i-shi'-ah) = Gift of the LORD; whom Jehovah lends; Jehovah exists; forgiven; (roots = [1] a gift; a present; [2]

Jehovah). Jah will lend; forgotten of Jah.

Ishijah (i-shi'-jah) = Same as Ishiah = Gift of the LORD; whom Jehovah lends; Jehovah exists; forgiven; (roots = [1] a gift; a present; [2] Jehovah). Jah will lend; forgotten of Jah.

Ishma (ish'-mah) = Desolateness; i.e., unfortunate; distinction; elevated; (root = to be desolate).

Ishmael (ish'-ma-el) = He will hear God; he will be heard of God; whom God hears; the Lord hears; God hears.

Ishmaelites (ish'-ma-el-ite) = Descendants of Ishmael = He will hear God; he will be heard of God; whom God hears; the Lord hears; God hears.

Ishmaiah (ish-ma-i'-ah) = He will hear the LORD; whom Jehovah hears; Jehovah hears.

Ishmeelite(s) (ish'-me-el-ites) = Same as Ishmael = He will hear God; he will

be heard of God; whom God hears; the Lord hears; God hears.

Ishmerai (ish'-me-rahee) = He will be kept of the LORD; whom Jehovah keeps; God keeps. They will be my keepers.

Ishod (i'-shod) = Man of beauty; man of splendor; man of glory; man of honor.

Ishpan (ish'-pan) = He will hide; cunning; (root= to cover; to hide). Firm; strong. He will make them prominent; he will lay them bare.

Ishtob [Tob] (ish'-tob) = Man of Tob = Distinguished. Good man.

Ishuah (ish'-u-ah) = He will be equal; equal; alike; level; self satisfied; (root = to be even; to be level; to be like).

Ishuai (ish'-u-ahee) = Level; equality. He will justify me.

Ishui (ish'-u-i) = Same as Ishuai = Level; equality. He will justify me.

Ismachiah (is-ma-ki'-ah) = Supported of the LORD; Jehovah supports; whom Jehovah upholds.

Ismaiah (is-ma-i'-ah) = Same as Ishmaiah = He will hear the LORD; whom Jehovah hears; Jehovah hears. Jah will hear.

Ispah (is'-pah) = He will be eminent; strong; (root = to be high; prominent). He will lay bare. Bald.

Israel (iz'-ra-el) = He will be a prince with God; prince with God; contender of God; he strives with God; soldier of God; God will rule; God ruled man; ruling with God; one that prevails with God.

Israelite(s) (iz'-ra-el-ites) = Descendants of Israel = He will be a prince with God; prince with God; contender of God; he strives with God; soldier of God; God will rule; God ruled man; ruling with God; one that prevails with God.

Israelitish (iz'-ra-el-i-tish) = Referring to Israel = He will be a prince with

God; prince with God; contender of God; he strives with God; soldier of God; God will rule; God ruled man; ruling with God; one that prevails with God.

Issachar (is'-sa-kar) = He is wages; he brings wages; he is hired; reward; there is here; (roots = [1] being; existence; that which is present; [2] to hire; to be rewarded).

Isshiah (is-shi'-ah) = Same as Ishiah = Gift of the LORD; whom Jehovah lends; Jehovah exists; forgiven; (roots = [1] a gift; a present; [2] Jehovah).

Isuah (is'-u-ah) = Level.

Isui (is'-u-i) = Same as Isuah = Level.

Italian (it-al'-yan) = Belonging to Italy = Calf-like.

Italy (it'-a-lee) = Calf-like.

Ithai (ith'-a-i) = Ploughman; being; existing. With me.

Ithamar (ith'-a-mar) = Land of palm; island of palms; palm-coast; palm tree.

Ithiel (ith'-e-el) = God is with me; God is; (roots = [1] El; [2] with; at; by; near).The Lord comes.

Ithmah (ith'-mah) = Bereavement; loneliness; purity; (root = to be solitary; bereaved). Orphanage; orphanhood.

Ithnan (ith'-nan) = Stable; i.e., firm. He will hire them; he will stretch out.

Ithra (ith'-rah) = Excellence; (root = abundance; excellent; that which is first).

Ithran (ith'-ran) = Exalted; very eminent; excellent; abundance.

Ithream (ith'-re-am) = Exalted of the people; abundance of the people; rest of the people; remainder of the people; remnant.

Ithrite (ith'-rite) = Descendants of Jether

[same as Ithra] = Excellence; (root = abundance; excellent; that which is first).

Ittahkazin [Eth Kazin] (it'-tah-ka'-zin) = Time of the judge; time of the chief; (roots = [1] time; season; opportunity; [2] a judge; a prince; [3] to cut off; to scrape off; to decide). To the due time of the prince.

Ittai (it'-ta-i) = Nearness of the LORD. Plowman; living. With me.

Ituraea (i-tu-re'-ah) = Past the limits. A province so named from Jetur.

Ivah (i'-vah) = Overturned. Produced. He is a perverter.

Iyyar = Second Jewish month (April - May).

Izehar (iz'-e-har) = Anointed; oil; bright one; olive oil.

Izeharites (iz'-e-har-ites) = Descendants of Izehar = Anointed; oil; bright one; olive oil.

Izhar (iz'-har) = Same as

Izehar = Anointed; oil; bright one; olive oil.

Izharites (iz'-har-ites) = Same as Izeharites = Descendants of Izehar = Anointed; oil; bright one; olive oil.

Izrahiah (iz-ra-hi'-ah) = Brought to light of the LORD; whom Jehovah brought to light; Jehovah is appearing; Jehovah does arise. Jah will arise (as the sun).

Izrahite (iz'-ra-hite) = He will be bright. He will arise.

Izri (iz'-ri) = Jehovah creates; balm. My imagination; my thought.

*J**esus Christ is Lord, to the glory of God the Father** (Philippians 2:11).

Jaakan (ja'-a-kan) = Intelligent; one who turns. Let him oppress them.

Jaakobah (ja-ak'-o-bah) = A helper; supplanter; supplanting; to Jacob. He will seek to over reach.

Jaala (ja'-a-lah) = Same as Jael - (the animal - Ibex) = Climber; a wild goat; chamois; gazelle; (root = to profit; to ascend). Doe; elevation.

Jaalah (ja'-a-lah) = Same as Jaala—(the animal— Ibex) = Climber; a wild goat; chamois; (root = to profit; to ascend). Doe; elevation.

Jaalam (ja'-a-lam) = He will be hid; he will hide; whom God hides; hidden; (root = to hide).

Jaanai (ja'-a-nahee) = The LORD hears; whom Jehovah answers; Jehovah answers. He will give my answers.

Jaareoregim [Jaare-Oregim] (ja'-a-re-or'-eg-im) = Tapestry of the weavers; forests of the weavers.

Jaasau (ja-a'-saw) = Made of the LORD; Jehovah makes. They will make him; they will perform.

Jaasiel (ja-a'-se-el) = Made of God; whom God created; God is maker. It will be done of God.

Jaazaniah (ja-az-a-ni'-ah) = He will be heard of the LORD; whom Jehovah hears; Jehovah does hearken.

Jaazer (ja-a'-zer) = Whom the Lord helps; whom (God) aids. Let him help.

Jaaziah (ja-a-zi'-ah) = He is comforted of the LORD; whom Jehovah strengthens; God consoles; God determines.

Jaaziel (ja-a'-ze-el) = He is comforted of God; whom God strengthens; God is determining; God is consoling.

Jabal (ja'-bal) = Leading; flowing; river; a river, moving or which glides away; (root = to flow; to bring; to lead; to carry).

Jabbok (jab'-bok) = Emptying; pouring out; running out (a river), (root = to empty; to make void; to pour out).

Jabesh (ja'-besh) = Dry; a dry place; arid; (root = to dry up; to wither).

Jabeshgilead [Jabesh Gilead] (ja'-besh-ghil'-e-ad) = Jabesh of Gilead. Jabesh = dry; a dry place; arid; and Gilead = perpetual fountain.

Jabez (ja'-bez) = He will cause pain; i.e., to his mother in his birth; causing pain; sorrow; trouble; he makes sorrow or height; (root = to grieve; to hurt; to pain). Whiteness swept away; mire swept away; shovel of mire.

Jabin (ja'-bin) = God discerns; he will understand; whom He (God) considered; he that understands; intelligent.

Jabneel (jab'-ne-el) =
Caused to be built of God;
may God cause to be built.

Jabneh (jab'-neh) = Will
be built; i.e., will be
prospered; which (God)
causes to be built.

Jachan (ja'-kan) = He
will stir up; troubled;
troublous; afflicting.

Jachin (ja'-kin) = He will
establish; founding; whom
(God) strengthens;
prepared.

Jachinites (ja'-kin-ites) =
Descendants of Jachin =
He will establish;
founding; whom (God)
strengthens.

Jacinth (ja'-cinth) =
Hyacinth; blue.

Jacob (ja'-cub) = He will
supplant; he that supplants;
he that follows after; a
heeler; one who trips up;
takes hold by the land;
supplanter; a detainer.

Jada (ja'-dah) = He
knows; wise; knowing.
The knower; i.e., the one
who knows.

Jadau (ja'-daw) = Beloved
of the Lord; favorite;
friend. My loves.

Jaddua (jad'-du-ah) =
Celebrated; known; i.e., of
God; skilled; very
knowing.

Jadon (ja'-don) = Whom
God will judge; he that
rules; he that abides. He
will strive (or judge).

Jael (ja'-el) = Same as
Jaala (the animal - Ibex) =
Climber; a wild goat;
chamois; gazelle; (root =
to profit; to ascend).To
help; benefit.

Jagur (ja'-gur) =
Lodging; (root = to
sojourn).

Jah (jah) = Poetic form of
Jehovah = He will be; i.e.,
the Eternal who always is;
the Eternal One; the name
of the LORD everlasting;
(root = to be; to breathe).
The independent One (a
shortened form of Jehovah).
Name signifies, He is. Used
in the sense of victor.

Jahath (ja'-hath) = He
will carry away; he will be
broken; (root = to be

broken). Revival; grasping. Union.

Jahaz (ja'-haz) = A round depressed place; a place trodden down.

Jahaza (ja-ha'-zah) = Same as Jahaz = A round depressed place; a place trodden down.

Jahazah (ja-ha'-zah) = Same as Jahaz = A round depressed place; a place trodden down.

Jahaziah (ja-ha-zi'-ah) = He will see the LORD; whom Jehovah watches over; Jehovah reveals. Jehovah sees. Jah will see.

Jahaziel (ja-ha'-ze-el) = He will be seen of God; whom God watches over; God sees; God reveals.

Jahdai (jah'-dahee) = He will be directed of the LORD; whom Jehovah directs; He (God) directs; guide; (root = to direct; to stretch out). He will be gladdened of God.

Jahdiel (jah'-de-el) = He will be made glad of God; whom God makes glad;

God makes glad; union of God; (root = to be glad; to rejoice).

Jahdo (jah'-do) = His union; union; (root = to unite; to join together). His enmity.

Jahleel (jah'-le-el) = Hope of God; hoping in God; God waits; God does grievously afflict; (root = to hope; to expect; to wait for).

Jahleelites (jah'-le-el-ites) = Descendants of Jahleel = Hope of God; hoping in God; God waits; God does grievously afflict; (root = to hope; to expect; to wait for).

Jahmai (jah'-mahee) = He will be guarded of the LORD; whom Jehovah protects. He will be my defenses; he will be my conceivings.

Jahzah (jah'-zah) = Same as Jahaz = A round depressed place; a place trodden down.

Jahzeel (jah'-ze-el) = He will allot of God; whom

God allots; God apportions; God distributes; (root = to divide; to apportion).

Jahzeelites (jah'-ze-el-ites) = Descendants of Jahzeel = He will allot of God; whom God allots; God apportions; God distributes; (root = to divide; to apportion).

Jahzerah (jah'-ze-rah) = He will be caused to return; may he bring back; may he lead back; Jehovah protects. He will be lead to the crown; he will be narrow-eyed.

Jahziel (jah'-ze-el) = Same as Jahzeel = He will allot of God; whom God allots; God apportions; God distributes; (root = to divide; to apportion).

Jair #1(ja'-ur) = He will enlighten; diffuse light; enlightens; shining; lightener. Jehovah enlightens, arouses or diffuses light.

Jair #2 (ja'-ur) = He will embroider. He will stir up.*The father of Elhanan.*

Jairite (ja'-ur-ite) =

Descendants of Jair #1 = He will enlighten; diffuse light; enlightens; shining; lightener. Jehovah enlightens, arouses or diffuses light.

Jairus (ja-i'-rus) = He will enlighten or diffuse light.

Jakan (ja'-kan) = Same as Akan = Torques; (root = to twist; to wrest).

Jakeh (ja'-keh) = Pious; fearing God; hearkening; obedience; (root = to be reverend; to fear God; to be pious).

Jakim (ja'-kim) = He (God) sets up; a setter up he raises up.

Jalon (ja'-lon) = Jehovah abides; abiding; passing the night; obstinate; (root = to lodge all night; to abide).

Jambres (jam'-brees) = Opposer; the sea with poverty.

James (james) = Supplanter.

Jamin (ja'-min) = Right hand; prosperity.

Jaminites (ja'-min-ites) =

Descendants of Jamin = Right hand; prosperity.

Jamlech (jam'-lek) = He will be made to reign; Jehovah rules; let him constitute.

Janna (jan'-nah) = He will answer.

Jannes (jan'-nees) = Full of pleasure; favor; impoverished. Be vexed; be oppressed.

Janoah (ja-no'-ah) = Rest. He will give rest.

Janohah (ja-no'-hah) = Same as Janoah = Rest. He will lead to rest.

Janum (ja'-num) = Sleep. He will slumber.

Japheth (ja'-feth) = Enlargement; extension; let him enlarge; he that persuades; beauty; (root = to enlarge).

Japhia (ja-fi'-ah) = Illustrious; splendid; shining; gleaming; which enlightens; (root = to shine). Causing brightness.

Jahplet (jaf'-let) = Jehovah causes to escape; whom God will free; may he deliver.

Japhleti (jaf'-let-i) = Will be liberated by the Lord; let him escape.

Japho (ja'-fo) = Beautiful; beauty; (root = to be beautiful; to adorn). To be fair to him.

Jarah (ja'-rah) = Same as Jehoadah = Whom Jehovah adorns; the LORD will adorn. Honey; one who unveils. Forest. Honey wood; honeycomb.

Jareb (ja'-reb) = He will plead; adverse; one who is contentious; avenger; revenger; wrangler; (root = to contend; to strive; to plead a cause). Let him contend.

Jared (ja'-red) = Descent; descending; he that descends; (root = to descend; to go down). A descender.

Jaresiah (ja-re-si'-ah) = He will be nourished of the LORD; whom Jehovah nourishes; God does nourish or plant; Jehovah gives a couch. Honey which is of Jah.

Jarha (jar'-hah) = Increasing moon; an adversary. The month of sweeping away(?).

Jarib (ja'-rib) = He will plead the cause; he does contend; adversary.

Jarmuth (jar'-muth) = High; height.

Jaroah (ja-ro'-ah) = New moon. To lunate (shine as the moon).

Jashen (ja'-shen) = Sleeping; shining.

Jasher (ja'-shur) = Same as Jesher = Uprightness; upright; just.

Jashobeam (jash-o'-be-am) = He will return among the people; the people return to God.

Jashub (ja'-shub) = He will return; turning back; he returns; (root = to return).

Jashubilehem [Jashubi Lehem] (jash'-u-bi-le'-hem) = He is restored by bread; giving bread; bread returns; returning to bread; turning back to Bethlehem. He will be restorer of bread (or of war).

Jashubites (jash'-u-bites) = Descendants of Jashub = He will return; turning back; he returns; (root = to return).

Jasiel (ja'-se-el) = Same as Jaasiel = Made of God; whom God created.

Jason (ja'-sun) = Healing; He that cares. Greco-Judean, Joshua = Jehovah is salvation; the LORD (is his) salvation; LORD of salvation.

Jasper (jas'-per) = He will be made bare; he will be made prominent.

Jathniel (jath'-ne-el) = He will be given of God; God gives; God bestows gifts; God is giving.

Jattir (jat'-tur) = Pre-eminent; lofty; excelling; (root = to exceed bounds).

Javan (ja'-van) = Supple; clay. He that deceives; a defrauder. The effervescing (one); mired.

126

Jazer (ja'-zur) = Same as Jaazer = Whom the Lord helps; whom (God) aids.

Jaziz (ja'-ziz) = He will bring abundance; he will shine; he moves about; shining; wanderer; (roots = [1] to move about; [2] a full breast; abundance; shining).

Jearim (je'-a-rim) = Forests.

Jeaterai (je-at'-e-rahee) = He will abound of the LORD; steadfast. My profits; my steps; my remainders.

Jeberechiah (je-ber'-e-ki'-ah) = He will be blessed of the LORD; whom Jehovah blesses; Jehovah does bless; Jehovah is blessing.

Jebus (je'-bus) = Treading down; a place trodden down; (root = to tread down with the feet; polluted).

Jebusi (jeb'-u-si) = Same as Jebus = Treading down; a place trodden down; (root = to tread down with the feet; polluted).

Jebusite(s) (jeb'-u-sites) = Descendants of Jebus = Treading down; a place trodden down; (root = to tread down with the feet; polluted).

Jecamiah (jek-a-mi'-ah) = Same as Jekamiah = He will be gathered of the LORD. Jah will establish; let Jah arise.

Jecholiah (jek-o-li'-ah) = Same as Jecoliah = Made strong of the LORD; Jehovah is strong; (root = to be able; to be strong). Is powerful. The prevailing of Jehovah.

Jechonias (jek-o-ni'-as) = Established of the LORD. Greek way of spelling Jeconiah = He will be established of the LORD; Jehovah establishes.

Jecoliah (jek-o-li'-ah) = Same as Jecholiah = Made strong of the LORD; Jehovah is strong; (root = to be able; to be strong). Is powerful.

Jeconiah (jek-o-ni'-ah) = He will be established of the LORD; Jehovah establishes; established by God; preparation of the LORD.

Jedaiah #1 (jed-a-i'-ah) = Praise of the LORD; Jehovah is praise; Jehovah knows; (root = to praise). *The son of Shimri and the son of Harumaph.* Praise thou Jah.

Jedaiah #2 (jed-a-i'-ah) = Known of the LORD.

Jediael (jed-e-a'-el) = Known of God; God knows. Know thou Jah.

Jedidah (je-di'-dah) = Beloved. Darling of Jehovah. Will be made known of God.

Jedidiah (jed-id-i'-ah) = Beloved of Jehovah; Jehovah is a friend; The beloved of Jah.

Jeduthun (jed'-u-thun) = A choir of praise; one who gives praise; praising; celebrating; friendship; (root = to confess; to praise). Full of love.

Jeezer (je-e'-zur) = Help. Contracted from Abiezer = my father will help; in

help; father of helps. Helpless; coast of help.

Jeezerites (je-e'-zur-ites) = Descendants of Jeezer = My father will help; in help; father of helps.

Jegarsahadutha [Jegar Sahadutha] (je'-gar-sa-ha-du'-thah) = The heap of witness; the heap of testimony. Chaldean: The field of terror.

Jehaleleel (je-hal-e'-le-el) = He will praise God; he praises God.

Jehalelel (je-hal'-e-lel) = Same as Jehaleleel = He will praise God; he praises God.

Jehdeiah (jeh-di'-ah) = He will be gladdened of the LORD; whom Jehovah makes glad; Jehovah inspires with joy; union of Jehovah.

Jehezekel (je-hez'-e-kel) = God does strengthen; God is strong. Same as Ezekiel = Strength of God; whom God will strengthen.

Jehiah (je-hi'-ah) = He

lives of the LORD; i.e., by the mercy of Jehovah; Jehovah lives; God is living.

Jehiel (je-hi'-el) = God lives; he lives of God; i.e., by the mercy of God. Jah shall save alive.

Jehieli (je-hi'-el-i) = He lives by mercy. Same as Jehiel = He lives of God; i.e., by the mercy of God; God lives.

Jehizkiah (je-hiz-ki'-ah) = Jehovah is strong; Jehovah does strengthen. Same as Hezekiah = The LORD my strength; the might of Jehovah; strength of the LORD.

Jehoadah (je-ho'-a-dah) = Jehovah unveils; Jehovah has adorned. Same as Jarah = Whom Jehovah adorns; the LORD will adorn.

Jehoaddan (je-ho-ad'-dan) = LORD of pleasure; Jehovah is beauteous. Jehovah is her ornament.

Jehoahaz (je-ho'-a-haz) = Whom Jehovah holds fast; Jehovah upholds; Jehovah

has laid hold; the LORD that sees; (root = to take hold of).

Jehoash (je-ho'-ash) = Jehovah supports; Jehovah has laid hold; Jehovah is strong; Jehovah hastens to build; the LORD gave; whom Jehovah supports; the substance of the LORD.

Jehohanan (je-ho'-ha-nan) = The LORD graciously gave; Jehovah is gracious; bestowed by the LORD.

Jehoiachin (je-hoy'-a-kin) = The LORD will establish; Jehovah has established.

Jehoiada (je-hoy'-a-dah) = The LORD knows; Jehovah knows; knowledge of the LORD.

Jehoiakim (je-hoy'-a-kim) = The LORD will set up; Jehovah has set up; the LORD will rise up.

Jehoiarib (je-hoy'-a-rib) = The LORD will contend; Jehovah will contend.

Jehonadab (je-hon'-a-dab) = The LORD gave spontaneously; Jehovah is bounteous; the LORD willing; Jehovah is liberal.

Jehonathan (je-hon'-a-than) = Jehovah has given; the LORD gave; LORD of giving; whom Jehovah gave.

Jehoram (je-ho'-ram) = The LORD exalts; Jehovah is high; Jehovah is exalted; the LORD celebrated.

Jehoshabeath (je-ho-shab'-e-ath) = Same as Jehosheba = The LORD's oath; Jehovah is the oath; Jehovah is her oath.

Jehoshaphat (je-hosh'-a-fat) = The LORD judges; i.e., he pleads for him; whom Jehovah judges; Jehovah is judge.

Jehosheba (je-hosh'-e-bah) = Same as Jehoshabeath = The LORD's oath; Jehovah is the oath; Jehovah is her oath.

Jehoshua (je-hosh'-u-ah) = Jehovah saves. Same as Joshua = Jehovah is salvation; the LORD (is his) salvation; LORD of salvation; the LORD saves.

Jehoshuah (je-hosh'-u-ah) = Same as Joshua = Jehovah is salvation; the LORD (is his) salvation; LORD of salvation; the LORD saves.

Jehovah (je-ho'-vah) = He will be; i.e., the Eternal who always is; the Eternal One; (root = to be; to breathe); the I AM THAT I AM; (He) was, is, will be, the LORD God. He is, He was. (There are but two tenses in Hebrew, the past and the future, with the latter denoting what is continued even in the present.)

Jehovah-Jireh (je-ho'-vah-ji'-reh) = The LORD will see; the LORD will provide; i.e., give a means of deliverance; (root = to see); the LORD will see and provide.

Jehovah-M'Kaddesh =

The LORD is my/our sanctification.

Jehovah-Nissi (je-ho'-vah-nis'-si) = The LORD is my/our banner or ensign; (root = something lifted up; to be seen afar off; a banner; a signal flag; an ensign).

Jehovah-Rohi = The LORD is my/our Shepherd.

Jehovah-Rophi = The LORD is my/our healing.

Jehovah-Sabaoth (je-ho'-vah-sab'-a-oth) = The LORD of warrior hosts.

Jehovah-Shalom (je-ho'-vah-sha'-lom) = The LORD is my/our peace; the peace of the LORD.

Jehovah-Shammah (je-ho'-vah-sham'-mah) = The LORD is there (ever present).

Jehovah-Tsidkenu = The LORD is my/our righteousness.

Jehozabad (je-hoz'-a-bad) = Whom the LORD gave; Jehovah gave; Jehovah has endowed.

Jehozadak (je-hoz'-a-dak) = The LORD has made just; Jehovah is just.

Jehu (je-hu) = The LORD; Jehovah is He; He is. He shall be (subsist).

Jehubbah (je-hub'-bah) = He will be hidden; hidden; (root = to hide oneself).

Jehucal (je-hu'-kal) = He will be made able; i.e., strengthened of the LORD; Jehovah is mighty; Jehovah is able. Jehovah will prevail; he will be prevailed over.

Jehud (je'-hud) = Praise. He will be praised.

Jehudi (je-hu'-di) = Praise of the LORD. A man of Judah; a Jew.

Jehudijah (je-hu-di'-jah) = Jewess (Jewess: a Jewish woman who is a believer; one who has crossed over—word now considered to be offensive by many); praised of the LORD. Jah will be praised.

Jehush (je'-hush) = He will gather together; to whom God hastens; collector;

(root = to assemble together).

Jeiel (je-i'-el) = Hidden of God; treasure of God; God snatches away; snatching away; (root = to remove away; to lay up).

Jekabzeel (je-kab'-ze-el) = God will assemble together; God gathers.

Jekameam (je-kam'-e-am) = He will gather together the people; he does assemble the people.

Jekamiah (jek-a-mi'-ah) = Jehovah is standing; Jehovah does gather; he will be gathered of the LORD. Let Jah arise; let Jah establish.

Jekuthiel (je-ku'-the-el) = God is mighty; reverence for God; the fear of God. Veneration of God; preservation of God.

Jemima (je-mi'-mah) = Dove; a little dove. Daily. He will spoil (mar) her.

Jemuel (je-mu'-el) = The day of God; God is light; desire of God. He will be made slumber of God.

Jephthae (jef'-thah-e) = Whom God sets free.

Jephthah (jef'-thah) = He will open; i.e., He will set free and liberate; He does open; He sets free; God opens; the breaker through. (root = to open; to ungirt; to unloose; to set free; to engrave).

Jephunneh (je-fun'-neh) = He will be beheld; i.e., cared for by God; for whom it is prepared; it will be prepared; he that beholds; appearing; regarding. He will be turned (prepared).

Jerah (je'-rah) = Moon; son of the moon. Lunar.

Jerahmeel (je-rah'-me-el) = He will obtain mercy of God; whom God loves; God have mercy; God has compassion; God is merciful; (root = to love; to show mercy; to show compassion).

Jerahmeelites (je-rah'-me-el-ites) = Descendants of Jerahmeel = He will obtain mercy of God; whom God loves; God have mercy; God has compassion; God is merciful; (root = to love; to show mercy; to show compassion).

Jered (je'-red) = Descent; flowing.

Jeremai (jer'-e-mahee) = He will be exalted of the LORD; Jehovah is high; dwelling in heights. Let me have promotions.

Jeremiah (jer-e-mi'-ah) = Elevated of the LORD; whom Jehovah has appointed; Jehovah is high; exalted of God. Jah will cast forth.

Jeremias (jer-e-mi'-as) = Whom Jehovah has appointed. Greek form of Jeremiah = Elevated of the LORD; whom Jehovah has appointed; Jehovah is high; exalted of God.

Jeremoth (jer'-e-moth) = High places; lifting up; elevation.

Jeremy (jer'-e-mee) = Shortened English form of Jeremiah = Elevated of the LORD; whom Jehovah has appointed; Jehovah is high; exalted of God.

Jeriah (je-ri'-ah) = Fear of the LORD; (root {feminine}.= fear; terror; reverence; filial fear; son or daughter of fear). Jehovah has founded; whom Jehovah regards.

Jeribai (jer'-ib-ahee) = Jehovah contends; he will contend;contentious.

Jericho (jer'-ik-o) = City of the moon; moon city; a fragrant place; sent (a city); (roots = [1] moon; [2] to breathe; to smell; to smell with pleasure; to delight in). Let him smell it.

Jeriel (je-ri'-el) = Founded of God; foundation of God; founded. May God teach.

Jerijah (je-ri'-jah) = Same as Jeriah = Fear of the LORD; Jehovah has founded; whom Jehovah regards; (root - fem. = fear; terror; reverence; son or daughter of fear). Teach thou Jah.

Jerimoth (jer'-im-oth) =

Heights. Same as Jeremoth = High places; lifting up; elevation. There shall be elevations.

Jerioth (je'-re-oth) = Curtains; tents; tent curtains; (roots = [1] a curtain; a tent; [2] to tremble; to be displeased; to be grieved).

Jeroboam (jer-o-bo'-am) = Whose people are countless; whose people are many; the people have become numerous; enlarged; struggler for the people; a wrangler among the people; (root = to become many; to be multiplied into myriads). Let the people contend; he will multiply the people.

Jeroham (je-ro'-ham) = He will obtain mercy; he finds mercy; love.

Jerubbaal (je-rub'-ba-al) = Let Baal plead; Baal strives; strives; let Baal defend his cause; he will content with Baal. Baal will be contended (with); Baal will be taught.

Jerubbesheth (je-rub'-be-sheth) = Contender with idol; let the idol of confusion defend itself. Same as Jerubbaal = Let Baal plead; Baal strives; strives; let Baal defend his cause; he will content with Baal. A teacher of Baal. Let the shame (-ful thing) contend.

Jeruel (je-ru'-el) = Same as Jeriel = Founded of God; foundation of God; founded. Fear ye God; taught of God.

Jerusalem (je-ru'-sa-lem) = Foundation of peace; founded in peace; teaching peace. Duel peace shall be taught; lay (set) ye double peace.

Jerusha (je-ru'-shah) = Possessed, namely by a husband; taken possession of or married; (root = to possess; to take possession; to inherit; to be a heir).

Jerushah (je-ru'-shah) = Same as Jerusha = Possessed, namely by a husband; taken possession of or married; (root = to possess; to take possession; to inherit; to be a heir).

Jesaiah (jes-a-i'-ah) = Jehovah is opulent; Jehovah has saved. Same as Isaiah = Salvation of the LORD. Save thou Jah.

Jeshaiah (jesh-a-i'-ah) = Same as Jesaiah = Jehovah is opulent; Jehovah has saved. Same as Isaiah = Salvation of the LORD.

Jeshanah (je-sha'nah) = Old; ancient. (as if withered).

Jesharelah (je-shar'-e-lah) = Upright towards God; right before God.

Jeshebeab (je-sheb'-e-ab) = Habitation of the father; father's seat; seat or dwelling of father; (root = to sit down; to tarry; to dwell in; to inhabit).

Jesher (je'-shur) = Same as Jasher = Uprightness; upright; just.

Jeshimon (jesh'-im-on) = The waste; a desolate place. The wilderness.

Jeshishai (jesh'-i-shahee)

= Jehovah is ancient; ancient of the LORD; i.e., a very old good man.

Jeshohaiah (je-sho-ha-i'-ah) = Depression of the LORD; whom Jehovah humbles. He will be bowed down of Jah.

Jeshua (jesh'-u-ah) = Same as Joshua = Jehovah is salvation; the LORD (is his) salvation; LORD of salvation; the LORD saves. Being saved. Jehovah is help.

Jeshuah (jesh'-u-ah) = Help. He will save; Jehovah is salvation.

Jeshurun (jesh'-u-run) = Upright; righteous; very upright.

Jesiah (je-si'-ah) = Jehovah exists. Same as Isaiah = Salvation of the LORD. He will be lent of Jehovah.

Jesimiel (je-sim'-e-el) = Made of God; i.e., created; Jehovah sits up; (root = to put; to set; to place; to make; to appoint).

Jesse (jes'-se) = Jehovah exists; firm; wealth; gift; my existence. My men.

Jesui (jes'-u-i) = Jehovah is satisfied. Same as Ishui = Level; equality.

Jesuites (jes'-u-ites) = Descendants of Jesui = Jehovah is satisfied. Same as Ishui = Level; equality.

Jesurun (jes'-u-run) = Same as Jeshurun = Upright; righteous.

Jesus (je'-zus) = Jehovah is salvation; Jehovah, my salvation; Savior. Greek form of Jehoshua.

Distinctive New Testament names given to Jesus are:

Emmanuel, Jesus, Christ (Hebrew: Messiah).

Descriptive Titles For Jesus:

They are listed alphabetically in this dictionary.

The ramifications of the name of Jesus are so great that the Bible is filled with descriptive titles for Jesus. Nearly three hundred of these are listed below with a few having the number of times the word is mentioned in the Scriptures in parentheses.

Advocate	1 John 2:1
Almighty (57)	Revelation 1:8
Alpha and Omega	Revelation 1:8; 21:6; 22:13
Altogether Lovely	Song of Solomon 5:16
Amen	Revelation 3:14
Ancient of Days	Daniel 7:22

Descriptive Titles For Jesus

Angel of His Presence	Isaiah 63:9
Anointed	Psalm 2:2
Apostle	Hebrews 3:1
Apple Tree	Song of Solomon 2:3
Approved of God	Acts 2:22
Author of Our Faith	Hebrews 12:2
Author of Salvation	Hebrews 5:9
Babe	Luke 2:16
Beginning of Creation of God	Revelation 3:14
Beginning and Ending	Revelation 1:8; 21:6; 22:13
Bishop of Souls	1 Peter 2:25
Branch	Zechariah 6:12; Isaiah 11:1
Branch of Righteousness	Jeremiah 33:15
Bread of Life	John 6:35
Bridegroom	Matthew 9:15; John 3:29
Bright and Morning Star	Revelation 22:16
Brightness of His Glory	Hebrews 1:3
Buckler	Psalm 18:2
Builder	Matthew 16:18
Bundle of Myrrh	Song of Solomon 1:13
Captain of Our Salvation	Hebrews 2:10

Captain of the Lord's Host	Joshua 5:15
Carpenter, Son of Mary	Mark 6:3
Carpenter's Son	Matthew 13:55
Chief Shepherd	1 Peter 5:4
Chief Cornerstone	1 Peter 2:6; Ephesians 2:20
Chief Shepherd	1 Peter 5:4
Chiefest Among Ten Thousand	Song of Solomon 5:10
Child	Luke 2:40
Chosen of God	Luke 23:35
Christ Jesus My Lord	Philippians 3:8
Christ of God	Luke 9:20
Christ the Lord	Luke 2:11
Christ; Son of the Living God	Matthew 16:16
Cluster of Camphire	Song of Solomon 1:14
Consolation of Israel	Luke 2:25
Counselor	Isaiah 9:6
Covenant of the People	Isaiah 42:6
Covert from Tempest	Isaiah 32:2
Creator of Israel	Isaiah 43:15
Day Star	2 Peter 1:19
Daysman	Job 9:33
Dayspring	Luke 1:78
Deliverer	Psalm 18:2; Romans 11:26

Descriptive Titles For Jesus

Desire of all Nations	Haggai 2:7
Dew	Hosea 14:5
Door	John 10:7, 9
Emmanuel	Matthew 1:23
End of the Law	Romans 10:4
Ensign of the People	Isaiah 11:10
Everlasting Father	Isaiah 9:6
Express Image of His Person	Hebrews 1:3
Faithful and True Witness	Revelation 3:14
Faithful and True	Revelation 19:11
Faithful Witness	Revelation 1:5
Finisher of Our Faith	Hebrews 12:2
First Begotten of the Dead	Revelation 1:5
First and the Last	Revelation 22:13
Firstborn of Every Creature	Colossians 1:15
Firstborn	Romans 8:29
Firstborn From the Dead	Colossians 1:18
Firstfruits	1 Corinthians 15:20
Forerunner	Hebrews 6:20
Fortress	Psalm 18:2
Foundation	Isaiah 28:16; 1 Corinthians 3:11
Fountain Opened (for sin)	Zechariah 13:1
Fountain of Living Waters	Jeremiah 2:13

Descriptive Titles For Jesus

Friend of Publicans and Sinners	Luke 7:34
Fruit of the Womb	Luke 1:42
Galilaean (KJV)	Luke 23:6
Glory of Thy People Israel	Luke 2:32
God of the Whole Earth	Isaiah 54:5
Good Shepherd	John 10:11
Good Master	Matthew 19:16,17; Mark 10:17
Governor of Nations	Psalm 22:28
Governor	Matthew 2:6
Great	Jeremiah 32:18
Greater Than Solomon	Matthew 12:42
Guide	Psalm 48:14
Head of the Body; the Church	Colossians 1:18
Head of the Church	Ephesians 5:23
Head of the Corner	1 Peter 2:7; Matthew 21:42
Head of All Principality and Power	Colossians 2:10
Head of Every Man	1 Corinthians 11:3
Healer	Matthew 14:14
Heir of All Things	Hebrews 1:2
Helper	Hebrews 13:6
Hiding Place	Isaiah 32:2

Descriptive Titles For Jesus

High Priest	Hebrews 3:1; 6:20; 7:26
High Priest Over the House of God	Hebrews 10:21
High Tower	Psalm 18:2
Higher Than the Heavens	Hebrews 7:26
Holy Child Jesus	Acts 4:27
Holy One	Psalm 16:10; Isaiah 43:15
Holy One of Israel (31)	Isaiah 41:14; 54:5
Holy One of God	Luke 4:34; Mark 1:24
Horn of My Salvation	Psalm 18:2
Horn of Salvation	Luke 1:69
Hope, My	Psalm 71:5
I AM	John 8:58
Image of Invisible God	Colossians 1:15
Immanuel	Isaiah 7:14
Immortal	1 Timothy 1:17
Intercessor	Hebrews 7:25
Invisible	1 Timothy 1:17
Jesus (977)	Matthew 1:21
Jesus is the Lord	1 Corinthians 12:3
Jesus Christ Our Savior	Titus 3:6
Jesus of Nazareth (17)	Luke 4:34
Jew	John 4:9

Judge of the Quick and the Dead	Acts 10:42
Judge of Israel	Micah 5:1
Just One	Acts 3:14
Just Man	Matthew 27:19
Justifier	Romans 3:26
King	Matthew 21:5
King of Glory	Psalm 24:8
King of the Jews (18)	John 18:39; 19:3
King of Israel	John 1:49
King of Saints	Revelation 15:3
King of kings (6)	1 Timothy 3:15; Revelation 17:14
King Eternal	1 Timothy 1:17
Lamb	Revelation 5:6; 15:3; 17:14
Lamb Slain	Revelation 13:8
Lamb Without Blemish and Spot	1 Peter 1:19
Lamb of God	John 1:29
Last Adam	1 Corinthians 15:45
Lawgiver	James 4:12
Leader and Commander of the People	Isaiah 55:4
Life	John 11:25
Lifter of My Head	Psalm 3:3
Light of Men	John 1:4

Light to Lighten the Gentiles	Luke 2:32
Light for the Gentiles	Isaiah 42:6; Acts 13:47
Light of the World	John 8:12
Lily of the Valley	Song of Solomon 2:1
Lion of the Tribe of Judah	Revelation 5:5
Living Bread	John 6:51
Living Stone	1 Peter 2:4
Lord (1131); LORD (6471)	Luke 24:3; Acts 2:36
Lord and Christ	Acts 2:36
Lord Both of the Dead and Living	Romans 14:9
Lord From Heaven	1 Corinthians 15:47
Lord God Almighty	Revelation 15:3
Lord of the Harvest	Matthew 9:38
Lord of the Sabbath	Luke 6:5
Lord of Hosts	Isaiah 54:5; Jeremiah 32:18
Lord of Lords	1 Timothy 6:15; Revelation 19:16
Lord Our Righteousness	Jeremiah 23:6
Love	1 John 4:16
Lowly	Zechariah 9:9
Man of Sorrows	Isaiah 53:3
Manna	John 6:57-58

Descriptive Titles For Jesus

Master (57)	Matthew 22:24; John 11:28
Master in Heaven	Colossians 4:1
Mediator	1 Timothy 2:5
Merciful, Faithful High Priest	Hebrews 2:17
Messenger	Malachi 3:1
Messiah	Daniel 9:25, 26
Messias (the Christ)	John 1:41
Mighty God	Isaiah 9:6; Jeremiah 32:18
Mine Elect	Isaiah 42:1
Minister of theCircumcision	Romans 15:8
Minister of Sanctuary	Hebrews 8:2
My Beloved	Song of Solomon 2:8; Matthew12:18
My Beloved Son	Matthew 17:5
My Strong Habitation	Psalm 71:3
Nail	Isaiah 22:23, 25
Name Above Every Name	Philippians 2:9
Nazarene	Matthew 2:23
New and Living Way	Hebrews 10:20
Offering; a Sacrifice to God	Ephesians 5:2
One Shepherd	John 10:16
One That Bringeth Good Tidings	Isaiah 41:27
Only Begotten of Father	John 1:14

Descriptive Titles For Jesus

Only Wise God	1 Timothy 1:17
Our Lord Jesus Christ (55)	Galatians 1:3
Our Peace	Ephesians 2:14
Overcomer	Revelation 17:14
Passover	1 Corinthians 5:7
Potentate	1 Timothy 6:15
Potter	Romans 9:21
Power and Wisdom of God	1 Corinthians 1:24
Precious Corner Stone	Isaiah 28:16
Precious	1 Peter 2:7
Priest	Hebrews 5:10; 7:17
Prince	Daniel 9:25; Acts 5:31
Prince of Life	Acts 3:15
Prince of Peace	Isaiah 9:6
Prince of the Kings of Earth	Revelation 1:5
Prophet	John 4:19; 7:40; Deuteronomy 18:18
Prophet of Nazareth	Matthew 21:11
Propitiation for Our Sins	1 John 2:2
Purifier of Silver	Malachi 3:3
Quickening Spirit	1 Corinthians 15:45
Rabbi; Son of God	John 1:49
Reconciler	2 Corinthians 5:19
Redeemer	Job 19:25; Isaiah 41:14; 54:5

Descriptive Titles For Jesus

Refiner	Malachi 3:3
Resurrection	John 11:25
Reward, Exceeding Great	Genesis 15:1
Rewarder	Hebrews 11:6
Righteous	1 John 2:1
Righteous Branch	Jeremiah 23:5
Righteous Man	Luke 23:47
Righteous Servant	Isaiah 53:11
Rock	Psalm 18:2; 28:1; 1 Corinthians 10:4
Rock of Offense	1 Peter 2:8
Root of David	Revelation 5:5; 22:16
Root of Jesse	Isaiah 11:10; Romans 15:12
Root Out of Dry Ground	Isaiah 53:2
Rose of Sharon	Song of Solomon 2:1
Salvation	Luke 2:30
Samaritan	John 8:48
Savior (Saviour, KJV) (29)	Luke 2:11; Acts 5:31
Savior (Saviour, KJV) of the World	John 4:42; 1 John 4:14
Scepter of Israel	Numbers 24:17

Descriptive Titles For Jesus

Second Man	1 Corinthians 15:47
Seed of the Woman	Genesis 3:14, 15
Servant	Isaiah 42:1; Philippians 2:7
Shadow from heat	Isaiah 25:4
Shepherd	Hebrews 13:20; 1 Peter 2:25
Shield, Thy	Genesis 15:1
Shiloh (rest, tranquility)	Genesis 49:10
Son of David	Matthew 9:27
Son of God (48)	Mark 1:1
Son of the Highest	Luke 1:32
Son of Joseph	John 6:42
Son of Man	Matthew 9:6; Mark 14:62; John 6:27
Son of the Blessed	Mark 14:61
Son of the Living God	Matthew 16:16
Star Out of Jacob	Numbers 24:17
Stem of Jesse	Isaiah 11:1
Stone	Isaiah 28:16; Matthew 21:42
Stone Cut Without Hands	Daniel 2:34, 35
Stone of Stumbling	1 Peter 2:8
Stranger in Jerusalem	Luke 24:18
Strength	Psalm 18:2
Stronghold (in the day of trouble)	Nahum 1:7

Descriptive Titles For Jesus

Sun of Righteousness	Malachi 4:2
Sure Foundation	Isaiah 28:16
Surety of a Better Testament	Hebrews 7:22
Teacher From God	John 3:2
Tender Plant	Isaiah 53:2
Testator	Hebrews 9:16, 17
The Child Jesus	Luke 2:27
The Christ (19)	Mark 14:61
The Lord's Christ	Luke 2:26
The Man	John 19:5
The Man, Christ Jesus	1 Timothy 2:5
The Word	John 1:1; 1:14
Thine Husband	Isaiah 54:5
Thy Maker	Isaiah 54:5
Thy Seed	Galatians 3:16
Tree of life	Genesis 2:9
Tried Stone	Isaiah 28:16
True God and Eternal Life	1 John 5:20
True Vine	John 15:1
True Light	John 1:9
Truth	John 14:6
Vine	John 15:5
Voice	Genesis 3:8
Way	John 14:6
Way of Holiness	Isaiah 35:8

Wonderful   Isaiah 9:6

Young Child   Matthew 2:11

Your King   Isaiah 43:15

Jether (je'-thur) = Abundance; excellence; pre-eminent. Same as Ithra = Excellence; (root = abundance; excellent; that which is first).

Jetheth (je'-theth) = A tent pin; nail; strengthener. A remnant.

Jethlah (jeth'-lah) = He (God) will exalt it; lofty. He will hang.

Jethro (je'-thro) = Same as Jether = Abundance; excellence; pre-eminent. Same as Ithra = Excellence; (root = abundance; excellent; that which is first).

Jetur (je'-tur) = An enclosure; defense; he that keeps. He will arrange; he will encircle.

Jeuel (je-u'-el) = Same as Jeiel = Hidden of God; treasure of God; God snatches away; snatching away; (root = to remove away; to lay up).

Jeush (je'-ush) = Same as Jehush = He will gather together; to whom God hastens; (root = to assemble together). He will succor.

Jeuz (je'-uz) = Counselor; counseling.

Jew (jew) = (An Israelite). Same as Judah = Praised; the LORD be praised; object of praise; praise of the LORD.

Jewess (jew'-ess) = a Jewish woman who is a believer—word now considered to be offensive by many; (root = Judah) = Praised; the LORD be praised; object of praise; praise of the LORD.

Jewish (jew'-ish) = Of or belonging to Jews.

Jewry (jew'-ree) = Old English name for Judea =

Praised; the LORD be praised; object of praise; praise of the LORD.

Jews (jews) = Inhabitants of Judea = Praised; the LORD be praised; object of praise; praise of the LORD.

Jezaniah (jez-a-ni'-ah) = Jehovah does harken; Jehovah does determine. He will prostitute (i.e., use illicitly the name of) Jehovah. Same as Jaazaniah = He will be heard of the LORD; whom Jehovah hears.

Jezebel (jez'-e-bel) = Noncohabitant; unchaste. Without obligation; i.e., (self) righteous; unmarried; chaste, free from carnal connection; (roots = [1] without; [2] to inhabit; to dwell together with).

Jezer (je'-zur) = Frame; form; i.e., of his parents; anything made; formation; (root = to form; to fashion; imagination).

Jezerites (je'-zur-ites) = Descendants of Jezer = Frame; form; i.e., of his parents; anything made;

formation; (root = to form; to fashion; imagination).

Jeziah (je-zi'-ah) = Jehovah unites; whom Jehovah assembles; he will be sprinkled of the LORD; i.e., purified or forgiven of the LORD; Jehovah exalts. He will be sprinkled of Jah.

Jeziel (je'-ze-el) = Assembly of God; God unites. Let him be sprinkled of God.

Jezliah (jez-li'-ah) = Jehovah unites; he will be drawn out of the LORD; i.e., preserved; deliverance. He will pour out suitably; he will cause her to flow forth.

Jezoar (je-zo'-ar) = Splendid. Whiteness.

Jezrahiah (jez-ra-hi'-ah) = Jehovah is shining; the LORD arises. Same as Izrahiah = Brought to light of the LORD; whom Jehovah brought to light; Jehovah shines forth.

Jezreel (jez'-re-el) = God sows; he will be sown of God; i.e., have a numerous progeny; God scatters; the

Lord sows; (root = to sow seed; to plant; to be made fruitful).

Jezreelite (jez'-re-el-ite) = Inhabitants of Jezreel = God sows; he will be sown of God; i.e., have a numerous progeny; God scatters; the Lord sows; (root = to sow seed; to plant; to be made fruitful).

Jezreelitess (jez'-re-el-i-tess) = (Feminine) - Inhabitants of Jezreel = God sows; he will be sown of God; i.e., have a numerous progeny; God scatters; the Lord sows; (root = to sow seed; to plant; to be made fruitful).

Jibsam (jib'-sam) = He will smell sweetly; i.e., be pleasant; fragrant; lovely; sweet.

Jidlaph (jid'-laf) = He will weep; weeping; he that distills; melting away; (root = to pour out tears; to drop tears; to weep).

Jimna (jim'-nah) = Same as Imna = He [God] will retain; whom (God) assigns; God does restrain;

withdrawing; holding back; (root = to withhold; to keep back; to deny).

Jimnah (jim'-nah) = Same as Imnah = Prosperity; he allots; success. Right handed; he will number.

Jimnites (jim'-nites) = Descendants of Jimnah = Same as Imnah = Prosperity; he allots; success. Right handed; he will number.

Jiphtah (jif'-tah) = Same as Jephthah = He will open; i.e., He will set free and liberate; God opens; (root = to open; to un-gird; to unloose; to set free; to engrave).

Jiphthahel [Iphtah El] (jif'-thah-el) = It will be opened of God; which God opens.

Joab (jo'-ab) = LORD Father; Jehovah is Father; Jehovah is a good Father; whose Father is the LORD; God the Father.

Joah (jo'-ah) = Jehovah is brother; God a friend.

Joahaz (jo'-a-haz) =

Jehovah helps; Jehovah has laid hold of. Same as Jehoahaz = Whom Jehovah holds fast; (root = to take hold of).

Joanna (jo-an'-nah) = Jehovah has been gracious; Jehovah has shown favor; the LORD is grace; the LORD give graciously.

Joash (jo'-ash) = Same as Jehoash = Jehovah supports; Jehovah has laid hold; Jehovah is strong; Jehovah hastens to build; the LORD gave; whom Jehovah supports; the substance of the LORD. God's existence. Jehovah has become man.

Joatham (jo'-a-tham) = The LORD is upright. Greek form of Jotham = The LORD is upright; LORD of integrity; (roots = [1] integrity; innocence; upright; [2] to complete; to make whole; to be upright).

Job (jobe) = The persecuted; hated; one ever returning to God; he

that weeps; a desert; (root = to persecute; to be an enemy). The cry of woe; I will exclaim.

Jobab (jo'-bab) = Howling; trumpet call; crying out; i.e., a desert; (root = to cry out; to shout). He will cause crying.

Jochebed (jok'-e-bed) = LORD of glory; glory of the LORD; Jehovah is glorious; Jehovah is (her/our) glory.

Joed (jo'-ed) = Jehovah is witness; LORD of witness; witness of the LORD; for whom Jehovah is witness.

Joel (jo'-el) = LORD of God; the LORD is God; Jehovah is might; Jehovah is God.

Joelah (jo-e'-lah) = God is snatching; removing of oaks; he helps. Let him be profitable; he will sweep away the strong.

Joezer (jo-e'-zer) = LORD of help; help of the LORD; Jehovah is help.

Jogbehah (jog'-be-hah) = Exalted; lofty; (root = to be high). He will be elevated.

152

Jogli (jog'-li) = Led into exile; an exile; exiled; (root = to be carried away). He will carry me captive.

Joha (jo'-hah) = Jehovah is living; haste. Lead thou, Jehovah.

Johanan (jo-ha'-nan) = Same as Jehohanan = The LORD graciously gave; Jehovah is gracious; bestowed by the LORD.

John (jon) = Jehovah has been gracious; Jehovah has graciously given.

Joiada (joy'-a-dah) = Jehovah sets up; Jehovah has known. Same as Jehoiada = The LORD knows; Jehovah knows.

Joiakim (joy'-a-kim) = Jehovah sets up; Jehovah establishes. Same as Jehoiakim = The LORD will set up; Jehovah has set up; the LORD will rise up.

Joiarib (joy'-a-rib) = Jehovah defends; Jehovah contends. Same as Jehoiarib = The LORD will contend; Jehovah will contend.

Jokdeam (jok'-de-am) = Possessed of the people. Burning of the people; let the people kindle.

Jokim (jo'-kim) = Jehovah sets up. Same as Jehoiakim = The LORD will set up; Jehovah has set up; the LORD will rise up.

Jokmeam (jok'-me-am) = Gathered of the people. He will establish the people.

Jokneam (jok'-ne-am) = Possessed of the people. The people will be purchased; the people will be lamented.

Jokshan (jok'-shan) = Sportsman; fowler; (root = to lay snares; to be a bird catcher).

Joktan (jok'-tan) = He will be small; little; small; dispute. Chaldean: Insignificant.

Joktheel (jok'-the-el) = Subdued of God. Absolved of God.

Jona (jo'-nah) = A dove.

Jonadab (jon'-a-dab) = Jehovah is liberal. Same as Jehonadab = The LORD gave spontaneously;

Jehovah is bounteous; the LORD willing.

Jonah (jo'-nah) = Dove; (roots = [1] to be weak; gentle; [2] to oppress; to destroy).

Jonan (jo'-nan) = God has been gracious.

Jonas (jo'-nas) = Same as Jona = A dove.

Jonathan (jon'-a-than) = Same as Jehonathan = The LORD gave; LORD of giving; whom Jehovah gave; the LORD gives.

Jonathelemrechokim (jo'-nath-e'-lem-re-ko'-kim) = The silent dove afar off; the dove of silence among strangers; literally: the dove of silence of distance.

Joppa (jop'-pah) = Same as Japho = Beautiful; beauty; (root = to be beautiful; to adorn). Fair to him.

Jorah (jo'-rah) = Autumnal rain; watering; (roots = [1] the first rain; the former rain; [2] to lay foundations; to sprinkle). Let him teach.

Jorai (jo'-rahee) = He will

be built up of the LORD. My early rain; my teachers.

Joram (jo'-ram) = Jehovah is high. Same as Jehoram = The LORD exalts; Jehovah is high; the LORD exalted.

Jordan (jor'-dan) = Descending; flowing down; (root = to go down; to flow down). Descending rapidly.

Jorim (jo'-rim) = He that exalts the LORD. A form of Joram = Same as Jehoram = The LORD exalts; Jehovah is high.

Jorkoam (jor'-ko-am) = Paleness of the people; spreading of the people.

Josabad (jos'-a-bad) = Same as Jehozabad = Whom the LORD gave; Jehovah gave. Jehovah is the one who bestows.

Josaphat (jos'-a-fat) = The LORD judges. Greek form of Jehoshaphat = The LORD judges; i.e., he pleads for him; whom Jehovah judges.

Josedech (jos'-e-dek) =

Jehovah is righteous.
Same as Jehozadak = The
LORD has made just;
Jehovah is just; the LORD
justifies.

Joseph (jo'-zef) = May
God add; he shall add;
increasing; (root = to add).

Jose (jo'-ze) = Same as
Joses = He that pardons.

Joses (jo'-zez) = He that
pardons.

Joshah (jo'-shah) =
Jehovah is a gift; Jehovah
is uprightness; aid;
Jehovah presents; (root =
being or setting upright;
aiding; uprightness; to
stand upright). He will be
prospered; let him subsist;
he will be made wise.

Joshaphat (josh'-a-fat) =
Jehovah judges.
Shortened form
Jehoshaphat = The LORD
judges; i.e., he pleads for
him; whom Jehovah
judges.

Joshaviah (josh-a-vi'-ah)
= Jehovah is equality;
Jehovah sits upright; set
upright of the LORD. He
will be prospered of Jah;
may Jah sustain him.

Joshbekashah (josh-bek'-
a-shah) = A seat in a hard
place; seat of hardship;
seat of hardness.

Joshua (josh'-u-ah) =
Jehovah is salvation; the
LORD (is his) salvation;
LORD of salvation; the
LORD saves.

Josiah (jo-si'-ah) =
Jehovah supports; given of
the LORD; whom Jehovah
heals; the fire of the
LORD; the spared of God.

Josias (jo-si'-as) = Whom
Jehovah heals. Greek form
of Josiah = Given of the
LORD; whom Jehovah
heals.

Josibiah (jos-ib-i'-ah) =
Jehovah causes to dwell;
he will be made to sit
down of the LORD; i.e., to
live tranquilly, or lead a
peaceable life; to whom
God gives a dwelling. Jah
will make to dwell.

Josiphiah (jos-if-i'-ah) =
Added of the LORD;
whom Jehovah will
increase; Jehovah will
increase. Jah will add.

Jotbah (jot'-bah) =

Pleasant; (root = to be good; to please; to do well to). She was good.

Jotbath (jot'-bath) = Goodness. Place of goodness.

Jotbathah (jot'-ba-thah) = Same as Jotbah = Goodness.

Jotham (jo'-tham) =Jehovah is upright; the LORD is upright; LORD of integrity; the integrity of God; (roots = [1] integrity; innocence; upright; [2] to complete; to make whole; to be upright). Jehovah is perfect.

Jozabad (joz'-a-bad) = Jehovah has bestowed; Jehovah has endowed. Same as Jehozabad = Whom the LORD gave; Jehovah gave.

Jozachar (joz'-a-kar) = Jehovah remembers; the LORD is remembered; whom Jehovah has remembered.

Jozadak (joz'-a-dak) = Jehovah is great; Jehovah is just. Same as Jehozadak = The LORD has made just; Jehovah is just.

Jehovah is the righteous (One).

Jubal (ju'-bal) = Joyful sound; music; jubilee; playing, ram's horn or a trumpet. He will be carried.

Jubilee (ju'-bi-lee) = Productive. He will be made able.

Jucal (ju'-kal) = Able. Same as Jehucal = He will be made able; i.e., strengthened of the LORD; Jehovah is mighty.

Juda (ju'-dah) = Same as Judah = Praised; the LORD be praised; object of praise; praise of the LORD.

Judaea (ju-de'-ah) = (fem. Land of Judaea). Same as Judea = Praised; the LORD be praised; object of praise; praise of the LORD.

Judah (ju'-dah) = Praised; the LORD be praised; object of praise; praise of the LORD. He shall be praised.

Judas (ju'-das)= Praise of the LORD. (Greek form of Judah).

Judas Iscariot (ju'-das Is-car'-e-ot) = Judas = Praise of the LORD: Iscariot = Man of Kerioth; a man of murder.

Jude (jood) = Praise of the LORD.

Judea (ju-de'-ah) = Land of Judah = Praised; the LORD be praised; object of praise; praise of the LORD.

Judith (ju'-dith) = Praised; the praised one.

Julia (ju'-le-ah) = Having curly hair.

Julius (ju'-le-us) = Downy; curly headed.

Junia (ju'-ne-ah) = Belonging to Juno. Latin: youthful; continue thou, Jah.

Jupiter (ju'-pit-ur) = A father of helps. (Roman mythology: chief god who ruled all gods).

Jushabhesed [Jushab-Hesed] (ju'-shab-he'-sed) = He will return love; whose love is

returned; loving kindness is returned. Mercy shall be restored.

Justus (jus'-tus) = Upright; just; righteous.

Juttah (jut'-tah) = It will be stretched out; extended; (root = to stretch out; to extend; to incline towards).

Know ye not that ye are the temple of God, and that the Spirit of God dwelleth in you? (1 Corinthians 3:16).

K

Kabzeel (kab'-ze-el) = God has gathered; God will assemble together.

Kadesh (ka'-desh) = Consecrated; sanctified. Apartness (set apart for a purpose).

Kadeshbarnea [Kadesh barnea] (ka'-desh-bar'-ne-ah) = Sacred desert of wandering; (roots = [1] a sodomite; a harlot; [2] to be holy; to be consecrated; to purify). A moving sanctuary. The son of wandering was set apart.

Kadmiel (kad'-me-el) = God is of old; eternity of God; going before of God; i.e., walking religiously and godly; (root = to precede; to go before; to come before; to prevent). Before (literally: in front of) God.

Kadmonites (kad'-mo-nites) = Oriental; Middle Easterners; ancients.

Kallai (kal'-la-i) = Jehovah is light; Jehovah is swift; lightly esteemed of God; swift. My swiftness.

Kanah (ka'-nah) = Place of reeds; i.e., full of reeds. He has purchased.

Kareah (ka'-re-ah) = Same as Careah = Bald.

Karkaa (kar'-ka-ah) = The floor; the ground; pavement.

Karkor (kar'-kor) = Soft and level ground; a plain. Battering down.

Karnaim = Same as Ashtaroth Karnaim = Ashtaroth of the two horns; the crescent moons (the new moon); two horns.

Kartah (kar'-tah) = City; (root = to meet any one; to be full; to lay beams; to build a city). Her meeting place.

Kartan (kar'-tan) = Two cities; double city. Their meeting place.

Kattath (kat'-tath) = Very small. Diminished.

Kedar (ke'-dar) = Powerful; dark skinned man; black-skinned; black skin; (root = to be dark; to be black; to mourn). Obscurity. Darkness.

Kedemah (ked'-e-mah) = Eastward; toward the east; eastern.

Kedemoth (ked'-e-moth) = Beginnings; ancients; (root = beginning; origin; pristine state). Confrontments. Eastern parts.

Kedesh (ke'-desh) = Sanctuary; holy place; (root = to be consecrated).

Kedeshnaphtali [Kedesh Naphtali] (ke'-desh-naf'-ta-li) = Same as Kedesh = Sanctuary; (root = to be consecrated): Naphtali = A struggle; my wrestling; my twisting; obtained by wrestling.

Kehelathah (ke-hel'-a-thah) = Assembly. Convocation.

Keilah (ki'-lah) = Fortress; enclosed; sling. Let the faint be alienated.

Kelaiah (kel-ah'-yah) = Congregation of the Lord; (roots = [1] to gather together; [2] to collect). Jehovah is light. Contempt.

Kelita (kel'-i-tah) = Same as Kelaiah = Congregation of the Lord; (roots = [1] to gather together; [2] to collect). Dwarf; crippled. Poverty. Lacking; stunted.

Kemuel (kem-u'-el) = Congregation of God; God stands; risen of God. Avenge ye God.

Kenan (ke'-nan) = One acquired; begotten. Same as Cainan = Possession. Their smith (fabricator).

Kenath (ke'-nath) = Possession.

Kenaz (ke'-naz) = Hunting; this possession; this nest.

Kenezite (ken'-e-zite) = Descendants of Kenaz = Hunting; this possession; this nest.

Kenite(s) (ken'-ites) = A nest; (roots = [1] a nest; abode, especially in a high rock; [2] to make a nest; to build a nest; to nestle). My purchase. A smith; a fabricator.

Kenizzites (ken'-iz-zites) = Same as Kenezite = Descendants of Kenaz = Hunting; this possession; this nest.

Kerenhappuch [Keren-Happuch] (ke'-ren-hap'-puk) = Beautifier or horn of paint; a horn reserved; the horn or child of beauty.

Kerioth (ke'-re-oth) = Cities. Readings.

159

Keros (ke'-ros) = Crook; the reed of a weaver's beam. Stooping.

Keturah (ket-u'-rah) = Incense; the smoke of incense.

Kezia (ke-zi'-ah) = Cassia; i.e., equally as precious; (root = to scrape; to peel off). Job 42:14 - "an excellent aromatic smell."

Keziz (ke'-ziz) = Cutting off; (root = to cut off; to amputate; to divide).

Kirbrothhattaavah [Kirbroth Hattaavah] (kib'-roth-hat-ta'-a-vah) = Graves of lust; (roots = [1] a grave; a sepulcher (sepulchre, KJV); [2] to bury; (3) to desire; to covet greedily; to lust).

Kibzaim (kib-za'-im) = Two heaps. Double gatherings.

Kidron (kid'-ron) = Same as Cedron = Very black; full of darkness, (intense form); turbid; (root = black). Great obscurity; wall. The mourner; the black one. (Brook and ravine near Gethsemane frequented by our Lord).

Kinah (ki'-nah) = Song of mourning; lamentation; (root = to lament).

Kir (kur) = A wall; a fortress; town; (roots = [1] a wall; a place fortified with a wall; [2] to dig; to cast out; to destroy).

Kirharaseth [Kir Haraseth] (kur-har'-a-seth) = Same as Kir = A wall; a fortress; town; (roots = [1] a wall; a place fortified with a wall; [2] to dig; to cast out; to destroy). A potsherd in the wall. (Also called the City of brick; City of dried earth).

Kirhareseth [Kir Hareseth] (kur-har'-e-seth) = Same as Kirharaseth. The wall is earthen.

Kirharesh [Kir Hareseth] (kur-ha'-resh) = Same as Kirharaseth. The wall is earthen.

Kirheres [Kir Hareseth] (kur-he'-res) = Same as Kirharaseth. The wall is earthen.

Kiriathaim (kir-e-a-thay'-im) = Same as Kirjathaim = Double city. Walled cities.

Kirioth (kir'-e-oth) = Same as Kerioth = Cities.

Kirjath (kur'-jath) = City; a walled city.

Kirjathaim (kur'-jath-a'-im) = Double city. Walled cities.

Kirjatharba [Kirjath Arba] (kur'-jath-ar'-bah) = City of Arba; (root = a city; a town). City of four.

Kirjatharim [Kiriath Jearim] (kur'-jath-a'-rim) = Contracted from Kirjath-jearim = City of woods; i.e., full of woods or trees. City of enemies; city of cities.

Kirjathbaal [Kirjath Baal] (kur'-jath-ba'-al) = City of Baal.

Kirjathhuzoth [Kirjath Huzoth] (kur'-jath-hu'-zoth) = A city of streets; i.e., a city that has many streets. City of broad ways.

Kirjathjearim [Kirjath Jearim] (kur'-jath-je'-a-rim) = Same as Kirjatharim = City of woods; i.e., full of woods or trees. The city of forests.

Kirjathsannah [Kirjath Sannah] (kur'-jath-san'-nah) = City of learning; (roots = Chaldean: To sweep away with a broom. Arab: learning; the law). City of thorns.

Kirjathsepher [Kirjath Sepher] (kur'-jath-se'-fer) = City of books; (root = to inscribe; to write; to number; to narrate).

Kish (kish) = Snaring; bird catching; (root = to ensnare). Power; straw; forage.

Kishi (kish'-i) = Snaring of the LORD; my snare; also called Kushaiah = The bow of Jehovah.

Kishion (kish'-e-on) = Very hard; hardness (intense form).

Kishon (ki'-shon) = Tortuous; winding about. Ensnarer.

Kislev = Ninth Jewish month (November - December)

Kison (ki'-son) = Same as Kishon = Tortuous; winding about.

Kithlish (kith'-lish) = Wall of man; fortified; (roots = [1] wall; [2] man).

Kitron (ki'-tron) = Knotty; (roots = [1] knotty; [2] to be bound). Burning. Incense-burner.

Kittim (kit'-timm) = They that bruise. Beaters down; crushers. Same as Chittim = Subduers; bruisers.

Koa (ko'-ah) = Prince. Alienation.

Kohath (ko'-hath) = Assembly; congregation; (root = to gather together; to collect together). Obedient. Waiting.

Kohathites (ko'-hath-ites) = Descendants of Kohath = Assembly; congregation; (root = to gather together; to collect together).

Kolaiah (ko-la-i'-ah) = The voice of the LORD; voice of Jehovah.

Korah (ko'-rah) = Ice; icy; hail. Baldness; bald.

Korahite (ko'-ra-hite) = Descendants of Korah = Ice; icy; hail; baldness; bald. Bold.

Korathites (ko'-ra-thites) = Descendants of Korah = Ice; icy; hail; baldness; bald. Bold.

Kore (ko'-re) = Partridge; a crier. Calling; happening.

Korhites (kor'-hites) = Same as Korah = Ice; icy; hail; baldness; bald. Bold.

Koz (coz) = The thorn.

Kushaiah (cu-shah'-yah) = Longer form of Kishi = The bow of Jehovah. Snare of Jehovah.

Love not the world, neither the things that are in the world. If any man love the world, the love of the Father is not in him (1 John 2:15).

L

Laadah (la'-a-dah) = Order; festival. For adornment.

Laadan (la'-a-dan) = Put in order; well ordered; festival-born. For their adornment.

Laban (la'ban) = White; glorious; (root = to be white; to be clean).

Lachish (la'-kish) = Obstinate; i.e., hard to be captured; impregnable. Swiftness. Walk of a man.

Lael (la'-el) = By God; devoted to God.

Lahad (la'-had) = In triumph or joy. Towards exultant shout. Oppression; oppressed; dark colored.

Lahairoi [Lahai Roi] (la-hah'-ee-roy) = To the living is sight. Same as BeerLahaiRoi = The well of the life of vision; the well of her that lives and of him that sees; i.e., preserves me in life; the well of the living who sees me.

Lahmam (lah'mam) = Because of violence; (roots = [1] to; because of; [2] to violate; to do violence; to take by violence). To the violent; their bread.

Lahmi (lah'mi) = A warrior; an eater; my war. My bread.

Laish (la'-ish) = Lion; an old lion.

Lakum (la'-kum) = Stopping up the way; i.e., a fortified place; fort. The rising up.

Lama (la'-mah) = Why.

Lamech (la'-mek) = Powerful; destroyer; One who overthrows; a strong young man; who is stuck. Reduced.

Laodicea (la-od-i-se'-ah) = Greek, laos - people; laity; and dicea - opinion; custom; opinion or custom of the people; = justice of the people; ruled by the people; rule of the majority; democratic; i.e., peoples right or opinions. The people's rights.

Laodiceans (la-od-i-se'-uns) = Inhabitants of Laodicea = Greek: laos - people; laity; and dicea - opinion; custom; opinion or custom of the people; = ruled by the people; rule of the majority; democratic (peoples right or opinions). The people's rights.

Lapidoth (lap'-i-doth) = Torches; i.e., having eyes of fire; enlightened; lightening flashes; (roots = [1] a torch; a lamp; [2] to flame; to shine). Flames.

Lasea (la-se'-ah) = Shaggy.

Lasha (la'-sha) = Fissure. Unto blindness (by covering the eyes).

Lasharon (lash'-ar-on) = Of the plain.

Latin (lat'-in) = The language spoken by Romans. Of Rome's strength.

Lazarus (laz'-a-rus) = God has ruled; without help. Greek form of Eleazar. The brother of Mary and Martha.

Leah (le'-ah) = Wearied; languid; weary; tired; (root = to be wearied; to labor; to be exhausted). Faint from sickness.

Lebanah (leb'-a-nah) = Moon; white; (root = white; i.e., poetic for the moon). A poetic designation for the moon.

Lebanon (leb'-a-non) = Very white; mountain of snow, (intense form); the white (mountain).

Lebaoth (leb'-a-oth) = Lionesses. Same as Bethlebaoth = House or place of lionesses; i.e., a place abounding in lions.

Lebbaeus (leb-be'-us) = Man of heart. A laver(?).

Lebonah (le-bo'-nah)= Frankincense, (from its whiteness).

Lecah (le'-cah) = Progress; journey; (root = to go through; to go on; to go forward; to go about). Addition.

Lehabim (le'-ha-bim) = Flames; scorching heat; flame-colored; (roots = [1] a flame; glittering steel; [2] to burn; to flame).

Lehi (le'-hi) = Jawbone; a cheek; (root = the cheek; the jawbone).

Lemuel (lem'-u-el) = By God; devoted to God; God is bright; with whom God.

Leshem (le'-shem) = Precious stone. Unto desolation.

Letushim (le-tu'-shim) = Artificers; one who hammers; those who sharpen; the hammered. Oppressed; struck. Sharpened ones; hammered ones.

Leummim (le-um'-mim) = Peoples; nations.

Levi (le'-vi) = Adhesion; joined; (root = to be joined; to cleave to; to lend to; to borrow). Associate. A companion.

Leviathan (le-vi'-ath-un) = A water monster. A coiled animal; their burrowing; their union.

Levites(s) (le'-vites) = Descendants of Levi = Adhesion; joined; (root = to be joined; to cleave to; to lend to; to borrow). Associate. A companion.

Leviticus = The book which treats of the affairs of the Levitical law. Called by the Jews = Law of the priests; Law of offerings.

Libertines (lib'-ur-tins) = Freedmen.

Libnah (lib'-nah) = Whiteness; transparency.

Libni (lib'-ni) = White; distinguished.

Libnites (lib'-nites) = Descendants of Libni = White; distinguished.

Libya (lib'-e-ah) = Same as Put = Extension. Grazing. Afflicted; weeping.

Libyans (lib'-e-uns) = Empty-hearted. Same as Put = Extension. Grazing.

Likhi (lik'-hi) = Jehovah is doctrine; characterized by knowledge; learned; fond of learning; (root = learning; doctrine; knowledge - which any one receives). My doctrine.

Linus (li'-nus) = Flax; nets. Linen.

Loammi [Lo-Ammi] (lo-am'-mi) = Not of my people; not my people.

Lod (lod) = Contention; strife. Travail; to bear.

Lodebar [Lo Debar] (lo-de'-bar) = Without pasture. Not a word; i.e., nothing.

Lois (lo'-is) = Agreeable; desirable. No standard bearer; no flight.

Loruhamah [Lo-Ruhamah] (lo-ru-ha'-mah) = Without mercy; not having obtained mercy. Not pitied.

Lot (lot) = Covering; veil; covered; concealed; myrrh; (roots = [1] a covering; a veil; [2] to cast over; to wrap in). A wrapping.

Lotan (lo'-tan) = Covering up; a covering; veiling.

Lubim(s) (lu'-bim) = Dwellers in a thirsty land; i.e., arid country.

Lucas (lu'-cas) = Same as Luke = Light giving; luminous.

Lucifer (lu'-sif-ur) = Light bearer; the shining one; shining. Howling.

Lucius (lu'-she-us) = Of the light; luminous; a noble.

Lud (lud) = Bending; strife. To the firebrands; travailing.

Ludim (lu'-dim) = Same as Lud = Bending; strife. To the firebrands; travailing.

Luhith (lu'-hith) = Tables; slabs; abounding in boards. Pertaining to the table.

Luke (luke) = Light giving; luminous.

Luz (luz) = Almond tree. A filbert. Perverse.

Lycaonia (li-ca-o'-ne-ah) = Wolf land. (A district of Asia Minor; ancient name of the city of Iconium).

Lycia (lish'-e-ah) = Wolfish.

Lydda (lid'-dah) = Greek form of Lod. Travail.

Lydia (lid'-e-ah) = Bending; brought forth. To firebrand; travailing.

Lydians (lid'-e-uns) = Same as Lud = Bending; strife.

Lysanias (li-sa'-ne-as) = Ending sorrow; ending sadness; drives away sorrow. Relaxing sadness.

Lysias (lis'-e-as) = He who has the power to set free; releaser.

Lystra (lis'-trah) = Ransoming; (The home of Timothy.)

Many are the afflictions of the righteous: but the LORD delivereth him out of them all (Psalms 34:19).

M

Maacah (ma'-a-kah) Same as Maachah = Oppression; compression; depression; (root = to press; to press into; to bruise). Squeezed. Pressure (literally: she has pressed).

Maachah (ma'-a-kah) = Oppression; compression; depression; (root= to press; to press into; to bruise). Squeezed. Pressure (literally: she has pressed).

Maachathi (ma-ak'-a-thite) Same as Maachah = Oppression; compression; depression; (root = to press; to press into; to bruise). Squeezed. Pressure (literally: she has pressed).

Maachathite(s) (ma-ak'-a-thites) = Inhabitants of Maachah = Oppression; depression; (root = to press; to press into; to bruise). Squeezed. Pressure (literally: she has pressed).

Maadai (ma'-a-dahee) = My unclothing; my slidings; my adornings.

Maadiah (ma-a-di'-ah) = Ornament of Jehovah. Adorned of Jah; shaken of Jah.

Maai (ma'-ahee) = Jehovah is compassionate; compassion; compassionate;

(root = bowels; heart; womb; belly). My bowels.

Maalehacrabbim (ma'-a-leh-ac-rab'-bim) = The going up of scorpions; ascent of scorpions.

Maarath (ma'-a-rath) = A place naked of trees; a treeless place; (root = to be naked; to make naked; to pour out).

Maaseiah (ma-a-si'-ah) = Refuge of the LORD; work of Jehovah; (root = a refuge; shelter; a hope). Jehovah is a refuge.

Maasiai (ma-a'-see-ahee) Same as Maaseiah = Refuge of the LORD; work of Jehovah; (root = a refuge; a shelter; a hope). My works.

Maath (ma'-ath) = Small; wiping away. From this time.

Maaz (ma'az) = Anger; wrath; counselor. Shutting.

Maaziah (ma-a-zi'-ah) = Consolation of the LORD; strength of Jehovah.

Macedonia (mas-e-do'-nee-ah) = Extended land. Tall(?).

Machbanai (mak'-ba-nahee) = Bond of the LORD; clothed with a cloak. He brought low my sons.

Machbenah (mak'-be-nah) = Bond; clad with a cloak. He brought low the building.

Machi (ma'-ki) = Decrease; (root = to pine away; to decrease; to become poor). My poverty.

Machir (ma'-kur) = Sold; a seller; salesman; (root = to sell; to betroth, a daughter; to sell oneself; i.e., to give oneself up).

Machirites (ma'-kur-ites) = Descendants of Machir = sold; a seller; salesman; (root = to sell; to betroth, a daughter; to sell oneself; i.e., to give oneself up).

Machnadebai (mak-nad'-e-bahee) = What is like the liberty of the LORD; i.e., how great is the liberty of the LORD; gift of the noble one. He brought low my willing ones.

Machpelah (mak-pe'-lah) = Double; a doubling; (root = to fold together; to double). One above another.

Madai (ma'-dahee) = Extended of the LORD; middle; (roots = [1] to measure; [2] Jehovah). My measures; my garments; what is enough.

Madian (ma'-de-an) = Contention; strife. Greek form of Midian = Strife; contention; (roots = [1] strife; contention; [2] to judge). A contender.

Madmannah (mad-man'-nah) = Dunghill; heap. Madmen (mad'-men) = A heap of dung. Garment of simulation.

Madmenah (mad-me'-nah) = Same as Madmannah = Dunghill; heap.

Madon (ma'-don) = Contention; strife; place of contention; (root = strife; contention; that which is contended for).

Magbish (mag'-bish) =

Congregating. Crystalizing.

Magdala (mag'-da-lah) = Tower; fortress.

Magdalene (mag'-da-leen) = Inhabitants of Magdala = Tower; fortress.

Magdiel (mag'-de-el) = Praise of God; honor of God; renown. My preciousness is God.

Magog (ma'-gog) = Expansion; increase of family; from the top. Overtopping; covering.

Magormissabib [Magor-Missabib] (ma'-gor-mis'-sa-bib) = Fear round about; fear or terror is about; (roots = [1] to terrify; to throw down; to cast to the ground; [2] round about; a compass about; seats set around; [3] to turn around; to turn about; to surround; to enclose).

Magpiash (mag'-pe-ash) = Killer of moths; moth slayer; cluster of stars. Plague of moths; the plague is consumed.

Magus (mag'-us) = Magician.

Mahalah (ma'-ha-lah) = Disease; sickness.

Mahalaleel (ma-hal'-a-le-el) = Praise of God; praiser of God; God is splendor.

Mahalath (ma'-ha-lath) = Harp; wind instrument; a musical instrument. Making sick; sickness; appeasing.

Mahalath Leannoth = Title of Psalms 53 and 88.

Mahali (ma'-ha-li) = Infirmity; weak; sick.

Mahanaim (ma-ha-na'-im) = Two hosts; two camps.

Mahaneh-dan (ma'-ha-neh-dan) = Camp of Dan.

Maharai (ma'-ha-rahee) = Impetuosity of the LORD; impetuous; hasty; (root = to hasten; to be quick; to be impetuous).

Mahath (ma'-hath) = Seizing; taking hold; instrument of seizing or dissolution; (root = to take hold of; to seize; to take away).

Mahavite (ma'-ha-vite) = Places of assembly. Declarers; propagators; living ones.

Mahazioth (ma-ha'-ze-oth) = Visions; vision of significance; (root = to contemplate; to see).

Mahershalalhashbaz [Maher-Shalal-Hash-Baz] (ma'-her-sha'-lal-hash'-baz) = Haste to the spoil; hasten the spoil; rush on the prey; the spoil hastens; the prey speeds; quick to the prey; to hasten the booty and hurry the spoil.

Mahlah (mah'-lah) = Disease; sick; ill; in pain; mildness.

Mahli (mah'-li) = Same as Mahali = Infirmity; weak; sick. My sickness.

Mahlites (mah'-lites) = Descendants of Mahli = Infirmity; weak; sick. My sickness.

Mahlon (mah'-lon) = Great infirmity; a sick person; painful; sick; weak; sickly; mild.

Mahol (ma'-hol) = Exultation; dancing; a dance; joy.

Makaz (ma'-kaz) = End; extremity; i.e., land's end. Cutting off.

Makheloth (mak'-he-loth) = Congregations; assemblies; choirs.

Makkedah (mak'-ke-dah) = A place of shepherds. A staff. Branding (spotting) place.

Maktesh (mak'-tesh) = Mortar; i.e., a hollow place; (roots = [1] a mortar; a hollow place; [2] to bray; to pound, in a mortar).

Malachi (mal'-a-ki) = Angel or messenger of the LORD; the messenger of Jehovah; my messenger.

Malcham (mal'-kam)= Most high king; their king; regnant; rule; by their king.

Malchiah (mal-ki'-ah)= Jehovah's king; Jehovah is king.

Malchiel (mal'-ke-el) = God's king; God is a king.

Malchielites (mal'-ke-el-ites) = Descendants of Malchiel = God's king.

Malchijah (mal-ki'-jah) = Same as Malchiah = Jehovah's king; Jehovah is king.

Malchiram (mal'-ki-ram) = King of height; my king is exalted; God is exalted.

Malchishua [Malki-Shua] (mal'-ki-shu'-ah) = King of help; king of aid. My king is salvation; king of opulence.

Malchus (mal'-kus) = King; counselor. Greek form of Malluch = Reigning; counselor; (root = to be king).

Maleleel (mal'-e-le-el) = Praise of God.

Mallothi (mal'-lo-thi) = Jehovah is speaking; Jehovah is splendid; I speak; (root = to speak; to utter). I have spoken.

Malluch (mal'-luk) = Reigning; counselor; (root = to be king). Kingly.

Mammon (mam'-mon) = Fullness. Wealth (as trusted in).

Mamre (mam'-re) = From seeing; from the vision;

fatness; vigor. Chaldean: Dignified. Causing fatness.

Manaen (man'-a-en) = Consoler; comforter.

Manahath (man'-a-hath) = Resting place; rest; gift; (root = to give; to distribute).

Manahethites (man'-a-heth-ites) = Inhabitants of Manahath = Resting place; rest; gift; (root = to give; to distribute).

Manasseh (ma-nas'-seh) = One who causes to forget; forgetting; forgetfulness; causing forgetfulness; (root = to forget; to be forgotten; to cause to forget).

Manasses (ma-nas'-seez) = Causing forgetfulness. Greek form of Manasseh = One who causes to forget; forgetting; forgetfulness; causing forgetfulness; (root = to forget; to be forgotten; to cause to forget).

Manassites (ma-nas'-sites) = Descendants of Manasseh = One who causes to forget; forgetting; forgetfulness; (root = to

forget; to be forgotten; to cause to forget).

Maneh (ma'-neh) = A weight. A coin; present.

Manoah (ma-no'-ah) = Rest; i.e., recreation; quiet; consolation of parents.

Maoch (ma'-ok) = Poor; oppression. Pressing; squeezing. Same as Maachah = Oppression; (root = to press; to press into; to bruise).

Maon (ma'-on) = Place of habitation; habitation.

Maonites (ma'-on-ites) = Inhabitants of Maon = Place of habitation; habitation.

Mara (ma'-rah) = Bitterness; bitter; sad. He was arrogant.

Marah (ma'-rah) = Bitterness; bitter. He rebelled.

Maralah (mar'-a-lah) = Place of concussions; i.e., a place obnoxious or subject to earthquakes; trembling. Causing shaking.

Maranatha (mar-an-a'-thah) = Our Lord comes;

even so, come Lord Jesus.

Marcus (mar'-cus) = A large hammer; polite. A defense(?).

Maresha (mar'-e-shah) = That which is at the head; i.e., leadership; capital. Headship; forget to be arrogant.

Mareshah (mar'-e-shah) = At the head; possession. Same as Maresha = That which is at the head; capital.

Mark = A large hammer; polite. (English form of Marcus).

Maroth (ma'-roth) = Bitterness; bitter fountains.

Marsena (mar'-se-nah) = Lofty; worthy. Bitter is the thorn bush.

Mars' Hill (marz-hill) = English form of Areopagus = Martial peak.

Martha (mar'-thah) = Dominant one; mistress; she was rebellious; (root = Chaldean: Feminine form of word meaning—lord; master). Lady.

Mary (ma'-ry) = Bitterness; rebellious; obstinate; (root = trouble; sorrow; disobedience; rebellion). Greek form of Miriam = Their rebellion.

Mary Magdalene = Mary = Bitterness; rebellious; obstinate; (root = trouble; sorrow; disobedience; rebellion). Greek form of Miriam = Their rebellion.

Magdala (mag'-da-lah) (Magdalene) = Tower; castle.

Maschil (mas'-kil) = Understanding. Giving understanding.

Mash (mash) = Drawn out. He departed; he felt (groped).

Mashal (ma'-shal) = Prayer; entreaty; (roots = [1] similitude; sentence; prayer; [2] to rule; to govern; to become like; to speak in proverbs). A parable; one who speaks in parables.

Masrekah (mas'-re-kah) = Vineyard; (root = to intertwine). Place of the choice vine.

Massa (mas'-sah) =
Bearing patiently; burden;
(root = to bear; to suffer;
to lift up; to take up; to
carry). A prophecy; a
burden (as something
undertaken to carry
through); Enduring.

Massah (mas'-sah) =
Temptation; (roots = [1]
temptation; trial; calamity;
[2] to prove; to try; to
venture). She fainted.

Mathusala (ma-thu'-sa-
lah) = When he is dead it
shall be sent. Greek form
of Methuselah = When he
is dead it shall be sent;
i.e., the flood; (root = to
send; to dismiss; to stretch
out; to be cast out).
Messenger of death. A
man of the javelin. It shall
be sent (deluge).

Matred (ma'-tred) =
Thrusting forward;
pushing forward; one who
expels; (root = a continual
dropping; a thrusting
dropping). Constant
pursuit; continuing.

Matri (ma'-tri) = Jehovah
is watching; rainy; rain;
(root = to rain; to pour

down rain; to be watered
with rain).

Mattan (mat'-tan) = A
gift.

Mattanah (mat'-ta-nah) =
Same as Mattan = A gift.
One who gives.

Mattaniah (mat-ta-ni'-ah)
= Gift of the LORD; gift
of Jehovah.

Mattatha (mat'-ta-thah) =
A gift. Greek form of
Mattaniah = Gift of the
LORD; gift of Jehovah.

Mattathah (mat'-ta-thah)
= Gift of Jehovah.

Mattathias (mat-ta-thi'-
as) = Gift of Jehovah.

Mattenai (mat'-te-nahee)
= Gift of the LORD;
liberal; bestowment; gift of
Jehovah. My gifts.

Matthan (mat'-than) = Gift.

Matthat (mat'-that) =
Another form of Matthan
= Gift.

Matthew (math'-ew) =
Gift of Jehovah.

Matthias (mat'-thias) =
Gift of God. Greek form
of Mattathias = Gift of
Jehovah.

Mattithiah (mat-tith-i'-ah) = Gift of the LORD.

Mazzaroth (maz'-za-roth) = Scattered; dispersed.

Meah (me'-ah) = A hundred.

Mearah (me'-a-rah) = A cave (from to strip, lay bare).

Mebunnai (me-bun'-nahee) = Building of the LORD; built; built up. My buildings.

Mecherathite (me-ker'-ath-ite) = Swordite (one who yields the sword); i.e., a soldier. He of the dug-out; he of the digging tool.

Medad (me'-dad) = Love. A measurer.

Medan (me'-dan) = Strife; contention; a striver; judgment. Discernment.

Mede(s) (meed) = Same as Madia = Extended of the LORD; (roots = [1] to measure; [2] Jehovah). My measure. My garment.

Medeba (med'-e-bah) = Flowing water. Waters of rest (quiet).

Media (me'-de-ah) = Same as Madai = Extended of the LORD; (roots = [1] to measure; [2] Jehovah). My measure. He of the measured; my garments.

Median (me'-de-an) = Same as Madai = Extended of the LORD; (roots = [1] to measure; [2] Jehovah). My measure.

Medeba = Water of rest; water of strength.

Megiddo (me-ghid'-do) = Place of troops; place of multitudes; (root = to crowd in great numbers in one place). Invading; gathering for cutting (self); his cutting-place.

Megiddon (me-ghid'-don) = Same as Megiddo = Place of troops; place of multitudes; (root = to crowd in great numbers in one place). The cutter; brander.

Mehetabeel (me-het'-a-be-el) = Benefited of God; God blesses; God is doing good; (root = to do good, to anyone).

Mehetabel (me-het'-a-bel) = Same as Mehetabeel = Benefited of God; God blesses; God is doing good; (root = to do good, to anyone). Whom God makes happy.

Mehida (me-hi'-dah) = A joining together; union; famous. Allegorist.

Mehir (me'-hur) = Price; wages; dexterity.

Meholathite (me-ho'-lath-ite) = Same as Abelmeholah = Meadow of dancing. Mourning for sickness.

Mehujael (me-hu'-ja-el) = Destroyed by God; struck by God; God is combating; blotted out by God; (root = to destroy; to wipe; to blot out; to abolish).

Mehuman (me-hu'-man) = Faithful. Their discomfiture.

Mehunim(s) (me-hu'-nims) = Descendants of Maon = Place of habitation.

Mejarkon [Me Jarkon] (me-jar'-kon) = Water of great greenness. Waters of yellowness. Waters of

mildew; waters of verdure.

Mekonah (me-ko'-nah) = Base; i.e., a foundation. A settlement.

Melatiah (mel-a-ti'-ah) = Delivered of the LORD; whom Jehovah freed; Jehovah has set free.

Melchi (mel'-ki) = Jehovah is my king.

Melchiah (mel-ki'-ah) = Jehovah's king.

Melchisedec (mel-kis'-e-dek) = King of righteousness; King of justice. Greek form of Melchizedek = King of righteousness; (roots = [1] king; [2] righteousness; rectitude; justice; [3] to be right; to be just; to justify). My King of righteousness.

Melchishua [Malki Shua] (mel'-ki-shu'-ah) = Same as Malchishua = King of help; king of aid.

Melchizedek (mel-kiz'-e-dek) = King of righteousness; (roots = [1] king; [2] righteousness; rectitude; justice; [3] to be right; to be just; to justify). My King of righteousness.

Melea (mel'-e-ah)=
Fullness. My dear friend;
object of care.

Melech (me'-lek) = King.

Melicu (mel'-i-cu) =
Counselor. Same as
Malluch = Reigning; (root
= to be king). My royalty;
they have made a king.

Melita (mel'-i-tah) =
Honey.

Melzar (mel'-zar) = The
overseer; steward. The
circumcised, he straitened.

Memphis (mem'-fis) =
Haven of good men; the
gate of the blessed.
Waving to and fro. Being
made fair. Greek:
blamable; encompassed.

Memucan (mem-u'-can)
= Impoverished. Their
poverty.

Menahem (men'-a-hem)
= Consoling; comforter; a
comforter; (root = to
lament; to comfort; to
comfort oneself; to take
revenge).

Menan (me'-nan) =
Consoling; comforting.
Soothsayer; enchanted.

Mene (me'-ne) = To
number; numbered; count.
He has numbered.

**Mene, Mene, Tekel,
Upharsin** [Mene, Mene,
Tekel, Parisn] (me'ne, te'-
kel, u'-far-sin) = God hath
numbered thy kingdom
and finished it.

Meonenim (me-on'-e-
nim) = Enchanters;
observers of times.

Meonothai (me-on'-o-
thahee) = Habitation of
the LORD; my
habitations.

Mephaath (mef'-a-ath) =
Beauty. The shining forth.

Mephibosheth (me-fib'-o-
sheth) = Exterminating the
idol; destroying shame;
utterance of Baal; (roots =
[1] to scatter; to
exterminate; [2] confusion;
shame; shameful thing;
idol). From my mouth
shame. Breathing shame.

Merab (me'-rab) =
Multiplication; increase. A
disputer.

Meraiah (mer-a-i'-ah) =
Lifted up of the LORD;
revelation of Jehovah;

stubbornness. Rebellion; provoking Jah.

Meraioth (me-rah'-yoth) = Rebellions; revelations.

Merari (me-ra'-ri) = Bitterness; bitter; unhappy.

Merarites (me-ra'-rites) = Same as Merari = Bitterness; bitter; unhappy.

Merathaim (mer-a-tha'-im) = Double rebellion. Double bitterness.

Mercurius (mer-cu'-re-us) = Messenger or herald of the gods, (Greek, also called Hermes). Eloquent; learned; shrewd; crafty.

Mered (me'-red) = Rebellion; rebellious.

Meremoth (mer'-e-moth) = Elevations; strong; (root = to be high).

Meres (me'-res) = Lofty; worthy. Moisture; fracture.

Meribah (mer'-i-bah) = Water of strife; chiding; contention. Strife.

Meribah Kadesh (mer'-i-bah ka'-desh) = Meribah = Water of strife; chiding; contention. Kadesh =

Consecrated; sanctified.

Meribbaal [Merib-Baal] (me-rib'-ba-al) = Contender against Baal. Rebellion of Baal. Baal is contentious.

Merodach (mer'-o-dak) = Death; slaughter. Your rebellion. Persian: poured myrrh.

Merodachbaladan [Merodach-Baladan] (mer'-o-dak-bal'-a-dan) = Merodach gives a son; the son of death. Mars is a worshiper of Baal. Merodach is not a lord; your rebellion; Baal is lord.

Merom (me'-rom) = A high place; exalted.

Meronothite (me-ron'-o-thite) = Joyful shouter.

Meroz (me'-roz) = Refuge. Of leanness.

Mesech (me'-sek) = Drawing out; (root = to draw; to draw one any where; to draw out; to take hold; to continue). Durability.

Mesha (me'-shah) = Retreat; deliverance; freedom; (root = to recede;

to depart; to remove). Salvation. (1 Chronicles. 8:9; Genesis 10:30; - waters of devastation; making to forget; equalizing; existing.)

Meshach (me'-shak) = Agile; expeditious. biting; waters of quiet. Who is what thou art(?)

Meshech (me'-shek) = Same as Mesech = Drawing out; (root = to draw; to draw one any where; to draw out; to take hold; to continue). Durability.

Meshelemiah (me-shel-e-mi'-ah) = Whom the LORD repays; i.e., rewards graciously; Jehovah repays; Jehovah recompenses.

Meshezabeel (me-shez'-a-be-el) = God sets free; liberated of God; God delivers; (root = to set free; to liberate).

Meshillemith (me-shil'-le-mith) = Recompense. Reconciliation.

Meshillemoth (me-shil'-le-moth) = Those who repay; retribution.

Meshobab (me-sho'-bab) = Returning; brought back; restored; delivered.

Meshullam (me-shul'-lam) = Repaying; those who repay; associate; friend. Reconciled.

Meshullemeth (me-shul'-le-meth) = Same as Meshullam (feminine) = Repaying; those who repay; retribution. Reconciliation.

Mesobaite (me-so'-ba-ite) = Congregation of the LORD. The one set up of Jah.

Mesopotamia (mes-o-po-ta'-me-ah) = Same as Aram = High; elevated; lifted up; magnified. Amidst the rivers. Aram of the rivers.

Messiah (mes-si'-ah) = The Anointed. (The Anointed One–Christ).

Messias (mes-si'-as) = Anointed. Greek form of Messiah, the anointed Christ.

Methegammah [Metheg Ammah] (me'-theg-am'-mah) = The bridle of the metropolis; (root = the head or blessing of anything; a foundation; a cubit). A bridle; a cubit length.

Methusael (me-thu'-sa-el) = Man who is of God. Asking for death. They died enquiring; they died who are of God;

Methuselah (me-thu'-se-lah) = When he is dead it shall be sent; i.e., the flood; (root = to send; to dismiss; to stretch out; to be cast out). Messenger of death. A man of the javelin. It shall be sent (deluge). Man of the dart.

Meunim (me-u'-nim) = Same as Maon = Place of habitation.

Mezahab (mez'-a-hab) = Offspring; the shining one; waters of gold.

Miamin (mi'-a-min) = From the right hand; on the right hand; fortunate.

Mibhar (mib'-har) = Most choice; i.e., best; choicest; youth choice.

Mibsam (mib'-sam) = Sweet odor; sweet smell; delight. Fragrant.

Mibzar (mib'-zar) = Defense; a fortress; a stronghold; fortified; (root = to fortify; to wall; to gather grapes; to restrain).

Micah (mi'-cah) = Who is like unto Jehovah? Who is like this(?)

Micaiah (mi-ka-i'-ah) = Who is like unto Jehovah?

Micha (mi'-cah) = Who is like Jehovah?

Michael (mi'-ka-el) = Who is like unto God?

Michah (mi'-cah) = Same as Micha = Who is like unto Jehovah?

Michaiah (mi-ka-i'-ah) = Same as Micha = Who is like unto Jehovah?

Michal (mi'-kal) = A little stream of water; brook; (root = to contain a little water). Who is all(?) Who is like Jehovah?

Michmas (mik'-mas) = Treasure; treasury; (root = to lay up in store). Poverty was melted; poverty of servile work.

Michmash (mik'-mash) = Same as Michmas =

Treasure; treasury; (root = to lay up in store). He that is removed. Poverty was felt; poverty has departed.

Michmethah (mik'-me-thah) = A hiding place. The poverty of the dead; the poverty of the reward.

Michri (mik'-ri) = Bought [of the LORD]; precious; Jehovah possess; valuable. My price.

Michtam (mik'-tam) = Writing. The poverty of the perfect; (blood) staining; i.e., deep dyeing.

Middin (mid'-din)= Measures; extensions; (root = to measure). From judgment; judging.

Midian (mid'-e-an) = Strife; contention; (roots = [1] strife; contention; [2] to judge). A contender.

Midianite(s) (mid'-e-an-ites) = Inhabitants of Midian = Strife; (roots = [1] strife; contention; [2] to judge).

Midianitish (mid'-e-an-i'-tish) = Referring to Midian = Strife; (roots = [1] strife; contention; [2]

to judge).

Migdalel [Migdal El] (mig'-dal-el) = Tower of God; i.e., a very high tower.

Migdalgad [Migdal Gad] (mig'-dal-gad) = Tower of fortune.

Migdol (mig'-dol) = Tower; (root = a tower; a castle; a lofty place; a town fortified with a tower).

Migron (mi'-gron) = Place of great conflict; a precipice. A threshing floor. Hurling down.

Mijamin (mij'-a-min) = Fortunate. Same as Miamin = From the right hand; on the right hand.

Mikloth (mik'-loth) = Staves; rods; sticks; (secondary meaning = To punish with a rod). Sprouts; triflings.

Mikneiah (mik-ne-i'-ah) = Possession of Jehovah; Jehovah is jealous.

Milalai (mil'-a-lahee) = Eloquent; i.e., the promise of the LORD; Jehovah is elevated; Jehovah is eloquent. My utterances.

Milcah (mil'-cah) = Queen. Chaldean: Counsel.

Milcom (mil'-com) = High king (intensive form). Their king. Reigning.

Miletum (mi-le'-tum) = Form of Miletus = Pure white fine wool. Cared for.

Miletus (mi-le'-tus) = Pure white fine wool. Cared for.

Millo (mil'-lo)= Rampart; a mound (filled with stones and earth); filled.

Miniamin (min'-e-a-min) = On the right hand; fortunate.

Minni (min'-ni) = Part. From me.

Minnith (min'-nith) = Small. Allotment. From her.

Miphkad (mif'-kad) = Place of meeting. Muster; apportionment.

Miriam (mir'-e-am) = Bitterness; their rebellion; rebellion. Star of the sea. Celebrated.

Mirma (mur'-mah)= Deceit; fraud; height.

Misgab (mis'-gab) = Refuge; height; (root = to be lofty; to be high; to exalt oneself).

Mishael (mish'-a-el) = Who is what God is; high place. Who asks(?)

Mishal (mi'-shal) = Enquiry. Same as Mashal = Prayer; entreaty; (roots = [1] similitude; sentence; prayer; [2] to rule; to govern; to become like; to speak in proverbs).

Misham (mi'-sham) = Their cleansing; swiftness; impetuous. Their regarding.

Misheal (mish'-e-al) = Same as Mashal = Prayer; entreaty; (roots = [1] similitude; sentence; prayer; [2] to rule; to govern; to become like; to speak in proverbs).

Mishma (mish'-mah) = Hearing; fame; report.

Mishmannah (mish-man'-nah) = Fatness; vigor; (root = to be fat; to cover with fat; to be fattened).

Mishraites (mish'-ra-ites) = A slippery place.

182

Touching evil (as removing or drawing out).

Mispar (mis'-par) = Number; i.e., a few; (root = to number).

Mispereth (mis-pe'-reth) = Writing; a narrative. Same as Mispar = Number; i.e., a few; (root = to number).

Misrephothmaim [Misrephoth Maim] (mis'-re-foth-mah'-yim) = The burning of waters; the burning upon the waters.

Mithcah (mith'-cah) = Sweetness; sweet fountain; (root = to be sweet; to be pleasant).

Mithnite (mith'-nite) = Strength. An athlete; literally, he of loins; a giver.

Mithredath (mith'-re-dath) = Given by the genius of the sun; given by Mithra, animating spirit of fire. Remainder of law; searching our of law.

Mitylene (mit-i-le'-ne) = Mutilated.

Mizar (mi'-zar) = Smallness; small;

diminutive; young.

Mizpah (miz'-pah) = A watch tower.

Mizpar (miz'-par) = Fear; writing. Same as Mispereth = Writing; a narrative. Number.

Mizpeh (miz'-peh) = Same as Mizpah = A watch tower.

Mizraim (miz'-ra-im) = Two distresses; fortresses. Two-fold Egypt; i.e., upper and lower Egypt. Oppressors; tribulations. Double straightness.

Mizzah (miz'-zah) = Terror; joy. From sprinkling.

Mnason (na'-son) = A diligent seeker. Solicitor; the number is safe.

Moab (mo'-ab) = Water of a father; i.e., seed, progeny; desire; progeny of a father; of the father. Waste; nothingness.

Moabite (mo'-ab-ite) = Inhabitants of Moab = Water of a father; i.e., seed, progeny; desire; progeny of a father; of the father. Waste; nothingness.

Moabitess (mo'-ab-i-tess) = Inhabitants of Moab (fem.) = Water of a father; i.e., seed, progeny; desire; progeny of a father; of the father. Waste; nothingness.

Moabitish (mo'-ab-i-tish) = Same as Moab = Water of a father; i.e., seed, progeny; desire; progeny of a father; of the father. Waste; nothingness.

Moadiah (mo-ad-i'-ah) = Festival of Jehovah. Same as Maadai = Jehovah is ornament; Jehovah is wavering; ornament of the LORD; adorned. The set time of Jah.

Moladah (mo-la'-dah) = Birth place; (root = to be born; birth; native land; kindred).

Molech (mo'-lek) = King; governing.

Molid (mo'-lid) = Begetting; begetter; (root = to be born). Causing to bring forth.

Moloch (mo'-loch) = Same as Molech = King; governing.

Morasthite (mo'-ras-thite) = Inhabitants of Moresheth-gath = Possession of Gath.

Mordecai (mor'-de-cahee) = Little man; bitter bruising; bitterly reduced. Bitterness of my oppresseion. A picture of the humanity of Jesus as our kinsman Redeemer (Esther 2:4-7; 10:1-3).

Moreh (mo'-reh) = Teacher; illustrious. Archer.

Moreshethgath [Moresheth Gath] (mor'-e-sheth-gath) = The possession of Gath.

Moriah (mo-ri'-ah) = Visible of the LORD; chosen of the LORD; provided by Jehovah. Instruction of God.

Mosera (mo-se'-rah) = Bonds.

Moseroth (mo-se'-roth) = Same as Mosera = Bonds.

Moses (mo'-zez) = Taken out of the water; saved out of the water; saved from the water; drawn out; drawn forth. A son.

Moza (mo'-zah) = Fountain; offspring; going forth.

Mozah (mo'-zah) = Same as Moza = Fountain; offspring; going forth. Wringing out.

Muppim (mup'-pim) = Anxieties; obscurities. Shakings; wavings.

Mushi (mu'-shi) = Proved of the LORD; drawn out; (root = to feel; to handle; to prove). Withdrawn. My yielding; my departure; depart thou.

Mushites (mu'-shites) = Inhabitants of Mushi = Proved of the LORD; drawn out; (root = to feel; to handle; to prove). Withdrawn. My yielding; my departure; depart thou.

Muthlabben (muth-lab'-ben) = Death to the son. (Psalm 9 title).

Myra (mi'-rah) = A balsam. Myrtle juice.

Mysia (miz'ye-ah) = Land of beach trees. Closure; abomination.

No good thing will he withhold from them that walk uprightly (Psalms 84:11).

Naam (na'-am) = Pleasantness; sweetness.

Naamah (na'-a-mah) = Pleasant; sweetness.

Naaman (na'-a-man) = Pleasantness; pleasant; delight; agreeable.

Naamathite (na'-a-math-ite) = Same as Naaman = Pleasantness; pleasant; delight; agreeable.

Naamites (na-'a-mites) = Descendants of Naaman = Pleasantness; pleasant; delight; agreeable.

Naarah (na'-a-rah) =

Handmaid; a girl; girl or child of the Lord; maiden; (root = a damsel; a young woman; a maiden).

Naarai (na'-a-rahee) = Pleasantness of Jehovah; child of the LORD; youthful. My boys; my shakings; my roarings.

Naaran (na'-a-ran) = Same as Naarah = Handmaid; a girl; (root = a damsel; a young woman; a maiden).

Naarath (na'-a-rath) = Same as Naarah = Handmaid; a girl; (root = a damsel; a young woman; a maiden). To maidenhood; maiden-place.

Naashon (na'-a-shon) = An enchanter; oracle; one that foretells. A diviner.

Naasson (na'-as-son) = Enchanter. Greek form of Naashon = An enchanter; oracle; one that foretells.

Nabal (na'-bal) = A fool; i.e., impious; foolish; prominence; (root = to be withered; to faint; to act foolishly; to despise).

Naboth (na'-both) = Fruits; prominence; productive; i.e., abundance; (root = to increase; to cause to germinate).

Nachon (na'-kon) = Smitten; stroke; (root = to smite; to strike; to break in pieces; to kill). Prepared. Established.

Nachor (na'-kor) = Noble; burning. Snorting.

Nadab (na'-dab) = Volunteer; i.e., willing; of one's free will; liberal; (root = to impel oneself).

Nagge (nag'-e) = Splendor of the sun. My shinings.

Nahalal (na'-ha-lal) = Pasture; i.e., where sheep were led; (root = to lead out; to lead to water; to provide for).

Nahaliel (na-ha'-le-el) = Torrents of God; (roots = [1] a river; a torrent; a valley; [2] God). Valley or river of God.

Nahallal (na'-hal-el) = Same as Nahalal = Pasture; i.e., where sheep were led; (root = to lead out; to lead to water; to provide for).

Nahalol (na'-ha-lol) = Same as Nahalal = Pasture; i.e., where sheep were led; (root = to lead out; to lead to water; to provide for).

Naham (na'-ham) = Consolation; i.e., to his parents; solace; (root = to comfort).

Nahamani (na-ham'-a-ni) = Repenting; (root = to repent). Comforter; compassionate.

Naharai (na'-ha-rahee) = Snorter; one who snores; snorting one.

Nahari (na'-ha-ri) = Same as Naharai = Snorter; one who snores; snorting one.

Nahash (na'-hash) = Serpent; oracle.

Nahath (na'-hath) = Letting down; descent; lowness; quiet; (root = to descend; to press down; to prostrate).

Nahbi (nah'-bi) = Hidden (of the LORD); Jehovah's protection; concealed. My hiding.

Nahor (na'-hor) = Snorting; breathing hard; slayer; inflamed; heated.

Nahshon (nah'-shon) = Enchanting; ominous. Same as Naashon = An enchanter; oracle; one that foretells.

Nahum (na'-hum) = Comforter; comforted; full of comfort; consolation; compassionate.

Nain (nane) = Pasture. Afflicted; beautiful.

Naioth (nah'-yoth) = Habitations; dwellings; (root = to sit down; to be decorous; to adorn).

Naomi (na'-o-mee) = Pleasant; pleasantness; agreeable; attractive; my joy; my bliss; pleasantness of Jehovah; (root = pleasantness; beauty; grace).

Naphish (na'-fish) = Refreshment; numerous; respiration; cheerful; (root = to take breath; to take rest).

Naphtali (naf'-ta-li) = A struggle; my wrestling; my

twisting; obtained by wrestling.

Naphtuhim (naf'-too-him) = Openings; (root = to open; to carve).

Narcissus (nar-sis'-sus) = Benumbing. Flower causing lethargy or astonishment. Narcotic.

Nashon (na'-shon) = Same as Naashon = An enchanter; oracle; one that foretells.

Nathan (na'-than) = Given [of God]; gift; given; he has given; (root = to give).

Nathanael (na-than'-a-el) = Gift of God.

Nathanmelech [Nathan Melech] (na'-than-me'-lek) = Gift of the king; placed of the king; i.e., constituted; the king is giver.

Naum (na'-um) = Comfort. Same as Nahum = Comforted; full of comfort; consolation; compassionate.

Nazarene (naz-a-reen') = A native of Nazareth = Branch. Preservation.

Nazareth (naz'-a-reth) = Branch. Preservation.

Nazarite(s) (naz'-a-rites) = One separated; to separate; to consecrate.

Neah (ne'-ah) = Wandering. Of a slope. A shaking.

Neapolis (ne-ap'-o-lis) = New city.

Neariah (ne-a-ri'-ah) = Servant of Jehovah; Jehovah has shaken; Jehovah drives away.

Nebai (ne'-bahee) = Fruit of the Lord; fruitful; (root = to bear fruit). Narrowing; projecting.

Nebaioth (ne-bah'-yoth) = High places; productive; husbandry. Prophecies; increasings.

Nebajoth (ne-ba'-joth) = Same as Nebaioth = High places; productive; husbandry. Prophetesses.

Neballat (ne-bal'-lat) = Folly in secret; (roots = [1] folly; [2] lot; secretly; enchantments).

Nebat (ne'-bat) = Aspect; an investigator;

cultivation; (root = to look; to behold; to regard). Behold; we speak idly.

Nebo (ne'-bo) = Mercury; interpreter; foreteller; (root = to speak; to prophesy; to sing; to be mad). A lofty place; height; fertile. His prophecy.

Nebuchadnezzar (neb-u-kad-nez'-zar) = Nebo is the god of fire. Nebo, protect the landmark; Nebo, defend the boundary. An entangled adversary. Confusing the lord of treasure; prophesy, the earthen vessel is preserved.

Nebuchadrezzar (neb-u-kad-rez'-zar) = Another way of spelling Nebuchadnezzar. Confusion of the abode of treasure; prophesy, the seer's vessel is preserved.

Nebushasban (neb-u-shas'-ban) = Nebo will save me; Nebo, save me. Worshiper of Mercury. Prophesy their deliverance.

Nebuzaradan (neb-u-zar'-a-dan) = Nebo gives posterity; Nebo hath an offspring. Mercury's

leader, lord; i.e., the leader whom Mercury favors. Winnowing over the threshold. Prophesy, the lord is estranged.

Necho (ne'-ko) = The lame; beaten; who was beaten. Conqueror. His smiting.

Nechoh (ne'-ko) = Same as Necho = The lame; beaten; who was beaten. Conqueror.

Nedabiah (ned-a-bi'-ah) = Spontaneous gift of the LORD; Jehovah is bountiful; Jehovah is willing.

Neginah (neg'-i-nah) = A stringed instrument. Harp-songs.

Neginoth (neg'-i-noth) = Stringed instruments. (Title to Psalms 4, 6, 54, 55, 67, and 76.) Harp-songs.

Nego (ne'-go) = Same as Nebo = Mercury; interpreter; foreteller; (root = to speak; to prophesy; to sing; to be mad). A lofty place; height; fertile.

Nehelamite (ne-hel'-am-ite) = Made fat; dreamer.

Nehemiah (ne-he-mi'-ah) = Jehovah comforts; Jehovah has consoled; the comfort of GOD; i.e., the aid of the LORD; (roots = [1] to comfort; [2] Jehovah).

Nehiloth (ne'-hi-loth) = Flutes. We will cause profanation; we shall divide the inheritance.

Nehum (ne'-hum) = Merciful; consolation. Comfort.

Nehushta (ne-hush'-tah) = Brass; bronze; a piece of brass.

Nehushtan (ne-hush'-tan) = A little brazen serpent; i.e., a contemptible piece of brass. Brazen. Enchanted.

Neiel (ne-i'-el) = Shaken of God; moved by God.

Nekeb (ne'-keb) = Cavern; (root = to bore; to perforate).

Nekoda (ne-ko'-dah) = Distinguished; a herdsman; herdsman; (roots = [1] a point; [2] to prick). Spotted.

Nemuel (ne-mu'-el) = Circumcision of God; God is spreading. They (were made to) slumber of God.

Nemuelites (ne-mu'-el-ites) = Descendants of Nemuel = Circumcision of God; God is spreading. They (were made to) slumber of God.

Nepheg (ne'-feg) = Sprout; bud; shoot; an offshoot. We will cease (grow numb).

Nephish (ne'-fish) = Same as Naphish = Refreshment; numerous; respiration; cheerful; (root = to take breath; to take rest).

Nephishesim (ne-fish'-e-sim) = Expansions; (root = to stretch out).

Nephthalim (nef'-tha-lim) = Wrestling. Greek form of Naphtali = A struggle; my wrestling; my twisting; obtained by wrestling. We will take the spoilers; refreshed of spices.

Nephtoah (nef-to'-ah) = Opening; opened; (root = to open).

Nephusim (ne-fu'-sim) =

190

Same as Nephishesim =
Expansions; (root = to
stretch out). Scatter spices.

Ner (nur) = Lamp; light;
brightness; (root = to give
light).

Nereus (ne'-re-us) =
Liquid. A water nymph
(ancient sea god).

Nergal (nur'-gal) = Mars
(the planet). Lion. A
slanderer. The lamp rolled.

Nergalsharezer [Nergal
Sharezer] (nur'-gal-sha-
re'-zur) = Nergal, protect
the king. Mars is the
brightest of light. Nergal
is the prince of fire. The
rolling lamp observed the
treasure.

Neri (ne'-ri) = Light of the
LORD.

Neriah (ne-ri'-ah) = Lamp
of Jehovah.

Nero (ne'-ro) = Brave.

Nethaneel (ne-than'-e-el)
= God gave; given of God;
God has given.

Nethaniah (neth-a-ni'-ah)
= Whom Jehovah gave;
Jehovah has given; the gift
of God; given of the LORD.

Nethinims (neth'-in-ims)
= The appointed;
appointed. Given ones.

Netophah (ne-to'-fah) =
A dropping; (root = to
drop; to prophesy).
Distillation.

Netophathi (ne-to'-fa-thi)
= Inhabitants of Netophah
= A dropping; (root = to
drop; to prophesy).
Distillation.

Netophathite (ne-to'-fa-
thite) = Same as Netophah
= A dropping; (root = to
drop; to prophesy).
Distillation.

Neziah (ne-zi'-ah) =
Overseer; pre-eminent;
pure; (roots = [1] to
conquer; to excel; [2] to
be over; to superintend; to
lead [in music]; [to be]
perpetual). Illustrious.

Nezib (ne'-zib) =
Garrison; (root = to put to
place; to fix; to establish).

Nibhaz (nib'-haz) = Lord
of darkness; i.e., the evil
demon. We shall utter
(what is) seen.

Nibshan (nib'-shan) =
Level; level and soft soil.

We shall prophesy quiet.

Nicanor (ni-ca'-nor) = Conqueror; victorious; I conquer. Untimely victory.

Nicodemus (nic-o-de'-mus) = Innocent blood; victor over the people. Conqueror of the populace.

Nicolaitanes (nic-o-la'-i-tans) = Destroyer of the people. Named after Nicolas = Conqueror of the people.

Nicolas (nic'-o-las) = (Nicolaus) Conqueror of the people (as a whole).

Nicopolis (ni-cop'-o-lis) = City of victory.

Niger (ni'-jur) = Black.

Nimrah (nim'-rah) = Same as Bethnimrah = House of pure water. Limpid (water). He was rebellious; leopardess.

Nimrim (nim'-rim) = Same as Bethnimrah = House of pure water. Clear waters. He was rebellious; leopardess.

Nimrod (nim'-rod) = Rebel; a rebel; to be rebellious; (root = to be rebellious; to be contumacious). Valiant; strong; he that rules. We will rebel.

Nimshi (nim'-shi) = Jehovah reveals; selected; drawn out (of the LORD); discloser. Woven.

Nineveh (nin'-e-veh) = Offspring's habitation; habitation of Ninus; a place of habitation; dwelling. Offspring of ease.

Ninevites (nin'-e-vites) = Inhabitants of Nineveh = Offspring's habitation; habitation of Ninus; a place of habitation; dwelling.

Nisan (ni'-san) = First Jewish month (March - April). Their flight.

Nisroch (nis'-rok) = Eagle; great eagle. A superintendent. Ensign of delicateness.

No (no) = Temple; portion; habitation or temple; (root = to sit; to dwell). Handsome. Disrupting; frustrating.

Noadiah (no-a-di'-ah) =

Jehovah has met; met with of the LORD; i.e., to whom the LORD manifested Himself; whom Jehovah meets; one to whom the LORD revealed Himself; assembled or ornament of the LORD.

Noah (no'-ah) #1 = Rest; comfort; comforter; (root = rest; comfort).

Noah (no'-ah) #2 = Motion; wandering; (root = to move to and fro; to wander; to shake; to wag [the head]). The second daughter of Zelophehad, born during the wanderings of Israel.

Naaman (na-a'-mon) = Temple of Amon = A nourisher; a nurse or a multitude. Faithful.

Nob (nob) = High place; noble. Fertile. Fruit; empty.

Nobah (no'-bah) = A barking; a loud voice.

Nod (nod) = Wandering; vagabond; flight; (root = to wander; to be a fugitive; to lament; to move the head).

Nodab (no'-dab) = Nobility. Liberal.

Noe (no'-e)= Rest. Greek form of Noah = Rest; comfort; a comforter; (root = rest; comfort).

Nogah (no'-gah) = Shining splendor; brightness; brilliance; shining; (root = to shine to illuminate; to cause to shine).

Nohah (no'-hah) = Rest.

Non (non) = Same as Nun = A fish; continuation; (root = to sprout; to put forth; to flourish).

Noph (nof) = Same as Memphis = To wave. Presentability.

Nophah (no'-fah) = A blast; windy; (root = to blow; to blow upon; to disperse). Breathing; blowing.

Nun (nun) = A fish; continuation; (root = to sprout; to put forth; to flourish). Perpetuity.

Nymphas (nim'-fas) = Spouse; bridegroom. Sacred to the muses. Bridal.

LORD Almighty, blessed is the man who trusts in you (Psalms 84:12, NIV).

Obadiah (o-ba-di'-ah) = A servant of the LORD; worshiper of Jehovah; (roots = [1] servant; [2] Jehovah).

Obal (o'-bal) = Stripped; bare of leaves; bare; inconvenience of old age. Hill. Heaping confusion.

Obed (o'-bed) = Serving; a servant who worships; worshiping (God).

Obededom [Obed Edom] (o'-bed-e'-dom) = Serving Edom; servant of Edom; a laborer of the earth.

Obil (o'-bil) = Overseer of camels; camel keeper; driver; leader; one who weeps. Causing mourning.

Oboth (o'-both) = Pythones; oracular serpents; familiar spirits; (root = a soothsayer; an invoker of the dead; one possessed with the devil; a bottle). Bottles (of skin). Necromancers.

Ocran (o'-cran) = Troubled; troublesome; troubler; to disturb; (root = to disturb; to bring evil upon; to be troubled).

Oded (o'-ded) = Setting up; established; aiding; he has restored; a sustainer.

Og (og) = Long-necked; a furrow; i.e., as long as a furrow. A circle. A hearth cake. Bread baked in ashes.

Ohad (o'-had) = Joined together; might; powerful; power. He shouted.

Ohel (o'-hel) = Tabernacle; tent; brightness of a tent; (root = a tent; a tabernacle).

Olivet (ol'-i-vet) = Place of olives.

Olympas (o-lim'-pas) = Bright; heavenly.

Omar (o'-mar) = Uppermost; mountaineer;

he that speaks; eloquent; talkative. I will say.

Omega (o'-me-gah) = Last letter in the Greek alphabet. Finality.

Omri (om'-ri) = Servant of the LORD; Jehovah apportions; (roots = [1] to serve; [2] Jehovah). Like a sheaf; a bundle of corn; impetuous.

On (on) = The sun; strength. Vigor; iniquity.

Onam (o'-nam) = Weariness; iniquity. Wealthy; strength. Their vigor (masculine); their iniquity.

Onan (o'-nan) = Iniquity; pain; strong. Their vigor (feminine); their iniquity.

Onesimus (o-nes'-i-mus) = Profitable.

Onesiphorus (o-ne-sif'-o-rus) = Bringing advantage. Profit bringing.

Ono (o'-no) = Strength; strong. His vigor; his iniquity.

Onycha (o-ny'-cha) = Whose travail; roaring (as a lion). (A spice.)

Onyx (o'-nyx) = Setting them equal; justifying them.

Ophel (o'-fel) = A hill; impregnable.

Ophir (o'-fur) = Abundance; precious; rich; fat. Reduced to ashes.

Ophni (of'-ni) = Man of the hill. My flying.

Ophrah (of'-rah) = Fawn; hind; hamlet. Dustiness; fawnlike (from its color).

Oreb (o'-reb) = Raven; crow. Cautious.

Oren (o'-ren) = Pine tree; i.e., tall and strong; strength.

Orion (o-ri'-on) = A fool.

Ornan (or'-nan) = Large pine; i.e., as tall as a great pine. Strong; that rejoices. Light was perpetuated; their fir tree.

Orpah (or'-pah) = Mane; i.e., neck of an animal; a fawn; a young doe; hind. (root = the neck or back of an animal). Hardened. Double minded.

Osee (o'-see) = Salvation. Same as Hosea = Jehovah

is help or salvation; salvation; causing to save.

Oshea (o-she'-ah) = God saves. Same as Hosea = Jehovah is help or salvation; salvation; causing to save.

Othni (oth'ni)= Lion of the LORD; i.e., most powerful; Jehovah is force; powerful. My seasonable speaking.

Othniel (oth'-ne-el) = Powerful one; lion of God; i.e., most powerful; powerful man of God. My season of God.

Ozem (o'-zem) = Strong; strength; one that fasts. I will hasten them.

Ozias (o-zi'-as) = Strength from the LORD; strength of Jehovah.

Ozni (oz'-ni) = Hearing; attentive; Jehovah hears.

Oznites (oz'-nites) = Descendants of Ozni = Hearing; attentive; Jehovah hears.

❦ ❧

Peace I leave with you, my peace I give unto you (John 14:27).

Paarai (pa'-ar-ahee) = Revelation; Jehovah is opening. Same as Naarai = Child of the LORD; youthful. My openings.

Pacatiana (pa-ca-she-a'-nah) = Dry; barren.

Padan (pa'-dan) = The plain of Aram. Their ransom.

Padanaram [Padan Aram] (pa'-dan-a'-ram) = Same as Padan = The plain of Aram. The ransom of Syria. Their ransom is high.

Padon (pa'-don) = Redemption; deliverances. Ransom.

Pagiel (pa'-ghe-el) = Prayer of God; i.e., answer

from God; praying to God; God meets; prevention of God; intervention of God; (root = to rush [upon]; to meet [with anyone]; to make peace; to cause to supplicate).

Pahathmoab [Pahath-Moab] (pa'-hath-mo'-ab) = Governor of Moab. Pit of Moab.

Pai (pa'-i) = Bleating; crying out; (root = to cry out). My groaning.

Palal (pa'-lal) = Judge; he has judged. Mediator; judge (as intervening).

Palestina (pal-es-ti'-nah) = The land of wanderers; land of strangers. Rolled in dust. Wallowing.

Palestine (pal'-es-tine) = Same as Palestina = The land of wanderers; land of strangers. Rolled in dust. Wallowing.

Pallu (pal'-lu) = Separated; distinguished; wonderful; (root = to separate).

Palluites (pal'-lu-ites) = Descendants of Pallu = Separated; distinguished;

wonderful; (root = to separate).

Palti (pal'-ti) = Deliverance of Jehovah. My escape.

Paltiel (pal'-te-el) = Deliverance of God; deliverer of the Lord.

Paltite (pal'-tite) = Descendant of Palti = Deliverance of Jehovah.

Pamphylia (pam-fil'-e-ah) = Of every tribe. (A costal region in the south of Asia Minor.)

Pannag (pan'-nag) = Preparation of affliction.

Paphos (pa'-fos) = Boiling; hot. (Known for its worship of Aphrodite or Venus.) Suffering.

Parah (pa'-rah) = Village of heifers; heifer. He increased.

Paran (pa'-ran) = Abounding in foliage; fruitful. Cavernous. Their beautifying.

Parbar (par'-bar) = Fertile in corn. Open apartment. He annulled the corn (word *corn* in

KJV us translated *wheat* in newer Bible versions).

Parmashta (par-mash'-tah) = Strong fisted; superior. Spoiled is the banquet.

Parmenas (par'-me-nas) = Standing firm; faithful; I abide.

Parnach (par'-nak) = Very nimble. The bullock we smote.

Parosh (pa'-rosh) = A flea; i.e., a cowardly man; a fugitive; fruit of the north.

Parshandatha (par-shan'-da-thah) = Of noble birth. Given to Persia; dung of impurity. Persian = Given by prayer. He repeatedly broke the decree.

Parthians (par-the'-uns) = A pledge. (Parthia was a rival power to Rome.)

Paruah (par'-u-ah) = Flourishing; increase; (root = to flourish; to bud; to cause to bud forth).

Parvaim (par-va'-im) = Oriental regions; eastern. (The country from which the gold was procured for

the decoration of Solomon's temple.) He broke their hooks(?).

Pasach (pa'-sak) = Torn asunder; a divider; limping. Your vanishing; your spreading out.

Pasdammim [Pas Dammim] (pas-dam'-mim) = 1 Chronicles 11:13, The border of blood. Extremity of Dammim; borders of Dammim. Vanishing of bloods; he spread our bloods. (Called Ephes-dammim in 1 Samuel 17:1).

Paseah (pa-se'-ah) = Lame; (root = to make lame). Vacillating; halting.

Pashur (pash'-ur) = Most noble; free; multiplies liberty; prosperity round about. Spreading over a hole. Increasing of white (linen).

Patara (pat'-a-rah) = Railing; reviling. (A city devoted to the worship of Apollo.) Suffering it seems(?). Scattered cursing.

Pathros (path'-ros) = Southern region; i.e.,

Egypt. A sprinkled, variegated piece. A morsel moistened.

Pathrusim (path-ru'-sim) = The south land. Inhabitants of Pathros = Southern region; i.e., Egypt. A sprinkled, variegated piece. A morsel moistened.

Patmos (pat'-mos) = My killing. Ancient Egyptian name was "Hahather," = The abode of Hather, the Egyptian Venus.

Patrobas (pat'-ro-bas) = One who pursues the steps of his father.

Pau (pa'-u) = Same as Pai = Bleating; crying out; (root = to cry out).

Paul (pawl) = Little.

Paulus (pawl-us) = Same as Paul = Little.

Pedahel (ped'-a-hel) = Redeemed of God; God redeemed; God delivers; God has saved.

Pedahzur (ped'-a-hel) = Redemption of strength; i.e., God; the Rock redeemed; the Rock

delivers; powerful.

Pedaiah (pe-dah'-yah) = Redemption of the LORD; whom Jehovah redeemed; Jehovah delivers.

Pekah (pe'-kah) = Open-eyed; watchfulness; a keen observer; (root = to open; to open one's eyes; to restore sight). Opening.

Pekahiah (pe-ka-hi'-ah) = Opening of the LORD; i.e., deliverance; whose eyes Jehovah opened; Jehovah has given sight.

Pekod (pe'-kod) = Visitation; i.e., punishment; (root = to visit; to set over; to punish).

Pelaiah (pel-a-i'-ah) = Distinguished of the LORD; whom Jehovah made distinguished; Jehovah has made illustrious; (roots = [1] to be distinguished; to consecrate; to be wonderful; [2] Jehovah). Distinguished of Jah.

Pelaliah (pel-a-li'-ah) = Judge of the LORD; whom Jehovah judged;

Jehovah judges.
Intervention of Jah.

Pelatiah (pel-a-ti'-ah) =
Deliverance of the LORD;
whom Jehovah delivered;
Jehovah delivers; Jehovah
and free.

Peleg (pe'-leg) = Division.
A channel (as a cleft,
dividing).

Pelet (pe'-let) =
Deliverance; liberation;
escape; (root = to deliver).

Peleth (pe'-leth) =
Swiftness; flight; (root =
to escape; to flee).
Separation.

Pelethites (pel'-e-thites) =
Runners.

Pelonite (pel'-o-nite) =
Such a one. A certain
(unnamed) one.

Peniel (pe-ni'-el) = The
face of God; God's face;
(root = to behold). Turn ye
(to) God.

Peninnah (pe-nin'-nah) =
Coral. A ruby.

Pentecost (pen'-te-cost) =
Fifty; fiftieth; the fiftieth
day.

Penuel (pe-nu'-el) = Same

as Peniel = The face of
God; God's face; (root =
to behold). Turn ye (to)
God.

Peor (pe'-or) = Opening;
(root = to open). Point. A
gaper.

Perazim (per'-a-zim) =
Breaches.

Peres (pe'-res) = Divided.

Peresh (pe'-resh) =
Excrement; i.e., that
which is sifted out;
distinction; (root = to
expand; to declare
distinctly; to pierce and
wound).

Perez (pe'-rez) = Breach;
bursting through; (root =
to break; to break forth; to
disperse).

Perezuzza [Perez Uzza]
(pe'-rez-uz'-zah) = Breach
of Uzza. (Uzza = Strength;
[root = to be strong]). The
breach was strengthened.

Perezuzzah [Perez
Uzzah] (pe'-rez-uz'-zah)
= Breach of Uzzah.
(Uzzah = Strength; [root =
to be strong]). The breach
was strengthened.

Perga (pur'-gah) = Earthy; (A city known for its worship of Diana.) Much earth; very earthy.

Pergamos (pur'-ga-mos) = Citadel; fortified; high tower; height; elevation. A root word from which we get our words bigamy and polygamy. Much marriage. (Idea of a marriage; i.e., mixture of the Church and the world.)

Perida (per-i'-dah) = Distinguished; separation; (root = to separate oneself; to be divided; to be dispersed). A recluse.

Perizzite(s) (per'-iz-zite) = Villagers; belonging to a village. Open; without walls. Rustic; squatter(?).

Persia (per'-she-ah) = A horseman. Divided.

Persian(s) (per'-she-un) = Same as Persia = A horseman. Belonging to Persia. Be divided.

Persis (pur'-sis) = One who takes by storm; that which divides.

Peruda (per'-u-dah) = Same as Perida =

Distinguished; (root = to separate oneself; to be divided; to be dispersed). A recluse.

Peter (pe'-tur) = A stone; a rock.

Pethahiah (peth-a-hi'-ah) = Loosed of the LORD; whom Jehovah looses; Jehovah has set free; (roots = [1] to open; [2] Jehovah). Opened of Jah.

Pethor (pe'-thor) = Interpretation of dreams. To interpret.

Pethuel (pe-thu'-el) = Ingenuousness of God; i.e., great simplicity of mind; God delivers; the noble-mindedness of God; (root = to be open; to be ingenuous; to persuade; to deceive). God's opening. Persuaded by God.

Peulthai (pe-ul'-thahee) = Wages of the LORD; deed of Jehovah; Jehovah works; full of work; (roots = [1] occupation; work wages; [2] Jehovah). My works; my wages.

Phalec (fa'-lek) = Division. Greek form of

Peleg = Division.

Phallu (fal'-lu) = Admirable. Wonderful.

Phalti (fal'-ti) = Deliverance of Jehovah; deliverance. My escape.

Phaltiel (fal'-te-el) = Deliverance of God.

Phanuel (fan-u'-el) = Vision of God. Greek form of Penuel = The face of God; God's face; (root = to behold). Turn ye to God.

Pharaoh (fa'-ra-o) = Son of the sun; mouth of the sun; sun; great house; voice of God; the king; the destroyer. A curtailer. (Title of rulers of Egypt.) His nakedness.

Pharaohhophra [Pharaoh Hophra] (fa'-ra-o-hof'-rah) = Pharaoh, the priest of the sun; priest of the sun. His nakedness; covering evil.

Pharaohnecho [Pharaoh Neco] (fa'-ra-o-ne'-ko) = Pharaoh the lame. His nakedness; he is smitten.

Pharaohnechoh [Pharaoh Neco] (fa'-ra-o-ne'-ko) = Pharaoh the lame. His nakedness; he is smitten.

Phares (fa'-rez) = Breach; rupture.

Pharez (fa'-rez) = Break forth violently.

Pharisee(s) (far'-i-see) = The separated. One who expounds.

Pharosh (fa'-rosh) = Same as Parosh = A flea; i.e., a cowardly man; a fugitive; fruit of the north.

Pharpar (far'-par) = Most swift; swift. Breaking asunder.

Pharzites (far'-zites) = Descendants of Pharez = Breaking forth violently.

Phaseah (fa-se'-ah) = Same as Paseah = Lame; (root = to make lame).

Phebe (fe'-be) = Moon; pure or radiant (as the moon).

Phenice (fe-ni'-se) = Palm tree. Palm land.

Phenicia (fe-nish'-e-ah) = Land of palms.

Phichol (fi'-kol) = Mouth of all; attentive; great; strong.

Philadelphia (fil-a-del'-fe-ah) = Brotherly love.

Philemon (fi-le'-mon) = Affectionate; friendly. One who kisses.

Philetus (fe-le'-tus) = Beloved; worthy of love; amiable.

Philip (fil'-ip) = Lover of horses; warrior.

Philippi (fil-ip'-pi) = Lover of horses. (A town named after Philip of Macedonia.)

Philippians (fil-ip'-pe-uns) = The people of Philippi = Lover of horses.

Philistia (fil-is'-te-ah) = The land of the Philistines = Same as Palestine = The land of wanderers. Land of strangers. Rolled in dust. Wallowing.

Philistim (fil-is'-tim) = Same as Palestine = The land of wanderers; land of strangers. Wanderers.

Philistine(s) (fil-is'-tin) = Same as Palestine = The land of wanderers; land of strangers. Rolled in dust. Wallowing.

Philologus (fil-ol'-o-gus) = Talkative; a lover of words; a lover of wandering. Lover of the word.

Phinehas (fin'-e-has) = Mouth of brass; face of trust. Serpent's mouth. Mouth of pity.

Phlegon (fle'-gon) = Zealous; burning.

Phrygia (frij'-e-ah) = Dry; barren. Parched.

Phurah (fu'-rah) = Branch; bough; beauty; bears fruit; (root = to adorn; to glorify; to boast). He was fruitful.

Phut (fut) = A bow. Extension; brow.

Phuvah (fu'-vah) = Mouth; utterance; a blast; scattered; (root = to puff; i.e., blow away; scatter into corners). He was scattered (as by a puff, a blow).

Phygellus (fi-jel'-lus) = Little fugitive; fugitive.

Pibeseth (pi-be'-zeth) = Portion of the spouse. Mouth of loathing.

Pihahiroth [Pi Hahiroth] (pi-ha-hi'-roth) = Mouth of caverns. The mouth of wrath; kindlings.

Pilate (pi'-lut) = Armed with a javelin; one armed with a dart. Close pressed (as a piece of felt).

Pildash (pil'-dash) = Lamp of fire; flame of fire. Steel.

Pileha (pil'-e-hah) = Servitude; ploughman; worship of plowing. Chaldean: To labor. Cleavage.

Piltai (pil'-tahee) = Jehovah causes to escape. Same as Palti = Deliverance of Jehovah. Whom Jehovah delivers. My escapes.

Pinon (pi'-non) = Ore; pearl. Same as Punon = Distraction; (root = to be perplexed). Darkness.

Piram (pi'-ram) = Like a wild ass; swift; (roots = [1] a wild ass; [2] to bear swiftly; to bear fruit).

Pirathon (pir'-a-thon) = Just revenge; (root = to make naked; to avenge; to become lawless). Leader.

Pirathonite (pir'-a-thon-ite) = Inhabitants of Pirathon = Just revenge; (root = to make naked; to avenge; to become lawless). Leader.

Pisgah (piz'-gah) = Divided rock; a part, boundary; (root = to divide; to cut up). Conspicuous. Survey.

Pisidia (pi-sid'-e-ah) = Pitchy. (A district of Asia Minor.) Persuasion of right.

Pison (pi'-son) = Great diffusion (of waters); flowing stream; (root = push; to frisk; to disperse; to multiply). Spread abroad. Increase.

Pispah (piz'-pah) = Dispersion; expansion. Disappearance.

Pithom (pi'-thom) = An enclosed place; (root = to shut in; to lock; to restrict). Mouth of integrity.

Pithon (pi'-thon) = Great enlargement. Simple;

harmless; gift of mouth. Mouth of a monster.

Pleiades (ple'ya-dez) = (A group of stars) named from the Hebrew word meaning *heap*. Greek: (Coming at) the sailing season; (root = to stow away).

Pochereth (po-ke'-reth) = Binding. Here the cutting off.

Pochereth of Zebaim = Retarding the gazelles; i.e., ensnaring them. Offspring of gazelles.

Pollux (pol'-lux) = Meaning uncertain - Castor and Pollux - twin sons of Zeus (Jupiter) and Leda.

Pontius (pon'-she-us) = Belonging to the sun. Of the sea.

Pontus (pon'-tus) = Sea.

Poratha (por'-a-thah) = Ornament. Having many chariots; fruitful. Frustration.

Porcius Festus = Porcius = Swinish. Festus = Festival, (Successor of Felix as governor of Judea.) Swinish festival.

Potiphar (pot'i-far) = Priest of the bull; a fat bull. Belonging to the sun; who is of the sun. My affliction was broken.

Potipherah [Potiphera] (po-tif'e-rah) = Priest of the sun; i.e., one who belongs to the sun; belonging to the sun. Affliction of the locks (of hair).

Praetorium (prae-to'-ri-um) = The chief magistrate's court.

Prisca (pris'-cah) = Ancient; primitive; (hence = worthy; venerable).

Priscilla (pris-sil'-lah) = Diminutive of Prisca = Ancient. Little old woman.

Prochorus (prok'-o-rus) = He that presides over the choir; leading in a chorus or dance; leader of singers.

Ptolemais (tol-e-ma'-is) = Warlike.

Pua (pu'ah) = Same as Phuvah = Mouth; utterance; a blast; scattered; (root = to puff; i.e., blow away; scatter into corners).

Puah (pu'-ah) #1 = Same as Phuvah = Mouth; utterance; a blast; scattered; (root = to puff; i.e., blow away; scatter into corners).

Puah (pu'-ah) #2 = Exodus 1:15; Splendor; splendid; light; child bearing; i.e., joy of the parents.

Publius (pub'-le-us) = Common. Popular. (The governor of Malita.)

Pudens (pu'-denz) = Shamefaced; bashful. Modest.

Puhites (pu'-hites) = Simple; openness; (root = a hinge).

Pul (pul) = Elephantine; strong. (A short name for Tiglathpileser.) Distinguishing.

Punites (pu'-nites) = Scattered. Distracted.

Punon (pu'-non) = Same as Pinon = Distraction; (root = to be perplexed). Darkness.

Pur (pur) = Poor.

Chaldean: A lot. Frustration.

Purim (pu'-rim) = Chaldean: Lots. Piece.

Put (put) = Same as Phut = A bow. Extension; brow. Afflicted.

Puteoli (pu-te'-o-li) = Wells.

Putiel (pu'-te-el) = Afflicted of God; contemned by God. God enlightens.

Pyrrhus (pir'-es) = Fiery-red; red-haired, (Acts 20:4, ASV).

Quicken thou me according to thy word (Psalms 119:25).

Quartus (quar'-tus) = The fourth.

Queen of heaven = The

queen of heaven was Astarte, the goddess of Venus; Called Ashtoreth by the Phoenicians and other Canaanites; she was regarded as the sister or consort of Baal. Together they were looked upon as symbolizing the generative powers of nature.

Remember me, O my God, for good (Nehemiah 13:31).

R

Raamah (ra'-a-mah) = Thundering; trembling; greatness; (root = to roar; to tremble; to thunder).

Raamiah (ra-a-mi'-ah) = Thunder of the LORD; Jehovah causes trembling; (root = thunder; raging). Thunder of Jah.

Raamses (ra-am'-seze) = Son of the sun. Thunder of the standard.

Rabbah (rab'-bah) = Great city; i.e., metropolis; capital city; great; (root = to be great; to multiply; to do much work). Populous.

Rabbath (rab'-bath) = Same as Rabbah = Great city; i.e., metropolis; capital city; great (root = to be great; to multiply; to do much work). Populous.

Rabbi (rab'-bi) = Master. My master.

Rabbith (rab'-bith) = Great; multitude; populous.

Rabboni (rab-bo-'ni) = Master; my chief master.

Rabmag (rab'-mag) = Most exalted; head of the magi; chief of the magicians. Chief soothsayer; much melting.

Rabsaris (rab'-sa-ris) = Grand master of the eunuchs; chief eunuch; the head chamberlain.

Rabshakeh (rab'-sha-keh) = Chief cupbearers.

Raca (ra'-cah) =

Worthless; empty; i.e., a senseless empty-headed man.

Rachab (ra'-kab) = Wide. Greek form of Rahab #2 = Spacious; broad; a wide place; (root = to be wide; to be spacious; to be expanded).

Rachal (ra'-kal) = Traffic; (root = to go about; to traffic).

Rachel (ra'-chel) = A ewe; a sheep; (root = to cherish).

Raddai (rad'-dahee) = Jehovah subdues; subduing; to subdue; to rule over; cutting under; (root = to subdue; to rule over). My subduings.

Ragau (ra'-gaw) = A friend.

Raguel (ra-gu'-el) = Friend of God; Jehovah is a friend; shepherd; (root = to feed; to shepherd; to use as a friend). Associate with God. Literally: tend ye God.

Rahab (ra'-hab) #1= Insolence; fierceness; (root = to rage; to be fierce; to make courageous). Job

9:13; Isaiah 3:5; Proverbs 6:3; Psalm138:3. A poetic name applied to Egypt, Psalms 87:4 and 89:10; Isaiah 30:7 and 51:9. Arrogance.

Rahab (ra'-hab) #2 = Spacious; broad; a wide place; (root = to be wide; to be spacious; to be expanded). Breadth. *A woman of Jericho,* Joshua 2:1; 3:6; 6:17, 23, 25.

Raham (ra'-ham) = Merciful; love; affection; pity; (roots = [1] a girl; a woman; [2] to compassionate).

Rahel (ra'-hel) = Same as Rachel = An ewe; a sheep; (root = to cherish).

Rakem (ra'-kem) = Variegated; friendship; embroidered; (root = to adorn with colors; to embroider).

Rakkath (rah'-kath) = A shore; (root = to beat; to spit out). Chaldean: The bank of a river. Leanness; her spitting.

Rakkon (rak'-kon) = Extreme shore; (intense form of Rakkath). Emaciation; spitting out.

Ram (ram) = High; exalted; elevated.

Rama (ra'-mah) = A hill. Greek form of Ramah = The height; lofty place; high place; i.e., a place especially consecrated to idols. Cast down.

Ramah (ra'-mah) = The height; lofty place; high place; i.e., a place especially consecrated to idols. Cast down.

Ramath (ra'-math) = The high place of the watchtower. The height.

Ramathaim (ram-a-tha'-im) = Double high place. The double height of the watchers.

Ramathaimzophim [Zophite] (ram-a-tha'-im-zo'-fim) = Ramathaim = The double eminence; double high place. Zophim = Watchmen; watchers; (root has force of looking out afar). The two places of Zophim. The double height of the watchers.

Ramathite (ra'-math-ite) = Inhabitants of Ramah =

The height; lofty place; high place; i.e., a place especially consecrated to idols. Cast down.

Ramathlehi [Ramath Lehi] (ra'-math-le'-hi) = (ra'-math) = The high place of the watchtower. Lehi = Jawbone; (root = the cheek; the jawbone). Delight of Lehi. Jaw-bone height.

Ramathmizpeh [Mizpah] (ra'-math-miz'peh) = Height of the watchtower. Height of Mizpeh. Mizpeh = A watchtower; (root has force of looking out afar).

Rameses (ram'-e-seze) = Son of the sun. Dissolving evil. Evil is the standard bearer.

Ramiah (ra-mi'-ah) = Placed of the LORD; Jehovah is high; exalted of Jehovah; (roots = [1] to throw; to place; i.e., in seats; to impose {tribute}; [2] Jehovah). Jah has exalted; loosed of Jah.

Ramoth (ra'-moth) = Heights; eminences; high places; (root = a lofty place). Coral.

Ramothgilead [Ramoth Gilead] (ra'-moth-ghil'-e-ad) = Heights of Gilead. Ramoth = Heights; eminences; high places; (root = a lofty place). Gilead = Perpetual fountain. A heap of testimony; a witness; mass of testimony; strong.

Rapha (ra'-fah) = He has healed; fearful; relaxation; giant; (roots = [1] to heal; to mend; to repair; to let down; [2] giant).

Raphu (ra'-fu) = Healed; feared; (root = to heal).

Reaia (re-ah'-yah) = Vision of the LORD; Jehovah has seen. Seen of Jah.

Reaiah (re-ah'yah) = Jehovah has seen; Jehovah has provided for. Same as Reaia = Vision of the LORD; Jehovah has seen. Seen of Jah.

Reba (Re'-bah) = Offspring; fourth; i.e., a fourth son; a fourth part; one who stoops.

Rebecca (re-bek'-kah) = Ensnarer. Greek form of Rebekah = A rope with a noose (to tie firmly); a tie rope for animals; (roots = [1] hitching place; stall; [2] tied up calf or lamb). A noose; captivating. Fattened.

Rebekah (re-bek'-kah) = A rope with a noose (to tie firmly); a tie rope for animals; (roots = [1] hitching place; stall; [2] tied up calf or lamb). A noose; captivating. Fattened.

Recah (re'-kah) = Rechah in KJV. (1 Chronicles 4:12). Spacious. Side. Uttermost part. Tenderness.

Rechab (re'-kab) = Horseman; a rider; (root = to ride). Companionship; square. Charioteer.

Rechabites (rek'-ab-ites) = Descendants of Rechab = Horseman; (root = to ride). Companionship; square. Charioteer.

Rechah (ray-kaw') = Spacious. Side. Uttermost part. Tenderness.

Red (Sea) = The weed; the weedy sea; i.e., the sea

of weed. To come to an end. Job 37:9 - A whirlwind.

Reelaiah (re-el-ah'-yah) = Trembling caused by Jehovah. Shaken of Jah.

Regem (re'-ghem) = Friend; friendship; (root = to heap together; to join together; to pile up). Stoning.

Regemmelech [Regem-Melech] (re'-ghem-me'-lek) = Friend of the king. Stoning of the king.

Rehabiah (re-hab-i'-ah) = Enlarging of the LORD; Jehovah enlarged; Jehovah is comprehensive; God is my extent.

Rehob (re'-hob) = Open space; width; street; a wide street; market place.

Rehoboam (re-ho-bo'-am) = Freer of the people; the people are enlarged; who enlarges the people; enlarges the people; i.e., sets them free; (roots = [1] a street; [2] a people).

Rehoboth (re'-ho-both) = Streets; wide; wide streets; wide spaces; roominess.

Rehum (re'-hum) = Pitied; beloved; merciful. Compassionate.

Rei (re'-i) = Jehovah is a friend; friend of God; friendly; sociable. My friend.

Rekem (re'-kem) = Same as Rakem = Variegated; friendship; embroidered; (root = to adorn with colors; to embroider).

Remaliah (rem-a-li'-ah) = Adorned of the LORD; whom Jehovah adorned; Jehovah increases; exaltation of the LORD; (roots = [1] to deck with gems; [2] Jehovah).

Remeth (re'-meth) = A high place. Elevation.

Remmon (rem'-mon) = Same as Rimmon = Pomegranate; very high; (roots = [1] a pomegranate; [2] to be high).

Remmonmethoar (rem'-mon-meth'-o-ar) = Stretching. The marked out pomegranate.

Remphan (rem'-fan) = The shrunken (as lifeless).

(An Egyptian idol worshiped by Israel.)

Rephael (re'-fa-el) = Healed of God; whom God healed; God is a healer; medicine of God. Enfeebling of the breath; healing of the breath.

Rephah (re'-fah) = Riches; healing. Healed of Jah; enfeebled of Jah.

Rephaiah (ref-a-i'-ah) = Jehovah heals; healed of the LORD; whom Jehovah healed.

Rephaim(s) (re-fa'-ims) = Same as Rapha = He has healed; fearful; relaxation; giant; (roots = [1] to heal; to mend; to repair; to let down; [2] giant). Healing. The dead; giants.

Rephidim (ref'-i-dim) = Props; supports; (root = to spread out; to strew). Joiners; solderers. Shrinking of hands.

Resen (re'-zen) = Bridle; (roots = [1] a curb; a bridle; [2] to bind).

Resheph (re'-shef) = Lightening; flame; haste.

Reu (re'-u) = Associate; i.e., of God; a friend; friendship. Feed ye.

Reuben (ru'-ben) = Behold a son; vision of the son.

Reubenite(s) (ru'-ben-ites) = Descendants of Reuben = Behold a son; vision of the son.

Reuel (re-u'-el) = Friend of God; God is a friend. Same as Raguel = Friend of God; (root = to feed; to shepherd; to use as a friend). Associate ye with God; tend ye God.

Reumah (re-u'-mah) = Exalted. Behold, what. Raised up; see you aught(?).

Rezeph (re'-zef) = Baking stone; i.e., a cake baked on the coals or stones. A stone. Burning; glowing.

Rezia (re-zi'-ah) = Jehovah is pleasing; delight; (root = to be delighted; to satisfy; to please). Haste.

Rezin (re'-zin) = Firm; stable; dominion; good will. A fugitive.

Delightsomeness.

Rezon (re'-zon) = Prince; noble; princeliness. To wax lean.

Rhegium (re'-je-um) = Breach; A passage (as broken through). (An Italian town located at the southern entrance to the straits of Messina.)

Rhesa (re'-sah) = Chieftain; will; course.

Rhoda (ro'-dah) = A rose.

Rhodes (rodes) = Rose.

Ribai (rib'-ahee) = Jehovah contends; judgement of the LORD; contentious; whom Jehovah defends; (roots = [1] contention; a forensic cause; [2] Jehovah). My strengths.

Riblah (rib'-lah) = Multitude of people; fertility. The strife ended; fruitful.

Rimmon (rim'-mon) = A pomegranate. Same as Remmon = Pomegranate; very high; (roots = [1] a pomegranate; [2] to be high).

Rimmonparez [Rimmon Perez] (rim'-mon-pa-'rez) = Pomegranate of the breach or rent .

Rinnah (rin'-nah) =A joyful cry; i.e., joy of parents; shout; a wild cry; strength.

Riphath (ri'-fath) = A crusher; i.e., of enemies; (root = to crush; to make to tremble). A stable. Bruising; shrivelling; healing. Genesis 10:3 - Slander; fault.

Rissah (ris'-sah) = Dew; (root = to temper; to moisten). Ruin.

Rithmah (rith'-mah) = Broom; juniper. Binding.

Rizpah (riz'-pah) = A baking stone; hot coal; a hot stone; (root = a baking stone; a tessellated [to lay out, inlay, or pave in a mosaic pattern] pavement). Pavement.

Roboam (ro-bo'-am) = Enlarger of the people. Greek form of Rehoboam = Freer of the people; the people are enlarged; who enlarges the people; enlarges the people; i.e., sets them free; (roots = [1] a street; [2] a people). Breakers loose.

Rogelim (ro'-ghel-im) = Same as Enrogel = Fountain of the fuller; fullers fountain. Footmen; they who tread upon.

Rohgah (ro'-gah) = Outcry; clamor; alarm. Copious rain. Fear cured; agitation.

Romamtiezer [Romamti-Ezer] (romam'-ti-e'-zur) = I have lifted up help; I have exalted help; highest place; (roots = to exalt oneself; [2] at the lifting up of yourself; [3] help). I have exalted the helper.

Roman(s) (ro'-muns) = Men of Rome = Strength; strong.

Rome (rome) = Strength; strong.

Rosh (rosh) = Head; chief; prince; the beginning; (root = a head; a chief; prince; beginning).

Rufus (ru'-fus) = Red.

Ruhamah (ru-ha'-mah) =

Compassionated; having obtained mercy.

Rumah (ru'-mah) = High; height. Exaltation.

Ruth (rooth) = Beauty; something worth seeing; (root = appearance; vision; the act of seeing; sight). Friendship; female friend. Trembling. Satisfied.

Salvation belongeth unto the LORD (Psalms 3:8).

Sabachthani (sa-bak'-tha-ni) = You have forsaken me. Have you forsaken me?

Sabaoth (sab'-a-oth) = Hosts, The LORD of.

Sabeans #1 (sab-e'-uns) = Inhabitants of Seba

Eminent. Drunkards.

Sabeans #2 (sab-e'-uns) = Joel 3:8 - They who come; go about (busybodies?).

Sabeans #3 (sab-e'-uns) = Job 1:15 - He who is coming.

Sabta (sab'-tah) = Same as Sabtah = Breaking through; i.e., terror to foes. He compassed the chamber.

Sabtah (sab'-tah) = Breaking through; i.e., terror to foes. He compassed the mark.

Sabtecha (sab'-te-kah) = Surrender. Same as Sabtah = Breaking through; i.e., terror to foes. He compassed the seat; he compassed the smiting.

Sabtechah (sab'-te-kah) = Beating; i.e., terror. He compassed the seat; he compassed the smiting.

Sacar (sa'-kar) = Wages; hire; reward.

Sadducees (sad'-du-sees) = Just; righteous. (Named after Zadok, founder of the sect.) The righteous.

Sadoc (sa'-dok) = Righteous; just. Greek form of Zadok = Just; righteous; upright; justified; (root = to be just).

Sala (sa'-lah) = Sprout - (Greek).

Salah (sa'-lah) = Sprout - (Hebrew). A missile; a weapon.

Salamis (sal'-a-mis) = A surging. Salt. (A city on the east end of the island of Cyprus.)

Salathiel (sa-la'-the-el) = I have asked for from God; I have asked God; ark or loan of God; (roots = [1] asked; [2] God).

Salcah (sal'-kah) = He lifted up the blind; straitened basket. Firm binding together.

Salchah (sal'-kah) = Same as Salcah = He lifted up the blind; straitened basket. Firm binding together.

Salem (sa'-lem) = At peace; perfect; (root = whole; perfect). Complete.

Salim (sa'-lim) = Peace.

Tossing.

Sallai (sal'-lahee) = Lifted up of the LORD; exaltation; (roots = [1] to lift up; [2] Jehovah). Weighed. My basket; my castings up.

Sallu (sal'-lu) = Elevated; weighed. They have raised up.

Salma (sal'-mah) = Garment; strength; firmness. Raiment.

Salmon #1 (sal'-mon) = Shady. His peace; peaceable. Clothing.

Salmon #2 (sal'-mon) = Psalm 68:14 - Image; resemblance.

Salmon #3 (sal'-mon) = Ruth 4:20 - Raiment; a garment.

Salmone (sal-mo'-ne) = Clothed. From the surging. (The east point of the island of Crete.)

Salome (sa-lo'-me) = Peace; peaceful; perfect. Very shady; i.e., shady character.

Salu (sa'-lu) = Weighed. Elevated; i.e., highly esteemed; unfortunate.

Samaria (sa-ma'-re-ah) = A watch mountain; a place of watching; (intense root = to watch). Guardianship.

Samaritan(s) (sa-mar'-i-tuns) = Inhabitants of Samaria = A watch mountain; a place of watching; (intense root = to watch).

Samgarnebo [Nebo-Sarsekim] (sam'-gar-ne'-bo) = Sword of Nebo. Be gracious, Nebo. Spice dragged away in his prophecy(?).

Samlah (sam'-lah) = Garment. Enwrapping.

Samos (sa'-mos) = A token; a sandy bluff. A height.

Samothracia (sam-o-thra'-she-ah) = A sign of rags. Height of Thrace.

Samson (sam'-sun) = A little sun. Splendid sun; i.e., great joy and felicity; like the sun; distinguished; strong; a perfect servant; sun-man.

Samuel (sam'-u-el) = Heard of God; i.e., asked of God; offering of God;

appointed by God; heard; (roots = [1] to hear; [2] God). His name by God. His name (is) of God(?).

Sanballat (san-bal'-lat) = Hate in disguise; the enemy is secret. Chaldean: A hidden branch. Hatred (or throne) in secret.

Sansannah (san-san'-nah) = Palm branch. Thorniness.

Saph (saf) = Tall; threshold; preserver; consummation; (roots = [1] expansion; a basin; threshold; [2] to stand at the threshold).

Saphir (sa'-fur) = Beautiful; (root = to be beautiful; to please).

Sapphira (saf-fi'-rah) = Sapphire; (root = beautiful; pleasant).

Sapphire (saf'-fire) = Telling out; recounting.

Sara (sa'-rah) = Princess. Greek form of Sarah = Princess; chieftainship; noblewoman; (roots = [1] a princess; a noble lady; [2] to lead; to fight). A ruler.

Sarah (sa'-rah) = Princess; chieftainness; noblewoman;

(roots = [1] a princess; a noble lady; [2] to lead; to fight). A ruler. Numbers 26:46 - the prince breathed.

Sarai (sa'-rahee) = Contentious; Quarrelsome. My ruler. My princesses.

Saraph (sa'-raf) = Serpent; burning. Fiery; fiery serpent.

Sardis (sar'-dis) = Remnant; builders rule; escaping ones; those who come out; (idea of restoration). Red ones(?).

Sardites (sar'-dites) = Descendants of Sered = Fear; (root = to fear; to tremble).

Sardius (sar'-di-us) = Ruddiness.

Sardonyz (sar'-do-nyx) = Ruddy.

Sarepta (sa-rep'-tah) = Smelting. Greek form of Zarephath = Workshop for melting and refining metals; refined; smelting house. She has refined.

Sargon (sar'-gon) = (God) appoints the king; the constituted king;

snares. Prince of the sun. Stubborn rebel.

Sarid (sa'-rid) = Survivor; escaped; (root = to flee; to escape). Remainder.

Saron (sa'-ron) = Full of darkness. Greek form of Sharon = A great plain. A place for singing. Rightness.

Sarsechim (sar'-se-kim) = Chief of the eunuchs; prince of the eunuchs. Prince of the coverts.

Saruch (sa'-ruk) = Branch. Greek form of Serug = Branch; shoot; (root = to intertwine). Interwoven.

Satan (sa'-tun) = Adversary.

Satyr (sa'-tyr) = A demon (in he-goat form, or as bristling with horror).

Saul (sawl) = Asked for; demanded; (root = to ask; to request; to inquire of). Required.

Sceva (see'-vah) = Left handed; I dispose. Mind reader.

Scythian (sith'-e-un) = Rude; rough.

Seba (se'-bah) = Eminent; old man. Drink thou.

Sebat (se'-bat) = Rest. Smite thou.

Secacah (se-ca'-cah) = Enclosure; (root = to cover; to protect; to fence round).

Sechu (se'-ku) = They hedged up. Watchtower.

Secundus (se-cun'-dus) = Second; secondary; favorable.

Segub (se'-gub) = Elevated; protected; fortified; (root = to exalt). Exalted (inaccessible).

Seir (se'-ur) = Rough; hairy; bristly; wooded; (root = [1] hairy; rough; a he-goat; [2] to shudder; to sweep away in a storm; to be fierce). Shaggy; goatlike.

Seirath (se'-ur-ath) = The hairy she-goat. Well wooded.

Sela (se'-lah) = Rock. Crag.

Selah (se'-lah) = Forte, a musical direction; pause. Pause and consider. Lift up; exalt. Make prominent.

Selahammahlekoth [Sela Hammahlekoth] (se'-lah-ham-mah'-le-koth) = Rock of division; rock of escapings; (root = division; fight; an order).

Seled (se'-led) = Exultation; burning; (root = to exalt). Recoil(?).

Seleucia (sel-u-si'-ah) = White light. Called after Seleucus.

Sem (sem) = Strengthen. Greek form of Shem = A name; i.e., celebrated, distinguished; (root = a name; a celebrated name).

Semachiah (sem-a-ki'-ah) = sustained of the LORD; whom Jehovah sustains; Jehovah supports.

Semei (sem'-e-i) = Hear; obey.

Senaah (sen'-a-ah) = Same as Hassenaah = Elevated, (idea of lifting up); thorny; the thorn hedge. Hated(?).

Seneh (se'-neh) = High; crag. Thorny.

Senir (se'-nur) = Coat of mail. Bear the lamp(?).

Sennacherib (sen-nak'-er-ib) = The thorn laid waste. San (the moon-god) has multiplied brethren; the moon god; destruction of the sword; a destructive branch.

Senuah (sen'-u-ah) = Light. Bristling. The violated. The hatred(?).

Seorim (se-o'-rim) = Fear; distress. Barley. Bearded ones.

Sephar (se'-far) = Numbering. Enumeration; census.

Sepharad (sef'-a-rad) = End of wandering; end of spreading out. Separated. (Possibly an Assyrian word signifying a "boundary.")

Sepharvaim (sef-ar-va'-im) = Enumeration; twofold. Scribes. 2 Kings 17:31 - Census of the sea.

Sepharvites (sef'-ar-vites) = Enumeration; twofold.

Serah (se'-rah) = Abundance. The prince breathed.

Seraiah (se-ra-i'-ah) =

Prince or soldier of the LORD; soldier of Jehovah; ruling with God; the LORD is my Prince; Jehovah is prince. Prevailing of Jehovah.

Seraphims (ser'-a-fims) = Burning ones.

Sered (se'-red) = Stubbornness subdued. Fear; deliverance; (root = to fear; to tremble).

Sergius (sur'-je-us) = Earth-born; born a wonder, (The proconsul of Cyprus.)

Serug (se'-rug) = Branch; shoot; firmness; (root = to intertwine). Interwoven.

Seth (seth) = Appointed; compensation; substitute; to replace.

Sethur (se'-thur) = Hidden; mysterious; secreted; (root = to hide; to be hid; to conceal).

Shaalabbin (sha-al-ab'-bin) = Place of foxes; earths of foxes. Hand of skill; jackal of discernment.

Shaalbim (sha-al'-bim) = He regarded the hearts; he

regarded the lions. Same as Shaalabim = Place of foxes; earths of foxes. Hand of skill; jackal of discernment.

Shaalbonite (sha-al'-bo-nite) = He regarded the hearts; he regarded the lions. Inhabitants of Shaalbim = Place of foxes; earths of foxes. Hand of skill; jackal of discernment.

Shaaph (sha'-af) = Who flew. Anger. Union; friendship.

Shaaraim (sha-a-ra'-im) = Two gates; (root = to separate; to estimate).

Shaashgaz (sha-ash'-gaz) = Who succored the cut-off. Servant of the beautiful. Beauty's servant.

Shabbethai (shab'-be-thahee) = Rest of the LORD; i.e., born on the Sabbath; Sabbath born; (root = to rest; to sit still; to cease; to remove). My Sabbaths.

Shachia (sha-ki'-ah) = Captive of the LORD;

(roots = [1] to take captive; [2] Jehovah). The return of Jah; taken captive of Jah.

Shaddai = Name for God, translated "Almighty" in KJV. See El Shaddai under **God.**

Shadrach (sha'-drak) = Rejoicing in the way. A tender breast; soft; tender. Decree of moon-god. The breast was tender.

Shage (sha'-ghe) = Wandering; erring; (root = to wander; to go astray; to err).

Shaharaim (sha-ha-ra'-im) = Two dawns; double dawns; (root = to break forth, as the dawn; to be curious; to seek).

Shahazimah (sha-haz'-i-mah) = To the proud ones; place of the proud. Lofty places.

Shalem (sha'-lem) = At peace; complete. Safe; perfect.

Shalim (sha'-lim) = Handfuls. Foxes.

Shalisha (shal'-i-shah) = Triangular; a third part;

(roots = [1] a third; triennial; [2] three; thrice). Third (place). Treble.

Shallecheth (shal'-le-keth) = Casting down; felling; (root = to cast; to cast down; to throw down).

Shallum (shal'-lum) = Retribution; recompense; spoilation; rewarder. Requital; restitution.

Shallun (shal'-lun) = They spoiled them; he spoiled the lodging. Retribution; spoilation.

Shalmai (shal'-mahee) = Jehovah is recompense; peace offering of the LORD; peaceful; (roots = [1] peace offerings; thank offerings; [2] to make peace; [3] Jehovah). My garments; my peace offerings.

Shalman (shal'-man) = He spoiled them; their peace-offering. Peaceable; a rewarder.

Shalmaneser (shal-man-e'-zer) = He spoiled them of the bond; their peace-offering of bondage. Fire-worshiper. Peace taken away; a withholder of rewards. The god Shalmana is chief; Shalmana be propitious.

Shama (sha'-mah) = Hearing; obedient; he has heard.

Shamariah (sham-a-ri'-ah) = Guarded of Jah.

Shamed (sha'-med) = Destroyer; watcher. Guardian; exterminator.

Shamer (sha'-mur) = Keeper; preserver. Guardian.

Shamgar (sham'-gar) = Destroyer. Here a stranger; cupbearer of a surprised stranger. The desolate dragged away.

Shamhuth (sham'-huth) = Notoriety; fame; renown; desolation of iniquity. Exaltation; desolation.

Shamir (sha'-mur) = Keeping; guarding. A thorn; a prison; oppression.

Shamma (sham'-mah) = Desert; desolation; fame; renown.

Shammah (sham'-mah) = Astonishment; desolation; loss; (root = to be astonished; to lay waste; to make desolate).

Shammai (sham'-mahee) = Astonishment of the LORD; celebrated; waste; (roots = [1] to be astonished; [2] Jehovah). My desolations.

Shammoth (sham'-moth) = Renown. Same as Shammah = Astonishment; desolation; loss; (root = to be astonished; to lay waste; to make desolate). Deserts. Desolations.

Shammua (sham-mu'-ah) = Hearing; i.e., of the Lord. Famous. A harkener (one who listens or harkens to God).

Shammuah (sham-mu'-ah) = Same as Shammua = Hearing; i.e., of the Lord. Famous. A harkener.

Shamsherai (sham'-she-rahee) = Heroic. He desolated my observers.

Shapham (sha'-fam) = He bruised them; he swept them bare. Youthful; vigorous. Bare; i.e., naked of trees; bald; (root = to be bald).

Shaphan (sha'-fan) =
Prudent; shy rock; badger
(coney); (unused root = to
be cunning; to hide).

Shaphat (sha'-fat) =
Judge; judges; he has
judged; (root = to judge).

Shapher (sha'-fur) =
Beauty; pleasantness.
Goodliness.

Sharai (sha'-rahee) =
Jehovah is deliverer;
liberated of the LORD;
free; my son; (roots = [1]
to loose; to set free; [2]
Jehovah). My observers;
my settings free.

Sharaim (sha-ra'-im) =
Same as Shaaraim = Two
gates; (root = to separate;
to estimate). Double gate.

Sharar (sha'-rar) =
Unyielding; an observer.
Hand; firm; strong; stay;
i.e., of family.

Sharezer (sha-re'-zur) =
He beheld treasure.
Protect or preserve the
king; (God) protect the
king. Prince of fire.
Splendor of brightness.

Sharon (sha'-run) =
Rectitude; observation. A
great plain. A place for
singing.

Sharonite (sha'-run-ite) =
Inhabitants of Sharon =
Rectitude; observation. A
great plain. A place for
singing.

Sharuhen (sha-ru'-hen) =
They beheld grace. A
pleasant dwelling place;
(roots = [1] to dwell; to
encamp; [2] grace; favor).

Shashai (sha'-shahee) =
Habitation of the LORD;
i.e., a servant of God;
noble; free; white;
pale.Whitish; my white
(ones); my linens.

Shashak (sha'-shak) =
Vehement desire; (root =
to run after; to desire; to
overflow). Activity;
runner; assaulter. The
rusher; the longed-for.

Shaul (sha'-ul) = Same as
Saul = Asked for;
demanded; (root = to ask;
to request; to inquire of).
Required.

Shaulites (sha'-ul-ites) =
Descendants of Shaul =
Same as Saul = asked for;
demanded; (root = to ask;

to request; to inquire of).
Required.

Shaveh (sha'-veh) =
Plain; (root = to be equal).
Equality.

Shaveh Kiriathaim (sha'-veh-kir-e-a-thay'-im) =
Plain of the double city.
Shaveh = plain:
Kiriathaim = (Same as
Kirjathaim) = Walled
cities; plain of the walled
city.

Shavsha (shav'-shah) =
The plain was vain.
Habitation; i.e., of the
Lord; nobility; splendor.

Sheal (she'-al) = Petition;
prayer; requesting; asking;
(root = to ask for).

Shealtiel (she-al'-te-el) =
I have asked of God. Same
as Salathiel = I have asked
for from God; I have
asked God; ark or loan of
God; (roots = [1] asked;
[2] God).

Sheariah (she-a-ri'-ah) =
Gate of Jehovah; Jehovah
is decider; Jehovah has
esteemed. Gate of Jah.

Shearjashub [Shear-Jashub] (she'-ar-ja'-shub)
= A remnant shall return;
i.e., from captivity; the
remnant shall return; (roots
= [1] residue; [2] to be left
over; to be let remain).

Sheba (she'-bah) #1 =
Main. He who is coming.

Sheba (she'-bah) #2 = An
oath. Captive.

Shebah (she'-bah) = The
place of an oath; to the
oath. Captive.

Shebam (she'-bam) =
Their hoar head. Sweet
smell; fragrance.

Shebaniah (sheb-a-ni'-ah)
= Jehovah is powerful;
Jehovah has dealt tenderly;
the LORD converts;
caused to grow up of the
LORD; whom Jehovah
hides; (root = [1] to be
tender;   delicate, as a
youth; [2] Jehovah). Who
is built of Jehovah; who is
discerned of Jehovah.

Shebarim (sheb'-a-rim) =
Fractures; terrors;
breaches; (roots = [1] a
fracture; a breach; terror;
[2] to break; to tear; to be
broken down).

Shebat = Eleventh Jewish month (January - February).

Sheber (she'-bur) = Breach; breaking; fracture.

Shebna (sheb'-nah) = Who built; tarry, I pray. Grown up; youth; youthfulness; tenderness; who rests himself; dwell here.

Shebuel (she-bu'-el) = Captive of God; God is renown; return, O God. Abide ye with God; led captive of God.

Shecaniah (shek-a-ni'-ah) = Inhabited of the LORD; habitation of the LORD; i.e., one of the LORD's people with whom He is pleased to dwell; Jehovah is a neighbor; Jehovah has dwelt; (roots = [1] to dwell; to inhabit; to be familiar with; [2] Jehovah).

Shechaniah (shek-a-ni'-ah) = Same as Shecaniah = Inhabited of the LORD; habitation of the LORD; i.e., one of the LORD's people with whom He is pleased to dwell; Jehovah is a neighbor;

Jehovah has dwelt; (roots =[1] to dwell; to inhabit; to be familiar with; [2] Jehovah).Jehovah dwells.

Shechem (she' kem) = Back; shoulder - literally, early rising; (root = the shoulder; the upper part of the back; a ridge of land). Diligence.

Shechemites (she'-kem-ites) = Same as Shechem = Back; shoulder- literally, early rising; (root = the shoulder; the upper part of the back; a ridge of land).

Shedeur (shed'-e-ur) = Breasts of light; breasts of fire; the Almighty is fire. Casting forth of fire; i.e., lighting, thunderbolt; giving forth of light; shedding of light; all mighty.

Shehariah (she-ha-ri'-ah) = Sought of the LORD; Jehovah seeks; Jehovah is the dawn; broken forth as the dawn; roots = [1] to chastise; to seek; to seek diligently; [2] Jehovah).

Shelah (she'-lah) #1 = Prayer; petition; peace; (root = request petition).

Shelah (she'-lah) #2 = Sent; shooting forth; i.e., of waters; (root = a weapon; a missile; a sprout). A son of Arphaxad, of the line of Shem. A descendant.

Shelanites (she'-lan-ites) = Descendants of Shelah #1 = Prayer; petition. *The third son of Judah.*

Shelemiah (shel-e-mi'-ah) = Repaid of the LORD; whom Jehovah repays; Jehovah is recompense; recompenses of God is my perfection; (roots = [1] retribution; remuneration; [2] Jehovah).

Sheleph (she'-lef) = Drawn out; i.e., selected; drawing out; (root = to draw out; to draw off). Peace-offering of Jehovah.

Shelesh (she'-lesh) = Triad; third. Might; tried. Triplicate; triplet.

Shelomi (shel'-o-mi) = Jehovah is peace; my peace; peaceful; (root = to be whole). My peace; peaceable.

Shelomith (shel'-o-mith) = Retribution; love of peace; peacefulness; (root = to be perfect). In 1 Chronicles 23:9-26; 25, 26 - pacifications.

Shelomoth (shel'-o-moth) = Retributions; (root = to be perfect).

Shelumiel (she-lu'-me-el) = Friend of God; God's peace; God my reward. (root = to be a friend).

Shem (shem) = A name; i.e., celebrated, distinguished; renown; name; (root = a name; a celebrated name).

Shema (she'-mah) = Hearing; fame; echo; repute; rumor (root = hearing; report; tidings).

Shemaah (shem'-a-ah) = One who harkens. The fame. Same as Shema = Hearing; fame; echo; repute; rumor; (root = hearing; report; tidings).

Shemaiah (shem-a-i'-ah) = Heard of the LORD; Jehovah has heard; Jehovah is fame; obeys the LORD. The hearkener of Jah.

Shemariah (shem-a-ri'-ah) = Guarded of the

LORD; Jehovah guards; God has kept; (roots = [1] to watch ov er; [2] Jehovah).

Shemeber (shem-e'-bur) = Splendor; heroism; name of wing; i.e., a winged name of great celebrity; soaring on high; (root = to mount up).

Shemer (she'-mur) = One kept by the Lord; custody; i.e., the object of watchfulness; guardian; (root = to watch). Guardianship.

Shemida (shem-i'-dah) = Fame of knowledge; fame of wisdom; science of the heavens; (root = to know). Name of knowledge; my name he knows.

Shemidah (shem-i'-dah) = Same as Shemida = Fame of knowledge; fame of wisdom; science of the heavens; (root = to know).

Shemidaites (shem'-i-dah-ites) = Descendants of Shemida = Fame of knowledge; fame of wisdom; science of the heavens; (root = to know).

Sheminith (shem'-i-nith) = Eighth. (A musical instrument with eight notes.)

Shemiramoth (she-mir'-a-moth) = Most exalted name; most high name; fame of the highest; height of the heavens.

Shemuel (shem-u'-el) = Same as Samuel = Heard of God; i.e., asked of God; (roots = [1] to hear; [2] God). His name by God.

Shen (shen) = Tooth; (root = a tooth; a sharp rock).

Shenazar (she-na'-zar) = Repetition of treasure. Light; splendor.

Shenir (she'-nur) = Same as Senir = Coat of mail. The fallow ground. Bear the lamp.

Shepham (she'-fam) = Their bareness. Same as Shapham = Youthful; vigorous. Bare; i.e., naked of trees; bald; (root = to be bald). Nakedness.

Shephathiah (shef-a-ti'-ah) = (1 Chronicles 9:8), Same as Shephatiah = Judge of the LORD; Jehovah is judge; whom Jehovah defends.

Shephatiah (shef-a-ti'-ah) = Judge of the LORD; Jehovah is judge; whom Jehovah defends.

Shephi (she'-fi) = My bareness; my prominence. High; i.e., eminent, illustrious; (root = a high place; high places). Baldness.

Shepho (she'-fo) = His bareness; his prominence. Unconcern; smoothness. Same as Shephi = High; i.e., eminent, illustrious; (root = a high place; high places).

Shephuphan (shef'-u-fan) = Their sinuosity; their bareness. Serpent; an adder.

Sherah (she'-rah) = Consanguinity; i.e., a female relation by blood. Near kinship.

Sherebiah (sher-e-bi'-ah) = Jehovah has made to tremble; Jehovah is originator; deliverance by the LORD; i.e., from captivity; heat of Jehovah; (roots = [1] to set loose; [2] Jehovah).

Sheresh (she'-resh) = Root; i.e., of the family; union.

Sherezer (she-re'-zur) = He beheld treasure. Same as Sharezer = Protect or preserve the king; (God) protect the king. Prince of fire. Splendor of brightness.

Sheshach (she'-shak) = Your fine linen. Confusion. A stopper of the way.

Sheshai (she'-shahee) = My fine linen (garments); Whitish; clothed in white; free; noble; (roots = [1] something white; [2] to be white).

Sheshan (she'-shan) = Their fine linen. Lily. Free; noble.

Sheshbazzar (shesh-baz'-zur) = Fine linen in the tribulation. Worshiper of fire. Rejoicing in distress. O sun-god, protect the son.

Sheth (sheth) = Same as Seth = Appointed; compensation substitute; to replace. Tumult. Numbers 24:17.

Shethar (she'-thar) = Who searches; appointed

searcher. Star; commander.

Shetharboznai [Shethar-Bozenai] (she'-thar-boz'-nahee) = Who searched my despisers. Star of splendor; i.e., brilliant star; starry splendor; bright star.

Sheva (she'-vah) = Habitation; i.e., of the Lord. Vanity; self-satisfying.

Shibboleth (shib'-bo-leth) = An ear of corn. A flowing stream or flood; (root = to flow). A branch.

Shibmah (shib'-mah) = Same as Shebam and Sibmah = Sweet smell; fragrant. Why hoary(?).

Shicron (shi'-cron) = Drunkenness; (root = to make oneself drunken).

Shiggaion (shig-gah'-yon) = Erratic. Irregular; inadvertency.

Shigionoth (shig-i'-o-noth) = Same as Shiggaion = Irregular; inadvertency. Wanderings.

Shihon (shi'-hon) = Desolation. Overturning; (root = to be laid waste; destruction). Ruin.

Shihor (shi'-hor) = Very black; turbid; (root = to become black).

Shihorlibnath [Shihor Libnath] (shi'-hor-lib'-nath) = Blackness of whiteness. River of glass; (roots = [1] to break forth; [2] transparency).

Shilhi (shil'-hi) = Armed (of the LORD); dart of the LORD; darter; one armed with darts; (roots = [1] a weapon; a dart; [2] to send; [3] Jehovah). My weapon (as sent).

Shilhim (shil'-him) = Missiles; sent one. Armed men; i.e., a fortress. Aqueducts.

Shillem (shil'-lem) = Recompense; retribution. Same as Shallum = Retribution. Rewarder. Requital.

Shillemites (shil'-lem-ites) = Same as Shallum = Retribution. Rewarder. Recompense.

Shiloah (shi-lo'-ah) = Sent; sending forth; sent forth; outlet of water.

Shiloh (shi'-loh) = Peace-bringer; bringer of prosperity. Pacificator; tranquillity; rest; (root = to be safe; secure). His descendant. *A name for the Messiah.*

Shiloni (shi-lo'-ni) = Sent one.

Shilonite(s) (shi'-lon-ite(s) = Same as Shiloh = Peace-bringer; bringer of prosperity. Pacificator; tranquillity; rest; (root = to be safe; secure). His descendant.

Shilshah (shil'-shah) = Might; heroism; triad; i.e., the third son.

Shimea (shim'-e-ah) = Splendor; something heard; hearing; rumor; (root = to hear). A report.

Shimeah (shim'-e-ah) = Same as Shimea = Splendor; something heard; hearing; rumor; (root = to hear). My reports. Appalment; desolation. 2 Samuel 13:3, 32 - Harkening.

Shimeam (shim'-e-am) = Their desolation. Astonishment; fame; rumor; (root = to be astonished).

Shimeath (shim'-e-ath) = Hearing; fame; famous. A report.

Shimeathites (shim'-e-ath-ites) = Responders; (descendants of Shimeah). A report.

Shimei (shim'-e-i) = One who harkens; my report. Jehovah is fame or famous; famous, of the LORD. My fame. My listener.

Shimeon (shim'-e-on) = A hearkening; hearing; an answering of prayer.

Shimhi (shim'-hi) = Same as Shimei = Jehovah is fame or famous; famous, of the LORD; My fame. My listener.

Shimi (shi'-mi) = Same as Shimei = Jehovah is fame or famous; famous, of the LORD; My fame. My listener.

Shimites she'-mites) = Descendants of Shimei = Jehovah is fame or famous; famous, of the LORD. My fame. My listener.

Shimma (shim'-mah) = A report. Fame; rumor.

Shimon (shi'-mon) = A waste; Tried; valuer. Great desert; (root = to lay waste).

Shimrath (shim'-rath) = Guardianship. Watch; watchfulness; guarding; ward; i.e., one in the hands of the Divine guardian of men; (root = to watch).

Shimri (shim'-ri) = Jehovah is watching; ward (of the LORD); watchful; (roots = [1] to watch; [2] Jehovah). My keeper; watchful.

Shimrith (shim'-rith) = Guarded; i.e., of the Lord; vigilant; (root = to guard). A Guardian.

Shimrom (shim'-rom) = Vigilant guardian; a guard or watch; (intense form of the root = to watch). Watch post.

Shimron (shim'-ron) = Same as Shimrom = Vigilant guardian; a guard or watch; (intense form of the root = to watch).

Watch post. Watchful.

Shimronites (shim'-ron-ites) = Descendants of Shimron = Vigilant guardian; a guard or watch; (intense form of the root = to watch). Watch post. Watchful.

Shimronmeron [Shimron Meron] (shim'-ron-me'-ron) = Guardian of arrogance. Same as Shimron = Vigilant guardian; a guard or watch; (intense form of the root = to watch). Watch post. Watchful.

Shimshai (shim'-shahee) = My minister; my suns. Jehovah is splendor or sunny; sun of the LORD; sunny.

Shinab (shi'-nab) = Tooth of the father; father's tooth. Hostile.

Shinar (shi'-nar) = Tooth of the city; change of city. Casting out; scattering all manner of ways. A shaken tooth; (Shinar = Hebrew word for Babylon in Joshua 7:21.)

Shiphi (shi'-fi) = Jehovah is fullness or abounding; eminent; nakedness;

abundant. My abundance.

Shiphmite (shif'-mite) = Inhabitants of Shapham = Bare; i.e., naked of trees; bald; (root = to be bald).

Shiphrah (shif'-rah) = He garnished; fairness. Beauty; (roots = [1] beauty; brightness; [2] to be bright). Prolific; to procreate.

Shiphtan (shif'-tan) = Their judgment. Judge; most just judge (intense form); judicial.

Shisha (shi'-shah) = Whiteness. Brightness; distinction; nobility.

Shishak (shi'-shak) = Greedy of fine linen; he who will give drink. Illustrious. A waterer.

Shitrai (shit'-ra-i) = My officers. Jehovah is deciding; scribe of the LORD; (roots = [1] to write; i.e., officers, magistrates; [2] Jehovah). Official.

Shittim (shit'-tim) = Same as Abelshittim = Plains; meadows of

acacias. Promoters of error.

Shiza (shi'-zah) = Splendor; vehement love; rising up; i.e., increase of family. Cheerful.

Shoa (sho'-ah) = Opulent. Noble; free; cry.

Shobab (sho'-bab) = Returning; restored; backsliding; apostate; (root = to return).

Shobach (sho'-bak) = Your turning back. Poured out; pouring; one who pours out; captivity; expansion.

Shobai (sho'-bahee) = My captive; my backslidings. Jehovah is glorious; recompense of the LORD; one who leads captive; (roots = [1] to return; to restore; [2] Jehovah). Bright.

Shobal (sho'-bal) = Flowing; shooting (forth); waving. Stream; wandering; travel.

Shobek (sho'-bek) = Forsaker; one who forsakes; free.

Shobi (sho'-bi) = Same as

Shobai = My captive; my backslidings. Jehovah is glorious; recompense of the LORD; one who leads captive; recompense of the LORD; (roots = [1] to return; to restore; [2] Jehovah). Taking captive.

Shocho (sho'-ko) = A hedge; fence; i.e., a strong fortification; (roots = [1] a branch; a hedge; [2] to fence about; to stop up the way). His hedge; his branch.

Shochoh (sho'-ko) = Same as Shocho = A hedge; fence; i.e., a strong fortification; (roots = [1] a branch; a hedge; [2] to fence about; to stop up the way). His hedge; his branch.

Shoco (sho'-ko) = Same as Shocho = A hedge; fence; i.e., a strong fortification; (roots = [1] a branch; a hedge; [2] to fence about; to stop up the way). His hedge; his branch.

Shoham (sho'-ham) = Their equalizing; justifying them. Onyx; beryl.

Shomer(sho'-mur) = Keeper or guarded (of the Lord); watchman; (root = to guard). Guarding.

Shophach (sho'-fak) = Extension; expansion. Same as Shobach = Poured out; pouring; one who pours out; captivity.

Shophan (sho'-fan) = Their bruising. Baldness.

Shoshannim (sho-shan'-nim) = Upon the lilies. Title of Psalms 45 and 69.

Shoshannim-Eduth (sho'-shan'-nim e'-duth) = Lilies of testimony. Title of Psalm 80.

Shua (shu'-ah) = Opulence; salvation. Wealth; rich; prosperity; noble; (root = to be rich).

Shuah (shu'-ah) = Prostration; affluence; depression; (root = to be bowed down). 1 Chronicles 4:11 - a pit.

Shual (shu'-al) = Jackal; a fox; a small pet.

Shubael (shu'-ba-el) = Same as Shebuel = Captive of God; God is renown; Return, O God.

Shuham (shu'-ham) = Pit digger; pitman; depression; (root = to bow down). Their pit.

Shuhamites (shu'-ham-ites) = Descendants of Shuham = Pit digger; pitman; depression; (root = to bow down).

Shuhite (shu'-hite) = Descendants of Shua = Wealth; rich; prosperity; noble; (root = to be rich).

Shulamite (shu'-lam-ite) = The perfect; the peaceful. Complete; (root = to be complete; [to have] peace) The rewarded.

Shumathites (shu'-math-ites) = The exalted. Garlic.

Shunammite (shu'-nam-mite) = Inhabitants of Shunem = Two resting places. Their sleep.

Shunem (shu'-nem) = Two resting places. Their sleep.

Shuni (shu'-ni) = Tranquility; quiet; fortunate; calm. My rest.

Shunites (shu'-nites) =

Descendants of Shuni = Tranquility; quiet; fortunate; calm. My rest.

Shupham (shu'-fam) = Their bareness. Serpent; (root = an adder).

Shuphamites (shu'-fam-ites) = Descendants of Shupham = Their bareness. Serpent; (root = an adder).

Shuppim (shup'-pim) = Bared ones. Serpent.

Shur (shur) = Rampart (as point of observation); beheld. A fort; i.e., a fortified city; a watcher; (roots = [1] a wall; [2] to look around).

Shushan (shu'-shan) = Lily.

Shushan-eduth (shu'-shan-e'-duth) = Lily of the testimony. Title of Psalm 60.

Shuthalhites (shu'-thal-hites) = Descendants of Shuthelah = Crashing; rending; (roots = [1] to make a crash; [2] to break). Plantation.

Shuthelah (shu'-the-lah) = Freshly appointed;

resembling rejuvenation. Crashing; rending; (roots = [1] to make a crash; [2] to break). Plantation; a plant.

Sia (si'-ah) = Departing. Council; assembly; congregation.

Siaha (si'-a-hah) = Same as Sia = Departing. Council; assembly; congregation.

Sibbecai (sib'-be-cahee) = My thickets. Jehovah is intervening; entangling; thicket of the LORD; (roots = [1] a wood; a thicket; [2] to intertwine).

Sibbechai (sib'-be-kahee) = Same as Sibbecai = My thickets. Jehovah is intervening; entangling; thicket of the LORD; (roots = [1] a wood; a thicket; [2] to intertwine).

Sibboleth (sib'-bo-leth) = A burden. Same as Shibboleth = An ear of corn. A flowing stream or flood; (root = to flow).

Sibmah (sib'-mah) = Same as Shebam = Sweet smell; fragrance.

Sibraim (sib'-ra-im) = Double purpose. Two-fold hope; two hills.

Sichem (si'-kem) = The shoulder blade. The shoulder (as place for burden).

Siddim (sid'-dim) = Cultivators; furrows. Plains; the plains; (roots = [1] a plain; [2] to harrow level).

Sidon (si'-don) = Hunting. Fishing; plenty of fish; (roots = [1] hunting; prey taken in hunting {or} fishing; [2] to lay snares). A place for hunting. Fortified.

Sidonians (si-do'-ne-uns) = Inhabitants of Sidon = Hunting. Fishing; plenty of fish; (roots = [1] hunting; prey taken in hunting {or} fishing; [2] to lay snares). A place for hunting. Fortified.

Sihon (si'-hon) = Sweeping away; i.e., a general who drives every thing before him; brush; great; (root = to sweep away). Self-possession.

Sihor (si'-hor) = Same as

Shihor = Very black; turbid; (root = to become black). Dark.

Silas (si'-las) = Woody. Shortened form of Silvanus = Lover of words. Of the forest; (root = Latin - wood).

Silla (sil'-lah) = He weighed; compared; weighing place. Heap of earth; highway; (root = to lift up).

Siloah (si-lo'-ah) = A missile (as sent). Sent; (root = to send; dart).

Siloam (si-lo'-am) = Same as Shiloah = Sent; sending forth; sent forth; outlet of water.

Silvanus (sil-va'-nus) = Lover of words. Of the forest; (root = Latin - wood).

Simeon (sim'-e-un) = Hearkening. Hearing with acceptance; hears and obeys; an obeyer; hearing; (root = to hear).

Simeonites (sim'-e-un-ites) = Same as Simeon = Hearkening. Hearing with acceptance; hears and obeys; an obeyer; hearing; (root = to hear).

Simon (si'-mun) = Same as Simeon = Hearkening. Hearing with acceptance; hears and obeys; an obeyer; hearing; (root = to hear).

Simri (sim'-ri) = Same as Shimri = Jehovah is watching; ward (of the LORD); watchful; (roots = [1] to watch; [2] Jehovah).

Sin (sin) = Clay; thorn; mire; (root = to be muddy or clayey).

Sina (si'-nah) = Thorny. Greek form of Sinai = Bush of the LORD. Pointed. My bushes.

Sinai (si'-nahee) = My thorns. Bush of the LORD. Pointed. My bushes.

Sinim (si'-nim) = Thorns.

Sinite (si'-nite) = Dwellers in a marshy land.

Sion #1 (si'-on) = Parched place (another name for Mt. Zion). Lifted up; (root = to lift up). Tumult; noise.

Sion #2 (si'-on) = Deuteronomy 4:28 - Elevation; a bearing;

carrying. *Another name for Mt. Hermon.*

Siphmoth (sif'-moth) = Lips; i.e., languages. Bare places.

Sippai (sip'-pahee) = My basins; my thresholds. Jehovah is preserver. Belonging to the doorstep.

Sirah (si'-rah) = Withdrawing. Turning aside.

Sirion (sir'-e-on) = Breastplate; a coat of mail; (roots = [1] a breastplate; [2] to shine; to glitter). Little prince.

Sisamai (sis'-a-mahee) = Water crane; swallow. Jehovah is distinguished. The sun. Fragrant.

Sisera (sis'-e-rah) = A crane of seeing; swallow of seeing. A field of battle; battle array; sea of horses; meditation; (root = to leap onward; to make an onset). Binding in chains. Found on a horse.

Sitnah (sit'-nah) = Accusation; hated; contention; (root = to lie in wait; to be an adversary). Hostility.

Sivan (si'-van) = Bright. Their covering(?). Second Jewish month (May - June).

Smyrna (smir'-na) = Bitterness; suffering. Myrrh.

So (so) = Concealed; conspicuous. Lifted up; (root = to lift up).

Socho (so'-ko) = Same as Shocho = A hedge; fence; i.e., a strong fortification; (roots = [1] a branch; a hedge; [2] to fence about; to stop up the way). His hedge; his branch.

Sochoh (so'-ko) = Same as Shocho = A hedge; fence; i.e., a strong fortification; (roots = [1] a branch; a hedge; [2] to fence about; to stop up the way). His hedge; his branch.

Socoh (so'-ko) = Same as Shocho = A hedge; fence; i.e., a strong fortification; (roots = [1] a branch; a hedge; [2] to fence about; to stop up the way). His hedge; his branch.

Sodi (so'-di) = My confidant. Jehovah

determines; acquaintance of God; a familiar acquaintance; an acquaintance; my secret; (roots = [1] a sitting together; an acquaintance; [2] to sit down, settle; [3] Jehovah).

Sodom (sod'-om) = Flaming; burning; (root = to burn). Mystery; their secret; (root = to hide). Fettered.

Sodoma (sod'-o-mah) = Burning. Greek form of Sodom = Flaming; burning; (root = to burn). Mystery; their secret; (root = to hide). Fettered.

Sodomites (sod'-om-ites) = Set apart ones (for unholy purposes); temple prostitutes. Persons who were as wicked as the men of Sodom, (The term identifies one of the sins of homosexuality.)

Solomon (sol'-o-mun) = Peaceable (intense form); peace; his peace. Peaceableness.

Son of God = The divinity of Christ.

Son of Man = The humanity of Christ.

Sopater (so'-pa-tur) = Saving father. Of good parentage; defends the father.

Sophereth (so-fe'-reth) = Registrar. Learning; writer; scribe; (root = to write).

Sorek (so'-rek) = Choice vine; noble vine; (roots = [1] a shoot, {or a} nobler {kind of vine}; [2] to intertwine).

Sosipater (so-sip'-a-tur) = Savior of his father. Saving father.

Sosthenes (sos'-the-neze) = Preserver of strength; of sound strength. Saving strength; strong savior.

Sotai (so'-tahee) = My swervings. Jehovah is turning back; drawn back of the LORD; deviator; one who turns aside; (roots = [1] to draw back; [2] Jehovah).

Spain (spane) = Scarceness.

Stachys (sta'-kis) = An ear of corn.

Stacte (stac'-te) = A drop.

Stephanas (stef'-a-nas) = Crowned.

Stephen (ste'-ven) = Wreath; crown.

Stoicks (sto'-ics) = Of the portico. (Followers of the Stoic philosophy.)

Suah (su'-ah) = Riches; distinction; sweepings; (root = to sweep away). Offal (the entrails of a butchered animal).

Succoth (suc'-coth) = Booths; tabernacles; (roots = [1] a booth; [2] to interweave; to cover).

Succothbenoth [Succoth Benoth] (suc'-coth-be'-noth) = Tabernacles of daughters; (roots = [1] daughters; maidens; [2] a daughter; [3] to build). The tabernacles built. The daughter's booths.

Suchathites (soo'-kath-ites) = Bush-men; hedgers. Dwellers in booths (or) tents.

Sukkiims (suk'-ke-ims) = Dwellers in tents. Thicket-men.

Sur (sur) = Turning aside. Go back; (roots = [1] removed; a degenerated branch; [2] to depart).

Susanchites (su'-san-kites) = Same as Susanna = Lily; a white lily. They of the lily. They of the place (Shushan).

Susanna (su-zan'-nah) = Lily; a white lily.

Susi (su'-si) = Jehovah is swift; rejoicing; horseman. My horse.

Sychar (si'-kar) = Drunken; hired.

Sychem (si'-kem) = Shoulder; diligence; (literally - early rising). Greek form of Shechem = Back; shoulder; (root =the shoulder; the upper part of the back; a ridge of land).

Syene (si-e'-ne) = Opening; key; i.e., of Egypt. Her veiling(?).

Syntyche (sin'-ti-ke) = Fortunate. Well-met.

Syracuse (sir'-a-cuse) = A Syrian hearing.

Syria (sir'-e-ah) = The highland; a citadel; (root =

to be elevated). Same as
Aram = High; elevated;
lifted up; magnified;
exalted. Exalted.

Syriack (sir'-e-ak) =
Language. The Syrian
language.

Syriadamascus (sir'-e-
ah-ma'-a-kah) = Syria =
The highland; a citadel.
Damascus = Activity;
moist with blood.

Syriamaachah [Aram
Maacah] (sir'-e-ah-da-
mas'-cus) = Syria = The
highland; a citadel.
Maachah = Oppression;
compression; depression;

Syrian(s) (sir'-e-un(s) =
Inhabitants of Syria = The
highland; a citadel; (root =
to be elevated). Same as
Aram = High; elevated;
lifted up; magnified;
exalted. 2 Chronicles 22:5
- lofty ones.

Syrophenician (sy'-ro-fe-
ne'-she-un) = Exalted
palm. Phoenician living in
Syria = The highland;   a
citadel; (root = to be
elevated). Same as Aram
= High; elevated; lifted
up; magnified.

*rust in the LORD,
and do good; so shalt
thou dwell in the land
(Psalms 37:3).*

Taanach (ta'-a-nak) = She
will afflict thee. Wandering
through. Castle.

Taanathshiloh [Taanath
Shiloh] (ta'-a-nath-shi'-lo)
= Shilo's opportunity;
Shilo's fig tree. Entrance
to Shiloh.

Tabbaoth (tab'-ba-oth) =
Rings; spots; (roots = [1] a
ring; a seal ring; [2] to
seal; to sink).

Tabbath (tab'-bath) =
Renowned; celebrated;
pleasantness; (root = to
spread a good report). You
were good.

Tabeal (tab'-e-al) = God

is good; the goodness of God; not scornful. Good for nothing.

Tabeel (tab'-e-el) = Same as Tabeal = God is good; the goodness of God; not scornful.

Taberah (tab'-e-rah) = Consuming; burning; (root = to consume with fire). You may burn.

Tabitha (tab'-ith-ah) = Same as Dorcas = Gazelle.

Tabor (ta'-bor) = You will purge. Stone-quarry; separated; (root = to sever; to point). Height. Purity.

Tabrimon (tab'-rim-on) = The pomegranate is good. Rimmon is god; goodness of Rimmon; (roots = [1] to be good; [2] the name of the idol, Rimmon).

Tachmonite (tak'-mun-ite) = You will make me wise. Same as Hachmonite = Very wise; (root = to be wise; to be cunning; to be skillful).Wisdom.

Tadmor (tad'-mor) = You will scatter myrrh. City of palms.

Tahan (ta'-han) = You

will decline; you will encamp. Supplication; i.e., of parents; (root = to be gracious). Camp. Preciousness; inclination.

Tahanites (ta'-han-ites) = Descendants of Tahan = You will decline; you will encamp. Supplication; i.e., of parents; (root = to be gracious). Camp. Preciousness; inclination.

Tahapanes (ta-hap'-a-neze) = You will fill hands with pity. The beginning of the age. Head of the land.

Tahath (ta'-hath) = Depression; humility. (roots = [1] that which is below; [2] to go down). Substitute. Subordinate.

Tahpanhes (tah'-pan-heze) = You will fill hands with pity. The beginning of the age; head of the land.

Tahpenes (tah'-pe-neze) = You will cover flight. Same as Tahpanhes = The beginning of the age; head of the age. Given of the serpent.

Tahrea (tah'-re-ah) = Separate the friend.

Delaying cries; i.e., a son slowly born; (roots = [1] to be tardy; to delay; [2] noise; outcry).Cunning; adroitness; flight.

Tahtimhodshi [Tahtim Hodshi] (tah'-tim-hod'-shi) = The lower ones of my new moon. Under the new moon.

Talitha (tal'-ith-ah) = Girl.

Talmai (tal'-mahee) = Abounding in furrows; furrows; i.e., as long as a furrow; ridges; my furrows; bold; spirited.

Talmon (tal'-mon) = Injurious oppression; oppressed (intense form); oppressor; violent. Outcast.

Tamah (ta'-mah) = Joy. Laughter. You will be fat (with inner joy).

Tamar (ta'-mar) = A palm tree; palm; (roots = [1] a palm tree; [2] to stand erect).

Tammuz (tam'-mu) = You shall be shriveled up. Hidden. Giver of the vine; sprout of life. Son of life. The meaning is much debated - Arabic root = The

heat of summer. Hebrew root = Burning. Syrian name given to the fourth Jewish month (June - July).

Tanach (ta'-nak) = Same as Taanach = Wandering through. Castle.

Tanhumeth (tan'-hu-meth) = Consolation; (root = to comfort).

Taphath (ta'-fath) = Distillation. Drop of myrrh; stacte; i.e., myrrh flowing spontaneously; a drop.

Tappuah (tap'-pu-ah) = You will cause to breathe. Apple; fruitful in apples; high place.

Tarah (ta'-rah) = You may breathe. Delay. Station.

Taralah (tar'-a-lah) = Release the curse. Reeling; (root = to tremble; to reel).

Tarea (ta'-re-ah) = Mark out a neighbor; chamber of a neighbor. Same as Tahrea = Delaying cries; i.e., a son slowly born; (roots = [1] to be tardy; to delay; [2] noise; outcry).

Tarpelites (tar'-pel-ites) =

They of the fallen (or wondrous) mountain.

Tarshish (tar'-shish) = She will cause poverty; she will shatter. Breaking; subjection; i.e., of enemies; hard; contemplation; (root = to break).

Tarsus (tar'-sus) = A flat basket.

Tartak (tar'-tak) = You shall be enchained. The moon; the mother of gods; (root = [Pehlv. language] - profound darkness; hero of darkness).

Tartan (tar'-tan) = Release the dragon. Great increase; military chief.

Tatnai (tat'-nahee) = Gift; overseer of gifts.

Tebah (te'-bah) = Confidence; i.e., of parents; (root = to confide in). Slaughter; slaughter of cattle; thick; strong.

Tebaliah (teb-a-li'-ah) = Baptized of the LORD; i.e., purified; whom Jehovah has immersed; Jehovah is protector; Jehovah has purified.

Tebeth (te'-beth) =

Goodness. Tenth Jewish month (December - January)

Tehaphnehes (te-haf'-ne-heze) = You will fill hands with pity. Same as Tahapanes = The beginning of the age. Head of the land.

Tehinnah (te-hin'-nah) = Grace; prayer; cry for mercy; entreaty; supplication.

Tekel (te'-kel) = Weighed.

Tekoa (te-ko'-ah) = Sound of trumpet; blowing a trumpet. Pitching (of tents); (root = to smite; to fix [by smiting]; to fix [one's tent]). Firm; settlement.

Tekoah (te-ko'-ah) = Same as Tekoa = Sound of trumpet; blowing a trumpet. Pitching (of tents); (root = to smite; to fix [by smiting]; to fix [one's tent]). Firm; settlement.

Tekoite(s) (te-ko'-ite(s)) = Inhabitants of Tekoah = Sound of trumpet; blowing a trumpet. Pitching (of tents); (root = to smite; to fix [by smiting]; to fix [one's tent]). Firm; settlement.

Telabib [Tel Abib] (tel-a'-bib) = Hill of ears of corn; (roots = [1] a hill; a heap of ruins; [2] an ear of corn).

Telah (te'-lah) = Rejuvenator; invigorator. Fracture; vigor.

Telaim (tel'-a-im) = Young lambs; lambs; i.e., spotted ones.

Telassar (te-las'-sar) = Weariness of the prince; hang thou the prince. Hill of Assur.

Telem (te'-lem) = Covering them; casting them out. Oppression; a lamb; (root = to oppress).

Telharesha [Harsha] (tel-ha-re'-shah) = Heap of artifice; heap of the artificer. Hill of plowing. Forest hill.

Telharsa [Tel Harsa] (tel-har'-sah) = Same as Telharesha = Heap of artifice; heap of the artificer. Hill of plowing. Forest hill.

Telmelah [Tel Melah] (tel-me'-lah) = Hill of salt; salt hill.

Tema (te'-mah) = Southerner. A desert; an untilled region; sun burnt; admiration.

Teman (te'-man) = Southern quarter; the south. On the right hand; perfect. Southward.

Temani (te'-ma-ni) = Descendants of Teman = Southern quarter; the south. On the right hand; perfect.

Temanite(s) (te'-man-ite(s) = Same as Teman = Southern quarter; the south. On the right hand; perfect.

Temeni (tem'-e-ni) = You shall go to the right hand; my right hand. Fortunate.

Terah (te'-rah) = You may breathe. Delay; i.e., slowly born. Chaldean: To delay. Wild goat; turning; wandering.

Teraphim (ter'-af-im) = Nourishers. Images; idols - literally: enfeeblers, or healers; avoidances.

Teresh (te'-resh) = Possession; you will

possess. Sever; austere; reverence.

Tertius (tur'-she-us) = The third; (root = Latin - the third).

Tertullus (tur-tul'-lus) = Triple-hardened. Liar; imposter.

Tetrarch = Ruler of a fourth part of a country.

Thaddaeus (thad-de'-us) = Sucking plenty. Breast; man of heart; one that praises.

Thahash (tha'-hash) = Badger; a seal; keep silent; reddish.

Thamah (tha'-mah) = You will be fat. Laughing; i.e., joy of parents; laughter; suppresses; combat.

Thamar (tha'-mar) = Palm tree. Greek equivalent of Tamar = A palm tree; palm; (roots = [1] a palm tree; [2] to stand erect).

Thara (tha'-rah) = Station. Greek form of Terah = Delay; i.e., slowly born. Chaldean: To delay. Wild goat; turning; wandering.

Tharshish (thar'-shish) = She will cause poverty or shattering. Same as Tarshish = Breaking; subjection; i.e., of enemies; hard; contemplation; (root = to break).

Thebez (the'-bez) = Brightness. Mire; clay. Whiteness; brilliancy.

Thelasar (the-la'-sar) = Same as Telassar = Weariness of the prince; hang thou the prince. Hill of Assur.

Theophilus (the-of'-il-us) = Loved by God; lover of God; friend of God.

Thessalonians (thes-sa-lo'-ne-uns) = Same as Thessalonica = Victory of falsity. Victory over the tossing of law; victory over falsity.

Thessalonica (thes-sa-lo-ni'-cah) = Victory of falsity. Victory over the tossing of law; victory over falsity.

Theudas (thew'-das) = Gift of God; he shall be praised. Praise. False teacher.

Thimnathah (thim'-nath-ah) = Portion. Same as Timnah = Portion assigned; i.e., separated; a portion; gift; (root = to divide). A portion there; you shall number there.

Thomas (tom'-us) = A twin.

Thummim (thum'-mim) = Perfection; completeness; truth.

Thyatira (thi-a-ti'-rah) = High tower; a castle; feminine oppression; odor of affliction.

Tiberias (ti-be'-re-as) = A place named after Tiberius = Son of Tiber; from the Tiber (as god-river).

Tiberius (ti-be'-re-us) = Son of Tiber; from the Tiber (as god-river).

Tibhath (tib'-hath) = Security; i.e., to dwell safely. Butchery. The slaughter place.

Tibni (tib'-ni) = Building of the LORD; (roots = [1] to build; [2] Jehovah). Made of straw; my straw; straw; intelligent.

Tidal (ti'-dal) = You shall be cast out of the Most High; you shall be cast out from heaven. Fear; reverence; i.e., of the object of fear; dread. Easing the yoke.

Tiglathpileser [Tiglath-Pileser] (tig'-lath-pi-le'-zur) = You will uncover the wonderful bond; you will carry away the wonderful bond. Mother of the gods (the son of the temple of Sarra). Hinders; binds; my strength is the god Ninib. Lord of the Tigris.

Tikvah (tik'-vah) = Expectation; strength. Hope.

Tikvath (tik'-vath) = You shall be gathered. Same as Tikvah = Expectation; strength.

Tilgathpilneser [Tilgath-pileser] (til'-gath-pil-ne'-zur) = Winepress heap of the wonderful bond; winepress heap of the distinguished captive. Same as Tiglathpileser = Mother of the gods (the son of the temple of

Sarra). Hinders; binds; my strength is the god Ninib. Lord of the Tigris.

Tilon (ti'-lon) = You shall murmur; you shall abide. Gift. Scorn.

Timaeus (ti-me'-us) = Highly prized. Polluted.

Timna (tim'-nah) = Restraint; restrained; unapproachable; inaccessible; (root = to restrain). You will withhold.

Timnah (tim'-nah) = Portion assigned; i.e., separated; a portion; gift; (root = to allot; to divide). You will withhold.

Timnath (tim'-nath) = Same as Timnah = Portion assigned; i.e., separated; a portion; gift; (root = to allot; to divide).

Timnathheres [Timnath Heres] (tim'-nath-he'-rez) = Portion of the sun.

Timnathserah [Timnath Serah] (tim'-nath-se'-rah) = Portion redundant; abundant portion; i.e., that which is left over and above; portion of the remainder.

Timnite (tim'-nite) = Inhabitants of Timnah = Portion assigned; i.e., separated; a portion; gift; (root = to allot; to divide).

Timon (ti'-mon) = Honorable; deemed worthy.

Timotheus (tim-o'-the-us) = Honoring God; zealot; to be honored of God; worshiping God; valued of God.

Timothy (tim'-o-thy) = Honoring God. English form of Timotheus = Honoring God; honored of God; worshiping God; valued of God.

Tiphsah (tif'-sah) = Passage; (root = to pass over). She shall pass over.

Tiras (ti'-ras) = He crushed the search. Desire; i.e., of parents.

Tirathites (ti'-rath-ites) = Openings; from a place (gate). Men of the gate; nourishers.

Tirhakah (tur-ha'-kah) = He searched out the pious; he searched out - the waiter. Exalted; brought forth.

Tirhanah (tur-ha'-nah) = A camp spy. Inclination; favor; kindness. Inhabiting a residence; i.e., a most secure dwelling place.

Tiria (tir'-e-ah) = Fear; (root = to fear). Foundation.

Tirshatha (tur'-sha-thah) = You shall possess there. The feared; (root = Persian - stern; severe). Chaldean: A driver out. Reverence; beholding the time.

Tirzah (tur'-zah) = Pleasantness; delight; (root = to delight [in any person or thing]). She is willing; liberal.

Tishbite (tish'-bite) = Captivity. Inhabitant of Tishbe = A captive; adding. You shall lead captive.

Tishri = Seventh Jewish month (September - October)

Titus (ti'-tus) = Nurse; rearer. Protected; honorable, from "I honor."

Tizite (ti'-zite) = You shall go forth.

Toah (to'-ah) = Prostration; low; depression; humility. Sinking.

Tob (tob) = Good (place); root = to be good).

Tobadonijah [Tob-Adonijah] (tob'-ad-o-ni'-jah) = Distinguished of my LORD-Jehovah; good is my LORD-Jehovah; My good God.

Tobiah (to-bi'-ah) = Distinguished of the LORD; Jehovah is good.

Tobijah (to-bi'-jah) = Goodness of Jehovah. Same as Tobiah = Distinguished of the LORD; Jehovah is good.

Tochen (to'-ken) = Portion cut out; a measure. Measurement.

Togarmah (to-gar'-mah) = Breaking bones; all bone; strong; (root = to break bones). Rugged. A strong hold. You will break her.

Tohu (to'-hu) = Humility; depression; lowly; inclined; that lives. Same as Toah = Prostration; low. They sank down.

Toi (to'-i) = Error; erring;

straying; wanderer; (root = to err; to go astray). Do thou mock.

Tola (to'-lah) = Little worm; scarlet (from the color of a worm); (root = [1] a worm; scarlet color; [2] to be clothed in scarlet.) Certain worms have a scarlet color and are used in dyeing cloth crimson or scarlet.

Tolad (to'-lad) = Generation; i.e., posterity; birth; (root = to bear). Let her bring forth; you may beget.

Tolaites (to'-lah-ites) = Descendants of Tola = Little worm; scarlet; (root = [1] a worm; scarlet color; [2] to be clothed in scarlet. Certain worms have a scarlet color and are used in dyeing cloth crimson or scarlet.

Topaz (to'-paz) = Affliction has fled away.

Tophel (to'-fel) = Unseasonable. Insipid. Lime.

Tophet (to'-fet) = A spitting (as object of contempt). Place of

burning; burning; a place abhorred; place of graves; detestable.

Topheth (to'-feth) = Spitting. Same as Tophet = Place of burning; burning; a place abhorred; place of graves; detestable.

Tou (to'-u) = Do you mock; do you stray away. Same as Toi = Error; erring; straying; wanderer; (root = to err; to go astray).

Trachonitis (trak-o-ni'-tis) = Rugged; rugged or stony tract; a heap of stones. Rocky region.

Troas (tro'-as) = A Trojan.

Trogyllium (tro-jil'-le-um) = A cache; i.e., a hole in the ground for preserving food. (A narrow channel used for shipping.)

Trophimus (trof'-im-us) = Master of the house; nourishing; well educated.

Tryphena (tri-fe'-nah) = Delicate; dainty one. Luxurious.

Tryphosa (tri-fo'-sah) = Luxuriating. Same as Tryphena = Delicate; dainty one.

Tubal (tu'-bal) = Flowing forth; i.e., increase and diffusion of a race; worldly possessions; (root = to flow; to bring forth). Production. Brought. You shall be brought.

Tubalcain [Tubal-Cain's] (tu'-bal-cain) = Flowing forth of Cain; i.e., increase of the race of Cain; production; forged work. You will be brought of Cain.

Tychicus (tik'-ik-us) = Fortuitous; fortunate.

Tyrannus (ti-ran'-nus) = Absolute rule; sovereign; a tyrant; despot.

Tyre (tire) = To distress. Rock; (root = to besiege). A bundle tied fast together; a flint.

Tyrus (ti'-rus) = To distress. Same as Tyre = Rock; (root = to besiege). A bundle tied fast together; a flint.

Use hospitality one to another without grudging (1 Peter 4:9).

Ucal (u'-cal) = I shall be completed; I shall be established. I shall prevail; power; overcame; consumed.

Uel (u'-el) = Will of God; (root = to desire). Desired of God.

Ulai (ul'-lah) = My leaders (mightiest). Pure water. Muddy water. Peradventure (perhaps).

Ulam (u'-lam) = Their leaders. First of all; i.e., a firstborn; foremost; porch; vestibule.

Ulla (ul'-lah) = He was taken up. Yoke; elevation; burden.

Ummah (um'-mah) = He was associated; juxtaposition. Union; i.e., community of inhabitants;

community; gathering.

Unni (un'-ni) = Afflicted (of the LORD); answering is with Jehovah; afflicted; depressed; poor; (roots = [1] to be depressed; [2] Jehovah). He was afflicted.

Upharsin (u-far'-sin) = And dividers. Divided.

Uphaz (u'-faz) = Desire of fine gold. Island of gold; glittering gold.

Ur (ur) = Light; fire; furnace; (root = to make light; to kindle).

Urbane (ur'-bane) = End of the way (Greek); of the city (Latin). Pleasant; refined; polite.

Uri (u'-ri) = Light (of the LORD); light of Jehovah; enlightened; fiery; burning; my furnace. My light.

Uriah (u-ri'-ah) = Jehovah is light; light of the LORD; light of Jehovah; the LORD my light.

Urias (u-ri'-as) = Jehovah is light. My light is Jah.

Uriel (u'-re-el) = A light or flame of God; God is

my light or fire; fire of God.

Urijah (u-ri'-jah) = Flame of Jehovah. Same as Uriah = Jehovah is light; light of the LORD; light of Jehovah; the LORD my light.

Urim (u'-rim) = Light; fire.

Uthai (u'thahee) = My helper (by teaching). Jehovah is help; Jehovah succors; opportune of the LORD; i.e., a son given in the season of the LORD; helpful; (roots = [1] to be in season; [2] Jehovah).

Uz (uz) = Counselor; counsel; firmness; (root = to consult). Also, Fertile; fruitful in trees; (root = to impress; to immerse oneself; i.e., the foot in the sand).

Uzai (u'-zahee) = Velocity of the Lord; robust. Hoped for. I shall have my sprinklings(?).

Uzal (u'-zal) = Going to and fro; wanderer; (root = to gad about). I shall be flooded.

Uzza (uz'-zah) = Strength; (root = to be strong). He was strengthened.

Uzzah (uz'-zah) = Same as Uzza = Strength; (root = to be strong). He was strengthened.

Uzzensherah [Uzzen Sherah] (uz'-zen-she'-rah) = Ear of Sherah; corner of Sherah.

Uzzi (uz'-zi) = The might of Jehovah; power of the LORD; (roots = [1] strength; power; [2] Jehovah). My strength.

Uzzia (uz-zi'-ah) = Power of the LORD; strength of Jehovah; might of Jehovah.

Uzziah (uz-zi'-ah) = Strength of the LORD; might of Jehovah; (roots = [1] power; strength; to become strong; [2] Jehovah).The LORD my strength.

Uzziel (uz-zi'-el) = Strength of God; power of God; God is strong; God my strength; roots = [1] strength; power; [2] God).

Uzzielites (uz-zi'-el-ites) = Descendants of Uzziel = Strength of God; power of God; God is strong; God

my strength; (roots = [1] strength; power; [2] God).

V erily, verily, I say unto thee, Except a man be born again, he cannot see the kingdom of God (John 3:3).

V

Vajezatha (va-jez'-a-thah) = White; sincere; pure. Strong as the wind; sincere. Born of Ized. And he sprinkled there.

Vaniah (va-ni'-ah) = And we were oppressed. God is praise; weak; distress; (root = to be weak; torpid; meek).

Vashni (vash'-ni) = Wherefore; sleep thou. Jehovah is praise; God is strong; gift (of God);

strong; (root = to give liberally). Changeable.

Vashti (vash'-ti) = Wherefore waste thou away; wherefore banquet thou. Beautiful; beautiful woman.

Vophsi (vof'-si) = Wherefore vanish thou. Fragrant; rich; addition (of the LORD); (roots = [1] to add; [2] Jehovah). Expansion.

Wisdom resteth in the heart of him that hath understanding (Proverbs 14:33).

You, being dead in your sins . . ., hath he quickened together with him, having forgiven you all trespasses" (Colossians 2:13).

(There are no entries for the letter "Y."

Wonderful—A miracle; a marvelous thing: or a wonderful counselor. A name given to Jesus in Isaiah 9:6.

Zion, which is the city of David (1 Chronicles 11:5).

Z

Zaanaim (za-an-a'-im) = Enormous migrations; wanderings; (root = to move one's tent).

Zaanan (za'-an-an) = Rich in flocks; place of flocks; (root = to abound in sheep and goats). Their flocks.

Zaanannim (za-an-an'-nim) = Same as Zaanaim = Enormous migrations; wanderings; (root = to move one's tent).

Zaavan (za'-av-an) = Great agitation (intense form); conquest; causing fear; disturbed; disquieted; (root = a removing; a commotion). Their removal; their disquiet.

Zabad (za'-bad) = Given; i.e., given of God; gift; endower; he has given a gift; present.

Zabbai (zab'-bahee) = Clemency of the LORD; pure; innocent; roving about; humming. My flittings; my wanderings (?).

Zabbud (zab'-bud) = Gift bestowed; i.e., bestowed by God; given; bestowed; (root = to bestow a gift). Well remembered; endowed.

Zabdi (zab'-di) = Jehovah gave; the gift of Jehovah; Jehovah is endower or dowry. My dowry.

Zabdiel (zab'-de-el) = Gift of God; the gift of God; my gift is God; God is endower; (root = [1] to bestow a gift; [2] God).

Zabud (za'-bud) = Gift bestowed; i.e., bestowed by God; endower; gift; given. (root = to bestow a gift).

Zabulon (zab'-u-lon) = A habitation. Greek form of Zebulun = Wished-for habitation; (root = [1] habitation; [2] to dwell with). Dwelling.

Zaccai (zac'-cahee) = Pure of the LORD; i.e., whom the LORD has cleansed; pure; innocent; (roots = [1] to be pure; to cleanse;[2] Jehovah). My pure ones.

Zacchaeus (zak-ke'-us) = Pure; justified.

Zacchur (zac'-cur) = Mindful; well remembered; pure; (root = to remember).

Zaccur (zac'-cur) = Same as Zacchur = Mindful; well remembered; pure; (root = to remember).

Zachariah (zak-a-ri'-ah) = Remembered of tne LORD; whom Jehovah remembers. Remember God. (root = to remember; to make mention of).

Zacharias (zak'-a-ri'-as) = Jehovah is renowned.

Zacher (za'-kur) = Remembrance; memorial; fame.

Zadok (za'-dok) = Just; righteous; upright; justified; (root = to be just).

Zaham (za'-ham) = Loathing; fatness; (root = to loathe). He loathed.

Zair (za'-ur) = Insignificant; lesser. Little; young; small; few; (root = to be small).

Zalaph (za'-laf) = The shadow beautified. Fracture; bruise; wound; purification; (root = to break).

Zalmon (zal'-mon) = Resemblance; image. Shady; ascent; (root = to be shady).

Zalmonah (zal-mo'-nah) = Representation; imagery. Same as Zalmon = Shady; ascent. Little image; (root = to be shady).

Zalmunna (zal-mun'-nah) = Shadow is withheld; a moving shadow; withdrawn from protection; shelter is denied.

Zamzummims (zam-zum'-mims) = Intriguers. Tribes making a noise; (root = to buzz; to make a noise). Devisers.

Zanoah (za-no'-ah) = To cast off. Stinking; marsh; bog; (root = to stink). Broken district.

Zaphnathpaaneah [Zaphnath-Paneah] (zaf'-nath-pa-a-ne'-ah) = Savior of the age; Savior of the world; giver of the nourishment of life; prince of the life of the age; revealer of a secret. The concealed treasure. Treasury of the glorious rest.

Zaphon (za'-fon) = North; north wind; i.e., a place exposed to the north wind; northward.

Zara (za'-rah) = A rising (as of the sun); brightness. Sprout.

Zarah (za'-rah) = Rising of light; i.e., joy of parents; (roots = [1] a rising {of light}; [2] to rise; dawn; sunrise). Shining; brightness.

Zareah (za'-re-ah) = Hornet; place of hornets. She was smitten with leprosy.

Zareathites (za'-re-ath-ites) = Same as Zorathites = Inhabitants of Zorah = A nest of hornets; i.e., a place of troublesome men; a place of hornets. She was smitten with leprosy.

Zared (za'-red) = Luxuriant growth of trees; exuberant growth; thick foliage. The stranger

subdued; the bond subdued.

Zarephath (zar'-e-fath) = Place of refining; she has refined. Refined; smelting house. Workshop for melting and refining metals.

Zaretan (zar'-e-tan) = Their distress. Narrowness of dwelling place; i.e., a small dwelling place. Cooling.

Zarethshahar [Zareth Shahar] (za'-reth-sha'-har) = Splendor of the morning; i.e., a town situated facing the rising sun; brightness of dawn.

Zarhites (zar'-hites) = Descendants of Zerah = Same as Zarah = Rising of light; i.e., joy of parents; (roots = [1] a rising {of light}; [2] to rise). Dawn. Shining.

Zartanah (zar'-ta-nah) = Same as Zaretan & Zarthan = Their distress. Narrowness of dwelling place; i.e., a small dwelling place. Cooling.

Zarthan (zar'-than) = Same as Zaretan = Their

distress. Narrowness of dwelling place; i.e., a small dwelling place. Cooling.

Zatthu (zath'-u) = Brightness of him. Ornament; beauty; lovely; pleasant.

Zattu (zat'-tu) = Same as Zatthu = Brightness of him. Ornament; beauty; lovely; pleasant.

Zavan (za'-van) = Same as Zaavan = Great agitation (intense form); conquest; causing fear; disturbed; disquieted; (root = a removing; a commotion). Their removal; their disquiet.

Zaza (za'-zah) = Brightness; fullness. Abundance; projection.

Zebadiah (zeb-ad-i'-ah) = Jehovah has endowed; gift of the LORD; given of the LORD; the LORD is my portion.

Zebah (ze'-bah) = Sacrifice; i.e., devoted to Moloch; victim; (root = to sacrifice).

Zebaim (ze-ba'-im) =

Hyenas; gazelles.

Zebedee (zeb'-e-dee) = Jehovah's gift; the gift of God.

Zebina (ze-bi'-nah) = Bought; one who is bought. Chaldean: To buy.

Zeboiim (ze-boy'-im) = Gathering of troops of soldiers; i.e., a military city.

Zeboim (ze-bo'-im) #1 = Same as Zeboiim = Gathering of troops of soldiers; i.e., a military city.

Zeboim (ze-bo'-im) #2 = Hyenas; gazelles.

Zebudah (ze-bu'-dah) = Bestowing a gift; given. Endowment.

Zebul (ze'-bul) = Habitation; (root = to inhabit; to dwell with).

Zebulonite (zeb'-u-lon-ite) = Descendants of Zebulun = Wished-for habitation; dwelling; (root = [1] habitation; [2] to dwell with).

Zebulun (zeb'-u-lun) = Wished-for habitation;

dwelling; (root = [1] habitation; [2] to dwell with).

Zebulunites (zeb'-u-lun-ites) = Same as Zebulonite = Descendants of Zebulun = wished-forhabitation; dwelling; (root = [1] habitation; [2] to dwell with).

Zechirah (zek-a-ri'-ah) = Jehovah remembers; Jehovah is renowned.

Zedad (ze'-dad) = Turned aside. A mountain; side of a mountain; steep place.

Zedekiah (zed-e-ki'-ah) = Jehovah is might; Jehovah is righteous; justice of the LORD; justice of Jehovah. My righteous God.

Zeeb (ze'-eb) = Wolf.

Zelah (ze'-lah) = Side; i.e., a place situated on the side of a mountain; (root = a rib; a side; a side chamber). Limping; one-sided.

Zelek (ze'-lek) = Fissure; i.e., an opening. Rent; a shadow.

Zelophehad (ze'lo'-fe-had) = First rupture; i.e., firstborn; the first born; fracture. Anxious for shade. Shadow of fear.

Zelotes (ze-lo'-teze) = Zealous; full of zeal.

Zelzah (zel'-zah) = Shade in the heat of the sun; a distinct shadow; double shadow. A clear (or dazzling) shadow.

Zemaraim (zem-a-ra'-im) = Two cuttings off; two fleeces. Double woolens.

Zemarite (zem'-a-rite) = Same as Zemaraim = Two cuttings off; two fleeces. Double woolens.

Zemira (ze-mi'-rah) = Song; i.e., of joy; a melody; (root = to sing). Causing singing.

Zenan (ze'-nan) = Same as Zaanan = Rich in flocks; place of flocks; (root = to abound in sheep and goats). Their flock.

Zenas (ze'-nas) = The gift of Zeus. Jupiter (as the father of gods).

Zephaniah (zef-a-ni'-ah) = Hid of the LORD; i.e.,

protected by the LORD; whom Jehovah hid; concealed of God; (roots = [1] to hide; to protect; [2] Jehovah). Watcher of the LORD. Treasured of Jehovah.

Zephath (ze'-fath) = A watch tower; (root = to look out).

Zephathah (zef'-a-thah) = Same as Zephath = A watch tower; (root = to look out). Place of watching.

Zephi (ze'-fi) = Expectation; i.e., hope of parents; watch tower; (root = to look out; to look for aid). Watch thou.

Zepho (ze'-fo) = Same as Zephi = Expectation; i.e., hope of parents; watch tower; (root = to look out; to look for aid). A watcher; watch; that sees. His watching.

Zephon (ze'-fon) = Earnest expectation; intense longing; a looking out; (root = to look out). Dark; wintry. A watcher; watchfulness.

Zephonites (zef'-on-ites)

= Descendants of Zephon = Earnest expectation; intense longing; a looking out; (root = to look out).

Zer (zur) = Flint. Strait.

Zerah (ze'-rah) = Rising; origin. Same as Zarah = Rising of light; i.e., joy of parents; (roots = [1] a rising {of light}; [2] to rise; dawn). Shining.

Zerahiah (zer-a-hi'-ah) = Rising of the light of the LORD; whom Jehovah caused to rise; The LORD is risen; Jehovah is appearing; Jehovah caused to spring froth.

Zered (ze'-red) = Dense forest. Same as Zared = Luxuriant growth of trees; exuberant growth.

Zereda (zer'-e-dah) = The adversary rules. Cooling; (root = to cool).

Zeredathah (ze-red'-a-thah) = Scene of the adversary's rule. Fortress; (root = to pierce).

Zererath (zer'-e-rath) = Oppression. Straightness.

Zeresh (ze'-resh) = Star of adoration. Persian: Star of Gold; gold. A stranger in want.

Zereth (ze'-reth) = Splendor; brightness; (root = to shine).

Zeri (ze'-ri) = Same as Jezer = Frame; form; i.e., of his parents; anything made; (root = to form; to fashion; imagination). Balm.

Zeror (ze'-ror) = Small bundle; bundle; that straitens; (root = [1] a small bundle; a bag; [2] to bind up; to shut up).

Zeruah (ze-ru'-ah) = Leprous; (root = to be leprous; to be stricken).

Zerubbabel (ze-rub'-ba-bel) = An offspring of Babel; born at Babylon; dispersed or begotten in Babylon; scattered in Babylon; the dispersed in Babylon; (root = to sow seed). Melted by Babylon.

Zeruiah (ze-ru-i'-ah) = Balsam from Jehovah. Cleft; (root = to cleave).

Troubled by God. Pierce ye Jah.

Zetham (ze'-tham) = Olive; place of olives; shining.

Zethan (ze'-than) = Olive tree (intense form); place of olives; shining.

Zethar (ze'-thar) = Very great; sacrifice; he that examines. This is the spy (searcher).

Zia (zi'-ah) = Shaking; i.e., fear; terror; terrified; motion; (root = to tremble).

Ziba (zi'-bah) = Plant; planter; plantation. Appointed.

Zibeon (zib'-e-un) = Dyed; a dyer; variegated; (root = divers colors). Wild robber; seizing prey.

Zibia (zib'-e-ah) = Female gazelle; strength.

Zibiah (zib'-e-ah) = Roe deer. Same as Zibia = Female gazelle; strength.

Zichri (zik'-ri) = Remembered (of the LORD); famous;

renowned. Memorable; do thou remember.

Ziddim (zid'-dim) = Sides; (root = to turn aside). Lying in wait.

Zidkijah (zid-ki'-jah) = Same as Zedekiah = Justice of the LORD justice of Jehovah. My righteous God. Jehovah is might.

Zidon (zi'-don) = Same as Sidon = Fishing; plenty of fish; (roots = [1] hunting; prey taken in hunting {or} fishing; [2] to lay snares). A place for hunting.

Zidonians (zi-do'-ne-uns) = Inhabitants of Zidon = Same as Sidon = Fishing; plenty of fish; (roots = [1] hunting; prey taken in hunting {or} fishing; [2] to lay snares).

Zif (zif) = Blossom; bloom. Brightness.

Ziha (zi'-hah) = Drought; dry; thirsty; sunniness; (root = to be dry). Causing dryness; parching.

Ziklag (zik'-lag) = Winding; bending; a

measure of oppression. Enveloped in grief.

Zillah (zil'-lah) = A shadow; shade; shadow of darkness or protection; (root = to be shady). He wasted.

Zilpah (zil'-pah) = A dropping; drop. Flippant mouth.

Zilthai (zil'-thahee) = Shadow of the LORD; i.e., under the LORD's protection; shady; (roots = [1] a shadow; [2] Jehovah).

Zimmah (zim'-mah) = Wicked device; planning; plan; purpose; counsel; consideration; (roots = [1] wickedness; wicked device; [2] to think evil). Lewdness.

Zimran (zim'-ran) = Celebrated; sung; a chanter; the singer.

Zimri (zim'-ri) = Song of the LORD; celebrated; vine. My psalm.

Zin = A low palm tree. Thorn.

Zina (zi'-nah) =

Abundance; (root = a full breast). Borrowed. Nourishing.

Zion (zi'-un) = Very dry; sunny; (root = a dry place). Parched place.

Zior (zi'-or) = Smallness; (root = to be small). Diminution.

Ziph (zif) = Refining place; melting place. Borrowed; (root = to borrow).

Ziphah (zi'-fah) = Borrowed; lent. Refinery.

Ziphims (zif'-ims) = Inhabitants of Ziph = Refining place; melting place. Borrowed; (root = to borrow). Smelters.

Ziphion (zif'-e-on) = Same as Zephon = Earnest expectation; intense longing; a looking out; (root = to look out). (to) the flow of song.

Ziphites (zif'-ites) = Same as Ziphims = Inhabitants of Ziph = Borrowed.

Ziphron (zif'-ron) = Sweet smell; fragrance.

Zippor (zip'-por) = A sparrow; little bird; a bird; (roots = [1] a little bird; [2] to chirp).

Zipporah (zip-po'-rah) = Same as Zippor (feminine) = A sparrow; a little bird; (roots = [1] a little bird; [2] to chirp).

Zithri (zith'-ri) = Protection of the LORD; protection of Jehovah; Jehovah's protection. My hiding place.

Ziz (ziz) = A flower. A blossom.

Ziza (zi'-zah) = Fertility; full breast; brightness. Same as Zina = Abundance; (root = a full breast). Exuberance; roving (as a beast).

Zizah (zi'-zah) = Same as Ziza/Zina = Fertility; full breast; brightness; abundance; (root = a full breast). Fullness.

Zoan (zo'-an) = A place of departure; a traveler; (roots = he moved tents; he loaded a beast of burden). Removal.

Zoar (zo'-ar) = Smallness; little; the younger (root = to be small). Bringing low.

Zoba (zo'-bah) = Statue; public place; a host; a plantation. A station; standing.

Zobah (zo'-bah) = Same as Zoba = Statue; public place; a host; a plantation. A station; standing.

Zobebah (zo-be'-bah) = Going slowly; walking slowly; slow moving. Sluggish; covered.

Zohar (zo'-har) = Whiteness; white; light; shining; distinction; (roots = [1] whiteness; [2] to be white).

Zoheleth (zo'-he-leth) = Serpent; the serpent stone; (root = to creep; to crawl). Serpents of the dust. Creepers of the dust.

Zoheth (zo'-heth) = Strong; corpulent. Releasing.

Zophah (zo'-fah) = A cruse; i.e., of water; (root = to spread out; to dilate).

A watch; expanse. Expanding.

Zophai (zo'-fahee) = Sweet; honey, (as dropping from the comb); honeycomb. Watcher. My honeycombs; my overflows.

Zophar (zo'-far) = Chirping; insolence; chatterer; (root = to turn, oneself about; to chirp; to twitter, as a bird). Sparrow. Departing early; a climber.

Zophim (zo'-fim) = Watchmen; watchers. Field of droppings; i.e., fertile.

Zorah (zo'-rah) = A nest of hornets; i.e., a place of troublesome men; a place of hornets.

Zorathites (zo'-rath-ites) = Inhabitants of Zorah = A nest of hornets; i.e., a place of troublesome men; a place of hornets.

Zoreah (zo'-re-ah) = Same as Zorah = A nest of hornets; i.e., a place of troublesome men; a place of hornets.

Zorites (zo'-rites) = Same as Zorathites = Inhabitants of Zorah = A nest of hornets; i.e., a place of troublesome men; a place of hornets.

Zorobabel (zo-rob'-a-bel) = Born at Babel; i.e., Babylon. Greek form of Zerubbabel = An offspring of Babel; born at Babylon; dispersed or begotten in Babylon; scattered in Babylon; the dispersed in Babylon; (root = to sow seed).

Zuar (zu'-ar) = Very small; smallness; little; (root = to be small). He was belittled.

Zuph (zuf) = Same as Zophai = Sweet; honey, (as dropping from the comb); honeycomb.

Zur (zur) = A rock; rock; stone. To besiege.

Zuriel (zu'-re-el) = Rock of God; God is the Rock; my Rock is God.

Zurishaddai (zu-re-shad'-da-i) = Rock of the Almighty; whose Almighty is the Rock; the Almighty is a Rock; my Rock is almighty.

Zuzims (zu'-zims) = Commotions; i.e., terrors; the wanderers. Chaldean: To arouse. Giants. Roving creatures.

Appendix A

The Religious Jewish Calendar

The Hebrews followed a lunar calendar. The month began when the thin crescent of the new moon was first visible at sunset. The day of the new moon that ushered in a new month was considered holy. The autumnal equinox was viewed as "*at the end of the year*" (Exodus 23:16, NIV), and the spring, or vernal equinox, was called "*the return of the year*" (1 Kings 20:26).

The Hebrews also commonly indicated the time of year by the season rather than by the names of the months. In Palestine the year divided loosely into the dry season (April - September) and the rainy season (October - March), and these were subdivided into seed-time (November - December) and harvest (April - June). We also find calendar designations by agricultural activities such as: "*wheat harvest*" (Genesis 30:14), "*barley harvest*" (2 Samuel 21:9), or the "*earing time*" (Exodus 34:12).

Nisan = First Jewish month (March - April). Begin Barley harvest. Before the Babylonian exile it was commonly called Abib.

Iyyar = Second Jewish month (April - May). Barley harvest.

Sivan = Third Jewish month (May - June). Wheat harvest.

Tammuz = Forth Jewish month (June - July).

Ab = Fifth Jewish month (July - August). Grape, fig, olives ripen.

Elul = Sixth Jewish

month (August -
September). Vintage
begins.

Tishri = Seventh Jewish
month (September -
October). Early rains,
plowing.

Heshvan = Eighth Jewish
month (October -
November). Wheat,
Barley sowing.

Kislev = Ninth Jewish
month (November -
December).

Tebeth = Tenth Jewish
month (December -
January). Rainy winter
months.

Shebat = Eleventh Jewish
month (January -
February). New year for
trees.

Adar = Twelfth Jewish
month (February -
March). Almonds
blooming.

Adar Sheni = Thirteenth
Jewish month (intercalary
month).

Appendix B

The Stones in the Breastplate

In Exodus 28:15-21 God instructed Moses to make a breastplate for the High Priest. In it were set four rows of three stones representing the twelve tribes of Israel. The Bible names for the stones are often difficult to relate to semiprecious and precious stones in today's world. Although commentators differ on some of the stones, our research causes us to believe these are the stones mentioned.

Row 1

Sardius Stone = a blood red stone (cornelian or ruby). It was the first stone in the breastplate and is the sixth stone in the foundation of the New Jerusalem. The name "Sardius" comes from the Hebrew - odem = redness (from the root word Adam, (ad'-um) = Earthy or red earth; of the ground; taken out of the red earth; (root = to be red; ruddy).

Topaz Stone = Chrysolite or perridot. This stone came from an Island in the Red Sea called "Topazos" (now, Zebirget). The island was frequently surrounded by fog. It was often sought for by navigators, hence it received its name, Topazin; in the native tongue = "to seek." The stone is green in color (often a pale green).

Carbuncle Stone = Translated from two Hebrew words: *ekdach*="fiery glow," and *barkath*=flashing or sparkling. The first word designates the deep red color found in the true carbuncle.

Row 2

Emerald Stone = (Garnet?) Green or

turquoise. A pure emerald is one of the rarest gems and a flawless emerald would be priceless. This is the fourth stone on the breastplate and the fourth stone in the foundation of the New Jerusalem. Emerald is also the description of the rainbow around the throne of God (Revelation 4:3).

Sapphire Stone = A hard, clear, deep blue type of corundum stone. It is next to the diamond in luster, beauty and hardness. It can be red in color like the ruby.

Diamond Stone = many scholars believe this to be onyx.

Row 3

Ligure Stone = Hebrew *leshem*; Greek *liqurion*. Both words mean "to attract." Perhaps the stone has a magnetic attractive quality. Could be the modern day Jacinth stone.

Agate Stone = Hebrew *cadcod*=ruddy or reddish. Is usually found in volcanic rocks.

Amethyst Stone = A rare variety of quartz. A six-sided purple crystal. It is the most highly valued stone in the quartz group.

Row 4

Beryl Stone = It was imported from the area of Tarshish. Today it is called aquamarine: A yellow, green, or bluish crystal. Interestingly, the wheels of Ezekiel's vision were the color of beryl (Ezekiel 1:16). The men of Daniel's vision were the color of beryl (Daniel 10:6), and Solomon and the king of Tyre wore jewelry of beryl (Song of Solomon 5:14; Ezekiel 28:13).The Chrysolite Stone, a golden yellow stone that is the seventh stone of the New Jerusalem (Revelation 21:20) is the same as the "beryl" of the Old Testament.

Onxy Stone = Today we call it Sardonyx. Comes from the Hebrew word *shoham* = to blanch; to make white.

Jasper Stone = This stone is very difficult to trace as the ancients called many stones jasper. It is a variety of quartz. Jade can be of two types: *nephrite*, which is the jade we usually see. The other family of jade is called *jadeite*. It looks like a green opal and has a depth and translucency that is difficult to describe. Jasper is the first foundation stone of the New Jerusalem, and the last stone in the High Priest's breastplate. It was jasper stones God chose to fit on the shoulder pads of the priests. On them the names of the twelve tribes were engraved.